The Journalist's
Moral Compass

The Journalist's Moral Compass

Basic Principles

Edited by
Steven R. Knowlton
and
Patrick R. Parsons

Foreword by Charles Bierbauer

PRAEGER

Westport, Connecticut
London

Library of Congress Cataloging-in-Publication Data

The Journalist's moral compass : basic principles / edited by Steven
   R. Knowlton and Patrick R. Parsons : foreword by Charles Bierbauer.
      p. cm.
   Includes index.
   ISBN 0–275–94537–5 (alk. paper)—ISBN 0–275–95153–7 (pbk.)
     1. Journalistic ethics—United States. 2. Freedom of the press—
United States. 3. Press—Economic aspects—United States.
I. Knowlton, Steven R. II. Parsons, Patrick R.
PN4888.E8J69 1995
174'.9097—dc20   93–4256

British Library Cataloguing in Publication Data is available.

Library of Congress Catalog Card Number: 93–4256
ISBN: 0–275–94537–5
     0–275–95153–7 (pbk.)

First published in 1995

Praeger Publishers, 88 Post Road West, Westport, CT 06881
An imprint of Greenwood Publishing Group, Inc.

Printed in the United States of America

The paper used in this book complies with the
Permanent Paper Standard issued by the National
Information Standards Organization (Z39.48–1984).

10 9 8 7 6 5 4

Contents

Foreword

Wh**at right do all these journalists have to harass mayors, police chiefs and tax collectors—not to mention everyone who runs afoul of the law, from the tax cheat to, perhaps, the president? Who are we—the journalists—to interrogate the accused?

Why should we be allowed to impose ourselves and our intrusive questions on the bereaved?

How is that right assumed and extrapolated from the First Amendment?

When they forbade any law "abridging the freedom of speech or of the press," what freedom did the Founding Fathers have in mind?

Freedom of the press has become a written-in-blood sanctity, an asylum, an electronic fence meant to halt the bloodhounds on the heels of the press. It is an assertive position taken by an unlicensed, unregulated and occasionally unloved assembly. We call ourselves journalists, reporters, columnists, commentators, broadcasters—even newshounds. While others sometimes call us things unfit to print, we demand the right to print—and to broadcast—virtually all we know in pursuit of the public's right to know. Uncensored, of course.

I'll admit to invoking that "public's right to know" from time to time in a journalism career that has spanned more than a quarter-century, automatically resorting to an unquestioned foundation in the First Amendment. But is that reflexive armor philosophically impenetrable? Have we worn it well? Would the pursuit of truth be any different without it?

In *The Journalist's Moral Compass*, Steven Knowlton and Patrick Parsons have presented us with the intellect of the ancients, revolutionaries, and contemporaries. It is a collection meant as much to provide questions as to answer them. But should journalists be as good at seeking out the questioning principles as simply asking the questions?

Would Locke set the press as the judge over prince or parliament? He does not say, but accords that power to the public. Are press and public one and the same?

How would the authors of Cato's letters apply their "reflections upon libelling" to today's political drama with its soap opera suggestions of sex and subversion? Is it "more pernicious" to sweep questions of character beneath the political carpet?

Would Robespierre have second thoughts about a fully unfettered press? (I'll take the question: I don't think so.)

So if we can get the blessings of Locke and "Cato" and Robespierre, and Plato grants us live, 24-hour coverage of the shadow play on the walls of his cave, let's "roll tape." "Start the presses."

Hold it.

Can we just do this? Sure, we have a moral imperative. It's in the book.

What about the moral compass? That's trickier. You want true moral or magnetic moral? How close do we have to get?

I think we at least set out in the right direction. Collectively, we are motivated by curiosity. It is essential to the nature of journalists. What else drives us?

We are skeptical, to say the least, disbelieving and often distrusting. Over time, we become cynical.

Adventure, travel and romance are diminishing attractions. Yes, the adrenaline pumps in combat and some of our ranks are ineluctably drawn to the worst situations. But too many of our number have perished in grubby conflicts to find glamour any more in being a war correspondent.

Travel, these days, is all airports, hotels, and conference halls. You don't look for a local cafe to read the newspapers. You look for one with a dataport to hook up your traveling electronic office—computers, printers, faxes.

Romance? Sometimes it finds you, but you're usually too tired to look for it.

Patriotism is low on the journalist's motivation list. With global audiences, a reporter cannot root for the home team. Should not? Not in print, not on the air. That's for the commentators and talk-show moralists. It's getting harder and harder to separate the journalist from the jingoist, but it's a demarcation worth fighting for. Our opinions and sympathies are for when the paper's been put down, the set turned off.

Ego? You bet. There's gratification in the byline. The TV appearances bring public recognition. As a television correspondent, I've been recognized on the streets of Venice, Athens, Moscow, and, occasionally, Washington. It's both amazing and frightening.

Money? It's a living; in some cases, it pays very well. It's also a business. For the most part, reporters have nothing to do with the business side and may view themselves at odds with owners and publishers whom, in some cases, they might prefer reporting on than reporting to.

How about truth? Does that motivate journalists? Yeah. Sure. Whatever truth is. It's a pursuit.

As I read through these treatises I found myself quarreling with Francis Bacon and his orderly progression from experience to axiomatic truth. Bacon dismisses the amassing of opinion, even the application of logic to the process. And did I detect a smirk when he rejects that most basic of journalistic thought processes: "much agitation and working of the wit?" Great thinkers from time to time ought to attend a city council meeting, wade through a Pentagon procurement order, or suffer a presidential campaign. Disorderly progressions are more often the raw material for journalists.

"Really?" is the recurrent margin note on my pages of Warren Breed's "Social Control in the Newsroom." Are we journalists that malleable? Can a cranky bunch of reporters unable to agree on the correct number of scoops to fuel the office coffee pot conform to an unenunciated editorial policy?

Yet I nod in deeply concerned agreement with Daniel Boorstin's warning of the "pseudo-events" that can capture television's eye and distort the viewer's. Thirty years ago—the equivalent of several ice ages at today's hyperpace—Boorstin caught on to what every political promoter now knows as a basic axiom. The camera has no peripheral vision and certainly no eyes in the back of its head. Some print reporters, unencumbered by instant deadlines, are more capable of 360-degree vision.

I cannot count how many pseudo-events I have covered. My nine years at the White House were an endless succession of them: campaign speeches, Rose Garden ceremonies, and most occasions of molehill dimension that were inevitably labeled "summits."

But the most pseudo of all events is the one misnamed "photo opportunity." It is most refined—and abused—at the presidential level. Prime Minister X of the Republic of Y comes calling on the president in the Oval Office. The press is invited to record the event on film and tape. In the brief two or three minutes while cameras whirr and click, a handful of reporters—the "pool"—pump questions, mostly at the U.S. president rather than at the obscure Prime Minister X. "You know I don't take questions at a photo opportunity," George Bush was inclined to say during his presidency. At least when, as was his prerogative, he chose not to.

But these impertinent reporters! How dare they embarrass the president before his distinguished guest! How dare they not? The reporters were, after all, invited to participate in the photo op, too. And reporters participate by asking questions as well as by observing. In fact, our bargain with the president's operatives was that if they wanted our cameras, they got our questions, too.

The photo opportunity has been, at times, the only opportunity the White House press corps has to determine or decipher policy. Presidents have remarkable devices for avoiding the press. In my time on the beat, ABC's Sam Donaldson matched his booming voice against the engines of Air Force One to shout questions at a conveniently hard-of-hearing President Ronald Reagan. UPI's Helen Thomas became a nagging conscience for one president after another with her unflagging questions about the poor, the Palestinians, and politics.

We risk seeming boorish, offensive and rude, and we are often chastised for being so. We are less often commended for our patience and perseverance with reluctant officials.

This is not just a Washington phenomenon, an inside-the-beltway confusion of camaraderie and confrontation. The late Frank Rizzo, while mayor of Philadelphia, once thrust a blunt finger in the direction of my chin with the admonishment: "You don't run this city and KYW doesn't run this city." He was right, of course. I didn't. But he was also wrong in assuming that was the goal for me or for my station.

It's almost too simple. Ask the question. Get the answer. Write the story.

The questions are getting tougher, though. Perhaps that's where the journalists in the highly competitive, technologically accelerated media of the late 20th century are running afoul.

Where did this running battle start? Try the demise of the presidency of Richard Nixon. The toughest of questions—"What did the president know and when did he know it?"—was posed by Sen. Howard Baker (R.-Tenn.) during the Watergate hearings. The sharpest from CBS's Dan Rather was actually a retort to Nixon's own query of Rather: "Are you running for something?" "No, sir, Mr. President," Rather shot back. "Are you?" It was a flippancy that underscored the diminished respect for the office holder. Subsequent presidents have paid in similar ways for Nixon's tarnish.

But other questions have been thrust into the realm of legitimacy. Extramarital sexual behavior is one, thanks to Democratic candidate Gary Hart's "catch me if you can" attitude in 1987. The press, loving a challenge, did. Since then, George Bush and Bill Clinton faced the same question in their campaigns. Many earlier presidents were spared questioning about even more questionable behavior at a time when it was accorded no more attention than a knowing wink.

Sex never loses its allure as a issue. The sin of the sixties—casual experimentation with drugs, usually marijuana—seems to have passed its peak. Clinton's "I didn't inhale" reduced it to a joke. Reporters scarcely ask anymore.

A reporter's question does not have to be whittled to skewering sharpness. Democrat Michael Dukakis's presidential bid was already adrift when Dukakis got hopelessly lost on a hypothetical question. Instead of rising to the bait thrown by CNN's Bernard Shaw—your wife's been raped, now how do you feel about the death penalty—Dukakis unemotionally explained away any chance for voter empathy. An unfair question? Not when the stakes are so high.

And so it goes from the Oval Office to the city council, from the Pentagon to the police chief, from the corporate suite to the corner store. The job does not differ much, only the venue.

It follows the knock on the door of a usually nondescript home where fate has done in a member of the household-violently. And to the first person who opens the door, you ask, "How do you feel?"

There's an easy answer that will suffice: "Go away."

And a reporter may secretly hope that no one will answer the door.

Who are we to ask? For that matter, who needs to know?

You may not find all the answers here. You'll probably find some new questions.

—Charles Bierbauer

Preface

This anthology is the result of the collaboration of two friends and colleagues who look at questions of journalistic principles from somewhat different perspectives. Knowlton is a 20-year veteran of newspaper and wire-service city rooms who returned to graduate school to study political history. Parsons is primarily a scholar trained as a sociologist, who thus tends to see journalism in the larger context of mass media studies.

Each now teaches news media ethics at Penn State University and through years of collaborative discussions, the sections of their courses have become increasingly similar. The idea for this book came out of those discussions. The premise was straightforward and simple in concept: Can we describe what, if anything, are the basic moral principles of contemporary American journalism? What, other than an often ill-thought-out reference to the First Amendment, gives the reporter the right to stick a mike in the face of a grieving widow and ask the classic stupid question: "How do you feel?" Does the public have, as journalists so often say, a "right to know"? If so, to know what? Everything? Some things? Who gets to decide? And how does that right, if there is one, square with the individual's right to privacy? How does one justify, morally, ruining a politician's career by revealing embarrassing details of a long-ago past?

The writings included in this volume are by no means comprehensive, but they try to frame the debate for these and other questions. Readers may well find that their favorite writers and favorite essays are missing. To keep this volume to a manageable length, the editors shortened substantially the essays they did include, and omitted many others entirely. What is left is certainly not exhaustive. We do believe, however, that the issues raised in this volume touch upon the most important arguments.

In the interest of brevity, introductory material has been kept to a minimum and included material has been edited extensively, sometimes ruthlessly. We believe we have not done violence to any writer's intent, although we are necessarily less confident that we have preserved each writer's prose style. Undoubtedly, great quantities of supporting evidence and context have been left out. Before readers discount or dismiss any of the arguments advanced here, we urge them to read the original work in its entirety.

A word on inclusive language is in order. Most of the authors in this book used "he" and "man" and similar sex-specific words throughout their writings, either because they believed that their topics were properly the concern of men only or because they believed that the terms could be defined broadly enough to include women as well. Although the former premise is now obsolete and the latter is specious, it would be anachronistic to talk about, say Thomas Hobbes's views on men and women in public life. It is one of the most dangerous pitfalls in the study of history to impose current thoughts and beliefs onto the past. When we discuss what Hobbes thought about "men" forming political institutions, we do not assume that he meant either to say or to imply "women and men," because, as far as we know, he did not.

No book is the product only of its listed authors and editors. Several colleagues offered helpful suggestions, and the book is better for their help. Especially helpful were suggestions by Professors Beth Barnes, Ronald Bettig, Mary Mander and John Spicer Nichols. Thanks also are due to Betty Jo Sanchez-Gunn, a fine journalist in her own right and a splendid research assistant. The faculty secretary, Betsy Hall, added many hours of expert typing to her regular duties without complaint or loss of efficiency. Also, machines can now read and process words, if you teach them how, so our thanks extend to Chet Smith at Penn State's Center for Academic Computing for teaching a scanner to handle some of the text and for teaching us to handle the scanner.

Thanks are due to Charles Bierbauer of CNN for shoving a copy of the typescript in with the rest of his luggage as he followed President Clinton to the Tokyo summit meeting and back. It seems appropriate that he took on the task of reading this book on journalism ethics in the midst of performing journalism's most crucial function, that of telling the sovereign people what their hired public servants are up to. His observations in the foreword are valuable, and his suggestions for improving the book's organization made it stronger and clearer.

To our wives and colleagues, Professors Karen Freeman and Susan Strohm, we offer undying gratitude for patience and understanding as this project consumed more time and attention than we thought it would. And to Karen, a talented and highly skilled copy editor, go special thanks for reading the entire manuscript and finding numerous problems of both style and substance that everyone else overlooked. Errors and imprecisions that remain are ours.

The Journalist's
Moral Compass

Introduction

This book is an introduction to the most important principles in American journalism, together with an overview of the most serious problems interfering with journalists' ability to live up to those principles. As any beginning reporting student soon discovers, journalism is not something to be memorized, nor even something to be learned in the way that traditional academic disciplines can be learned. Even a first course in journalism requires a great deal of analytical thinking: How does this fact relate to that one? Which of these two pieces of information is the more important? That analysis quickly encompasses questions of ethical propriety: Is this story fair? What would make it more so? What information does the public need to know, and which details are just gratuitous pandering? American journalism has profound intellectual and moral principles at its heart. This book examines the most significant of those principles.

What is it that should drive reporters, editors, anchors, columnists and all the others to do what they do? Are they in the news business to bolster their egos? That is part of it, of course, for the ego gratification in journalism can be enormous. Is it the money? Hardly, although salaries in the profession are not the embarrassment they used to be. It is travel and adventure? In part, to be sure, but most journalists are neither foreign nor White House correspondents, and many of those who are eventually tire of life on the road. Is it, as cynics have suggested, just the chance to hobnob with the rich and powerful, while taking none of the risk or responsibility? Doubtless, these and other motives drive journalists to excellence, yet there is more. Simply put, journalism is a career in which acting on the highest of moral principles not only does not interfere with achieving professional excellence, but defines it. What are those principles? Albert Camus, the French journalist and author, identified much of the profession's guiding spirit in 1957 when, on accepting the Nobel Prize for Literature, he said of journalists: "Whatever our personal frailties may be, the nobility of our calling will always be rooted in two commitments difficult to observe: refusal to lie about what we know and resistance to oppression."

Few reporters keep Camus's essays or Cato's letters on their desks, and few editors wrestle on deadline with whether Adam Smith makes any sense in a post-industrial world. Yet it is also true that good journalists have strongly held beliefs, deeply rooted in ethics, political science, and history. Those beliefs powerfully shape what they do.

This book lays no claim to presenting all possible views and interpretations of journalists' behavior and motivations. Nor does it claim that all journalists think or act alike, or that they are all equally competent or principled, any more than one could say the same for all architects or dancers or police officers. But the example of a bad cop, or a stupid one, does not invalidate the argument that most police officers believe in the rule of law, in personal courage, in organizational discipline, and so on.

This volume is not a survey of all the things journalists might believe. It is, in a sense, more old-fashioned than that. The editors unapologetically declare that some values endure longer than others and that some are more important than others. Further, the editors are interested in more than what journalists *do* believe; they are interested in what they *should* believe.

The arguments offered by this book are presented in three sections. The first section deals with politics—the relation of the press to the state. This section puts the First Amendment in context and is the section that news professionals will almost certainly find most familiar. In the words of Milton and Mill, of Locke and of Lippmann, the case is made for the role a free press can and should make in a democratic society. This section also explores the origins of the most substantial philosophical counterweight to the journalist's instinct to publish, the individual's right to privacy. That argument, like that for a free press itself, has its philosophical roots in Lockean political theory.

The second section deals with the problems of truth and objectivity. It is here that writers from Plato to Suzanne Pingree argue about the difficulties surrounding questions of truth. Whose truth are we talking about? Is there a Truth, or just a lot of little truths? It has been a long time since anyone argued that journalism should deal *only* with politics, narrowly defined, but what else are journalists obliged to do? After all, politics, along with all the other most powerful institutions (including the news business itself), used to be the exclusive province of well-off white males, but is no longer. What are journalists' obligations to those whose sense of truth and reality is vastly at variance with the mainstream?

The third section looks at economics and the daunting influence money has had on journalism. It has been true since the earliest days of journalism that money has a tremendous influence on what journalists do, just as it has an influence on what nearly everyone else does. Many critics, amateur and professional, from within the business and from without, have argued that the influence of money is so pervasive that all other considerations are trivial. There is too much evidence to the contrary to believe that is true. We hope and believe that a reasonable discussion of the nature of the problem can help journalists and journalists-in-training to recognize that there is often a problem of conflicting loyalties between the truth and the dollar and to arm themselves to fight the good fight. Many a tight-fisted publisher has been shamed into doing the right thing, making it doubly important for tomorrow's journalists to know that what they produce is not just another commodity like hair spray and soap, but something far more important.

By nearly any standard, American journalists today are more principled than ever before, despite the self-serving carping from politicians who would obviously rather shoot the messenger than deal with the message. There is no doubt that contemporary readers and viewers are more aware of journalism's shortcomings than were their predecessors. Yet it is also true that those readers and viewers both demand more from journalists and get more than even a generation ago. In part, that is because the public is increasingly sophisticated, better able to distinguish good reporting from bad, and is thus more critical of shoddy work. And in part, it is because there are more critics than ever before, both in the industry and in the academy, who earn their living finding fault with the press. For all that, and perhaps in large measure because of all that, this generation of journalists and journalists-in-training spends more time and energy on concern with ethical issues than any generation in American history. That is not because today's journalists are inherently smarter or nobler than their predecessors. And it is certainly not because the challenges are easier or simpler. On the contrary, the problems, particularly those stemming from economic pressures, may be more daunting than ever before. Today's journalists are better at the moral dimension of what they do because they are better trained and more well-grounded in the history and the philosophy of their craft. To borrow from Newton (who, in turn, borrowed from the Roman poet Lucan), reporters and editors can see farther today because they have the luxury of standing upon the shoulders of giants. This book represents a gathering of those giants, and its readers are invited to climb up.

We begin with what journalists say they believe in, as reflected in the Code of Ethics of the nation's leading organization of working professionals, the Society of Professional Journalists. Other professional groups, such as broadcasters, have their own codes of ethics as well, but the SPJ code is the broadest in scope. It is only about 800 words long, but it contains a surprising number of ideas and concepts, which show up in the rest of the book.

Society of Professional Journalists: Code of Ethics
1987

T he Society of Professional Journalists believes the duty of journalists is to serve the truth.

We believe the agencies of mass communication are carriers of public discussion and information, acting on their Constitutional mandate and freedom to learn and report the facts.

We believe in public enlightenment as the forerunner of justice, and in our Constitutional role to seek the truth as part of the public's right to know the truth.

We believe those responsibilities carry obligations that require journalists to perform with intelligence, objectivity, accuracy, and fairness.

To these ends, we declare acceptance of the standards of practice here set forth:

I. Responsibility

The public's right to know of events of public importance and interest is the overriding mission of the mass media. The purpose of distributing news and enlightened opinion is to serve the general welfare. Journalists who use their professional status as representatives of the public for selfish or other unworthy motives violate a high trust.

II. Freedom of the Press

Freedom of the press is to be guarded as an inalienable right of people in a free society. It carries with it the freedom and the responsibility to discuss, question, and challenge actions and utterances of our government and of our public and private institutions. Journalists uphold the right to speak unpopular opinions and the privilege to agree with the majority.

III. Ethics

Journalists must be free of obligation to any interest other than the public's right to know the truth.

1. Gifts, favors, free travel, special treatment or privileges can compromise the integrity of journalists and their employers. Nothing of value should be accepted.

2. Secondary employment, political involvement, holding public office, and service in community organizations should be avoided if it compromises the integrity of journalists and their employers. Journalists and their employers should conduct their personal lives in a manner that protects them from conflict of interest, real or apparent. Their responsibilities to the public are paramount. That is the nature of their profession.

3. So-called news communications from private sources should not be published or broadcast without substantiation of their claims to news values.

4. Journalists will seek news that serves the public interest, despite the obstacles. They will make constant efforts to assure that the public's business is conducted in public and that public records are open to public inspection.

5. Journalists acknowledge the newsman's ethic of protecting confidential sources of information.

6. Plagiarism is dishonest and unacceptable.

IV. Accuracy and Objectivity

Good faith with the public is the foundation of all worthy journalism.

1. Truth is our ultimate goal.

2. Objectivity in reporting the news is another goal that serves as the mark of an experienced professional. It is a standard of performance toward which we strive. We honor those who achieve it.

3. There is no excuse for inaccuracies or lack of thoroughness.

4. Newspaper headlines should be fully warranted by the contents of the articles they accompany. Photographs and telecasts should give an accurate picture of an event and not highlight an event out of context.

5. Sound practice makes clear distinction between news reports and expressions of opinion. News reports should be free of opinion or bias and represent all sides of an issue.

6. Partisanship in editorial comment that knowingly departs from the truth violates the spirit of American journalism.

7. Journalists recognize their responsibility for offering informed analysis, comment, and editorial opinion on public events and issues. They accept the

obligation to present such material by individuals whose competence, experience and judgment qualify them for it.

8. Special articles or presentations devoted to advocacy or the writer's own conclusions and interpretations should be labeled as such.

V. Fair Play

Journalists at all times will show respect for the dignity, privacy, rights, and well-being of people encountered in the course of gathering and presenting news.

1. The news media should not communicate unofficial charges affecting reputation or moral character without giving the accused a chance to reply.

2. The news media must guard against invading a person's right to privacy.

3. The media should not pander to morbid curiosity about details of vice and crime.

4. It is the duty of news media to make prompt and complete correction of their errors.

5. Journalists should be accountable to the public for their reports and the public should be encouraged to voice its grievances against the media. Open dialogue with our readers, viewers, and listeners should be fostered.

VI. Pledge

Adherence to this code is intended to preserve and strengthen the bond of mutual trust and respect between American journalists and the American people.

The Society shall—by programs of education and other means—encourage individual journalists to adhere to these tenets, and shall encourage journalistic publications and broadcasters to recognize their responsibility to frame codes of ethics in concert with their employees to serve as guidelines in furthering these goals.

Part I—Politics:
The Press and the State

Congress shall make no law respecting an establishment of religion, or prohibiting the free exercise thereof; or abridging the freedom of speech, or of the press; or the right of the people peaceably to assemble, and to petition the Government for a redress of grievances.
—First Amendment
U.S. Constitution

I n 45 words, the founding generation set themselves and those who followed on a course unequaled in human history. At the time the First Amendment was ratified in December 1791, political thinkers, some of whose arguments are on the pages that follow, had been arguing for more than a century that ordinary citizens—the farmers, surveyers, tradespeople, artisans and the rest—were capable of governing their own lives. And in those 45 words—indeed, in only 13 if one omits for the moment the religion and assembly clauses— the framers undertook the boldest political experiment in history. A breakaway colony from the world's most powerful nation was just setting itself up as an independent sovereign state. It had staggering potential for wealth and was not burdened by centuries of European dynastic tradition. Under such auspicious circumstances, the framers committed themselves, and us, to trying to build a society of, by and for its people. There had been many other experiments in building utopian societies in the past, of course, and many would follow, but never before or since on such a grand scale. And as we are inundated daily with reminders that our computers and our satellites and our fiber-optic networks make our era an information age, it is important to note that in 1791, the builders of this bold political experiment declared a new vision for humankind. The absolute key to realizing this new vision, they said, was a free flow of information.

Hence, journalism's most important function, the one for which it was given constitutional protection, is a political one. It is a critically important happenstance of history that the American system of government, and with it the American system of journalism, came into being during a brief slice of history called the Enlightenment. This was the era in the middle of the eighteenth century in which leading intellectuals believed the power of the rational mind was not merely king, but more powerful than kings.

Of course, there had been newspapers by broad definition for centuries, even millennia, testifying to the human mind's chronic hunger for knowledge. But in the eighteenth century, when the belief in the power of knowledge reached new heights, the gathering and disseminating of information took on even greater importance. For the founding generation, those who designed the United States system of government during the very peak of the Enlightenment, the essential information for the people to know was of a very particular sort. The crucial information, the founders believed, was knowledge about government itself. The fundamental principle of the political order they were designing was that they and their successors would not be in charge of it. Instead, the citizenry would remain in charge—the people in whose name and on whose behalf they, the governors, did their work. By today's standards, the founding generation's concept of universal sovereignty was woefully inadequate, but nowhere on the planet had ultimate political power been left in as many hands as in the American experiment. The founding generation was fully aware of the historically corrupting influence of political power, and there was no guarantee that the American system would work. To give it a chance, they adopted a new model of political power-sharing proposed by a French nobleman, Charles Louis de Secondat, baron de Montesquieu. In Montesquieu's model, political power was to be divided among three branches of government, each branch helping to keep track of the other two. And as something of a fail-safe, or backup, system, the founders of the American system asked the newspaper press to watch over all three branches and report its findings back to the sovereign people. There was no guarantee that a free flow of information would make the system work, of course, but without such a flow, it was thought impossible. That was the reason the founders provided the powerful protection of the First Amendment and the reason they heavily subsidized newspapers with cheap postage and other benefits.

Over time, many readers and viewers have asked—and sometimes demanded—that journalism take on other social and cultural roles, and the industry has responded, sometimes well, sometimes poorly. But the fundamental mission remains that of keeping the government honest through critical and public scrutiny of the governors. This reader in the guiding principles of American journalism begins, therefore, where the institution itself began, with the most profound political thinkers of the Enlightenment. The essays in this section deal with fundamental questions of popular government: What is the origin of political power? What is the proper relationship between the state and its citizens? How much can and should citizens know about what their government is doing? Who is going to tell them? And who, if anyone, is going to watch over the watchdogs and make sure they are getting it right? What do we do if they get it wrong? Who is the final arbiter of which is which?

Chapter 1
John Milton
1608-1674

J ohn Milton, the great seventeenth-century English poet, is
often afforded pride of place among journalists for his ringing
defense of a free press contained in his 1644 masterpiece,
Areopagitica. Yet the short pamphlet was not so much a
philosophical declaration of proto-First Amendment principles as it
was a diatribe against those who had dared to criticize an earlier
pamphlet he had written. No doubt he was sincere, but the
circumstances surrounding the writing of this great work were hardly
the loftiest.

In 1643, when Milton was already a mature man of thirty-five
and a well-known London poet, he quite unexpectedly married a
seventeen-year-old country girl named Mary Phillips. After a month
of marriage, Milton tired of his new bride and sent her back to her
father. Some months later, Milton changed his mind and sent a
servant to fetch her. When she did not return to London with the
servant, Milton dashed off a pamphlet of indignant invective, arguing
for vastly liberalized divorce laws.

The pamphlet caused quite a stir, including denunciations from
the pulpit and demands that it be burned. The notoriety attracted the
notice of the Stationers' Company, the small fraternity of printers
who had enjoyed near total control of the printing industry in Britain
for nearly a century. Under law, anyone who wanted to publish either
had to be a member of the Stationers' Company or else get the
company's permission, or license, to publish. In this way, printers
enjoyed a virtual monopoly on the growing publishing trade, and
government got important censoring work from company printers.
But Milton had not taken his divorce pamphlet to a member of the
Stationers' Company for printing, nor had he received their

permission to print it elsewhere. Thus, the pamphlet was unlicensed, a situation roughly akin to a bootleg audiotape or a floppy disk of pirated software. Milton responded with the *Areopagitica*, denouncing the censors and the licensers in bitter and brilliant terms. It is important to note that Milton's argument was largely a religious one, in which he equated freedom of thought with orthodox Anglicanism and narrow dogmatism with Roman Catholicism.

At the time, the British Parliament was unmoved by Milton's argument. The practice of licensing, what we now call prepublication censorship, was not lifted until after England's Glorious Revolution half a century later. But Milton's soaring testament to freedom of thought has sounded down the centuries.

Areopagitica
1644

I t is of greatest concernment in the Church and Commonwealth, to have a vigilant eye how books demean themselves as well as men; and thereafter to confine, imprison, and do sharpest justice on them as malefactors: for books are not absolutely dead things, but do contain a potency of life in them to be as active as that soul was whose progeny they are; nay they do preserve as in a vial the purest efficacy and extraction of that living intellect that bred them. I know they are as lively, and as vigorously productive, as those fabulous dragon's teeth; and being sown up and down, may chance to spring up armed men. And yet on the other hand unless wariness be used, as good almost kill a man as kill a good book; who kills a man kills a reasonable creature, God's image; but he who destroys a good book, kills reason itself, kills the image of God, as it were in the eye. Many a man lives a burden to the earth; but a good book is the precious life-blood of a master spirit, embalmed and treasured up on purpose to a life beyond life. 'Tis true, no age can restore a life, whereof perhaps there is no great loss; and revolutions of ages do not oft recover the loss of a rejected truth, for the want of which whole nations fare the worse. We should be wary therefore what persecution we raise against the living labours of public men, how we spill that seasoned life of man preserved and stored up in books; since we see a kind of homicide may be thus committed, sometimes a martyrdom, and if it extend to the whole impression, a kind of massacre, whereof the execution ends not in the slaying of an elemental life, but strikes at that ethereal and fifth essence, the breath of reason itself, slays an immortality rather than a life. . . .

Dionysius Alexandrinus was, about the year 240, a person of great name in the Church for piety and learning, who had wont to avail himself much against heretics by being conversant in their books; until a certain Presbyter laid it scrupulously to his conscience, how he durst venture himself among those defiling volumes. The worthy man, loath to give offence, fell into a new debate with himself what was to be thought; when suddenly a vision sent from God, it is his own Epistle that so avers it, confirmed him in these words: Read any books whatever come to thy hands, for thou art sufficient both to judge aright, and to examine each matter. To this revelation he assented the sooner, as he confesses, because it was answerable to that of the Apostle to the Thessalonians, Prove all things, hold fast that which is good. And he might have added another remarkable saying of the same author: To the pure all things are pure, not only meats and drinks, but all kind of knowledge whether of good or evil: the knowledge cannot defile, nor consequently the books, if the will and conscience be not defiled. For books are as meats and viands are, some of good, some of evil substance; and yet God in that unapocryphal vision, said without exception, Rise, Peter, kill and eat, leaving the choice to each man's discretion. Wholesome meats to a vitiated stomach differ little or nothing from unwholesome; and best books to a naughty mind are not unappliable to occasions of evil. Bad meats will scarce breed good nourishment in the healthiest concoction; but herein the difference is of bad books, that they to a discreet and judicious reader serve in many respects to discover, to confute, to forewarn, and to illustrate. . . .

Good and evil we know in the field of this world grow up together almost inseparably; and the knowledge of good is so involved and interwoven with the knowledge of evil, and in so many cunning resemblances hardly to be discerned, that those confused seeds which were imposed on Psyche as an incessant labour to cull out, and sort asunder, were not more intermixed. It was from out the rind of one apple tasted, that the knowledge of good and evil as two twins cleaving together leapt forth into the world. And perhaps this is the doom which Adam fell into of knowing good and evil, that is to say of knowing good by evil. As therefore the state of man now is what wisdom can there be to choose, what continence to forbear without the knowledge of evil? He that can apprehend and consider vice with all her baits and seeming pleasures, and yet abstain, and yet distinguish, and yet prefer that which is truly better, he is the true warfaring Christian. I cannot praise a fugitive and cloistered virtue, unexercised and unbreathed, that never sallies out and sees her adversary, but slinks out of the race, where that immortal garland is to be run for, not without dust and heat. Assuredly we bring not innocence into the world, we bring impurity much rather: that which purifies us is trial, and trial is by what is contrary. . . . Since therefore the knowledge and survey of vice is in this world so necessary to the constituting of human virtue, and the scanning of error to the confirmation of truth, how can we more safely, and with less danger scout into the regions of sin and falsity then by reading all manner of tractates, and hearing all manner of reason? And this is the benefit which may be had of books promiscuously read. . . .

If we think to regulate printing, thereby to rectify manners, we must regulate all recreations and pastimes, all that is delightful to man. No music must be heard, no song be set or sung, but what is grave and Doric. There must be licensing dancers, that no gesture, motion, or deportment be taught our youth but what by their allowance shall be thought honest; for such Plato was provided of. It will ask more than the work of twenty licensers to examine all the lutes, the violins, and the guitars in every house; they must not be suffered to prattle as they do, but must be licensed what they may say. And who shall silence all the airs and madrigals, that whisper softness in chambers? . . .

Many there be that complain of divine Providence for suffering Adam to transgress, foolish tongues! when God gave him reason, He gave him freedom to choose, for reason is but choosing; he had been else a mere artificial Adam, such an Adam as he is in the motions. We ourselves esteem not of that obedience, or love, or gift, which is of force: God therefore left him free, set before him a provoking object, ever almost in his eyes; herein consisted his merit, herein the right of his reward, the praise of his abstinence. Wherefore did He create passions within us, pleasures round about us, but that these rightly tempered are the very ingredients of virtue? They are not skilful considerers of human things, who imagine to remove sin by removing the matter of sin. . . .

[Licensing is] the greatest discouragement and affront that can be offered to learning and to learned men. It was the complaint and lamentation of prelates, upon every least breath of a motion to remove pluralities, and distribute more equally Church revenues, that then all learning would be for ever dashed and discouraged. But as for that opinion, I never found cause to think that the tenth part of learning stood or fell with the Clergy: nor could I ever but hold it for a sordid and unworthy speech of any Churchman who had a competency left him. If therefore ye be loath to dishearten utterly and discontent, not the mercenary crew of false pretenders to learning, but the free and ingenuous sort of such as evidently were born to study, and love learning for itself, not for lucre, or any other end, but the service of God and of truth, and perhaps that lasting fame and perpetuity of praise which God and good men have consented shall be the reward of those whose published labours advance the good of mankind, then know, that so far to distrust the judgment and the honesty of one who hath but a common repute in learning, and never yet offended, as not to count him fit to print his mind without a tutor and examiner, lest he should drop a schism, or something of corruption, is the greatest displeasure and indignity to a free and knowing spirit that can be put upon him. What advantage is it to be a man over it is to be a boy at school, if we have only escaped the ferular, to come under the fescu of an *imprimatur*? if serious and elaborate writings, as if they were no more than the theme of a grammar lad under his pedagogue, must not be uttered without the cursory eyes of a temporizing and extemporizing licenser. . . .

Well knows he who uses to consider, that our faith and knowledge thrives by exercise, as well as our limbs and complexion. Truth is compared in Scripture to a streaming fountain; if her waters flow not in a perpetual progression, they sicken into a muddy pool of conformity and tradition. A man may be a heretic in the truth; and if he believe things only because his pastor says so, or the Assembly so determines, without knowing other reason, though his belief be true, yet the very truth he holds becomes his heresy. There is not any burden that some would gladlier post off to another, than the charge and care of their religion. There be, who knows not that there be of Protestants and professors who live and die in as arrant an implicit faith as any lay Papist of Loretto. . . .

For if we be sure we are in the right, and do not hold the truth guiltily, which becomes not, if we ourselves condemn not our own weak and frivolous teaching, and the people for an untaught and irreligious gadding rout, what can be more fair, than when a man judicious, learned, and of a conscience, for aught we know, as good as theirs that taught us what we know, shall not privily from house to house, which is more dangerous, but openly by writing publish to the world what his opinion is, what his reasons, and wherefore that which is now thought cannot be found? Christ urged it as wherewith to justify Himself, that He preached in public; yet writing is more public than preaching; and more easy to refutation, if need be, there being so many whose business and profession merely it is, to be the champions of Truth; which if they neglect, what can be imputed but their sloth, or inability?

Thus much we are hindered and disinured by this curse of licensing towards the true knowledge of what we seem to know. For how much it hurts and hinders the licensers themselves in the calling of their ministry, more than any secular employment, if they will discharge that office as they ought, so that of necessity they must neglect either the one duty or the other, I insist not, because it is a particular, but leave it to their own conscience, how they will decide it there.

There is yet behind of what I purposed to lay open, the incredible loss and detriment that this plot of licensing puts us to, more than if some enemy at sea should stop up all our havens and ports, and creeks, it hinders and retards the importation of our richest merchandise, Truth; nay it was first established and put in practice by antichristian malice and mystery on set purpose to extinguish, if it were possible, the light of Reformation, and to settle falsehood; little differing from that policy wherewith the Turk upholds his *Alcoran*, by the prohibition of printing. 'Tis not denied, but gladly confessed, we are to send out thanks and vows to heaven, louder than most of nations, for that great measure of truth which we enjoy, especially in those main points between us and the Pope, with his appurtenances the prelates: but he who thinks we are to pitch our tent here, and have attained the utmost prospect of reformation, that the mortal glass wherein we contemplate, can show us, till we come to beatific vision, that man by this very opinion declares, that he is yet far short of Truth.

Truth indeed came once into the world with her divine Master, and was a perfect shape most glorious to look on: but when He ascended, and His Apostles after Him were laid asleep, then straight arose a wicked race of deceivers, who as that story goes of the Egyptian Typhone with his conspirators, how they dealt with the good Osiris, took the virgin Truth, hewed her lovely form into a thousand pieces, and scattered them to the four winds. From that time ever since, the sad friends of Truth, such as durst appear, imitating the careful search that Isis made for the mangled body of Osiris, went up and down gathering up limb by limb still as they could find them. We have not yet found them all, Lords and Commons, nor ever shall do, till her Master's second coming; He shall bring together every joint and member, and shall mould them into an immortal feature of loveliness and perfection. Suffer not these licensing prohibitions to stand at every place of opportunity forbidding and disturbing them that continue seeking, that continue to do our obsequies to the torn body of our martyred saint. We boast our light; but if we look not wisely on the sun itself, it smites us into darkness. Who can discern those planets that are oft combust, and those stars of brightest magnitude that rise and set with the sun, until the opposite motion of their orbs bring them to such a place in the firmament, where they may be seen evening or morning. The light which we have gained, was given us, not to be ever staring on, but by it to discover onward things more remote from our knowledge. It is not the unfrocking of a priest, the unmitring of a bishop, and the removing him from off the Presbyterian shoulders that will make us a happy nation, no, if other things as great in the Church, and in the rule of life both economical and political be not looked into and reformed, we have looked so long upon the blaze that Zuinglius and Calvin hath beaconed up to us, that we are stark blind. There be who perpetually complain of schisms and sects, and make it such a calamity that any man dissents from their maxims. 'Tis their own pride and ignorance which causes the disturbing, who neither will hear with meekness, nor can convince, yet all must be suppressed which is not found in their *Syntagma*. They are the troublers, they are the dividers of unity, who neglect and permit not others to unite those dissevered pieces which are yet wanting to the body of Truth. To be still searching what we know not, by what we know, still closing up truth to truth as we find it (for all her body is homogeneal, and proportional), this is the golden rule in theology as well as in arithmetic, and makes up the best harmony in a church; not the forced and outward union of cold, and neutral, and inwardly divided minds. . . .

God is decreeing to begin some new and great period in His Church, even to the reforming of Reformation itself: what does He then but reveal Himself to His servants, and as His manner is, first to His Englishmen; I say as His manner is, first to us, though we mark not the methods of His counsels, we are unworthy. Behold now this vast city; a city of refuge, the mansion house of liberty, encompassed and surrounded with His protection; the shop of war hath not there more anvils and hammers waking, to fashion out the plates and instruments of armed Justice in defence of beleaguered Truth, than there be pens and heads there, sitting by their studious lamps, musing, searching, revolving new notions and ideas wherewith to present, as with their homage and their fealty, the approaching Reformation: others as fast reading, trying all things, assenting to the force of reason and convincement. What could a man require more from a nation so pliant and so prone to seek after knowledge? What wants there such a towardly and pregnant soil, but wise and faithful labourers, to make a knowing people, a nation of prophets, of sages, and of worthies? Where there is much desire to learn, there of necessity will be much arguing, much writing, many opinions; for opinion in good men is but knowledge in the making. Under these fantastic terrors of sect and schism, we wrong the earnest and zealous thirst after knowledge and understanding which God hath stirred up in this city. What some lament of, we rather should rejoice at, should rather praise this pious forwardness among men, to reassume the ill-deputed care of their religion into their own hands again. A little generous prudence, a little forbearance of one another, and some grain of charity might win all these diligences to join, and unite in one general and brotherly search after Truth; could we but forego this prelatical tradition of crowding free consciences and Christian liberties into canons and precepts of men. . . . For now the time seems come, wherein Moses the great prophet may sit in heaven rejoicing to see that memorable and glorious wish of his fulfilled, when not only our seventy Elders, but all the Lord's people are become prophets. No marvel then though some men, and some good men too perhaps, but young in goodness, as Joshua then was, envy them. They fret, and out of their own weakness are in agony, lest those divisions and subdivisions will undo us. The adversary again applauds, and waits the hour; when they have branched themselves out, saith he, small enough into parties and partitions, then will be our time. Fool! he sees not the firm root, out of which we all grow, though into branches. . . .

Methinks I see in my mind a noble and puissant nation rousing herself like a strong man after sleep, and shaking her invincible locks: methinks I see her as an eagle mewing her mighty youth, and kindling her undazzled eyes at the full midday beam; purging and unscaling her long-abused sight at the fountain itself of heavenly radiance, while the whole noise of timorous and flocking birds, with those also that love the twilight, flutter about, amazed at what she means, and in their envious gabble would prognosticate a year of sects and schisms.

What should ye do then, should ye suppress all this flowery crop of knowledge and new light sprung up and yet springing daily in this city, should ye set an oligarchy of twenty engrossers over it, to bring a famine upon our minds again, when we shall know nothing but what is measured to us by their bushel? Believe it, Lords and Commons, they who counsel ye to such a suppressing, do as good as bid ye suppress yourselves; and I will soon show how. If it be desired to know the immediate cause of all this free writing and free speaking, there cannot be assigned a truer than your own mild, and free, and human government; it is the liberty, Lords and Commons, which your own valorous and happy counsels have purchased us, liberty which is the nurse of all great wits; this is that which hath rarefied and enlightened our spirits like the influence of heaven; this is that which hath enfranchised, enlarged and lifted up our apprehensions degrees above themselves. Ye cannot make us now less capable, less knowing, less eagerly pursuing of the truth, unless ye first make youselves, that made us so, less the lovers, less the founders of our true liberty. We can grow ignorant again, brutish, formal, and slavish, as ye found us; but you then must first become that which ye cannot be, oppressive, arbitrary, and tyrannous, as they were from whom ye have freed us. That our hearts are now more capacious, our thoughts more erected to the search and expectation of greatest and exactest things, is the issue of your own virtue an abrogated and merciless law, that fathers may dispatch at will their own children.... Give me the liberty to know, to utter, and to argue freely according to consciences, above all liberties....

And now the time in special is, by privilege to write and speak what may help to the further discussing of matters in agitation. The Temple of Janus with his two controversal faces might now not insignificantly be set open. And though all the winds of doctrine were let loose to play upon the earth, so Truth be in the field, we do injuriously by licensing and prohibiting to misdoubt her strength. Let her and Falsehood grapple; who ever knew Truth put to the worst, in a free and open encounter? Her confuting is the best and surest suppressing. He who hears what praying there is for light and clearer knowledge to be sent down among us, would think of other matters to be constituted beyond the discipline of Geneva, framed and fabricked already to our hands. Yet when the new light which we beg for shines in upon us, there be who envy and oppose, if it come not first in at their casements. What a collusion is this, whenas we are exhorted by the wise man to use diligence, to seek for wisdom as for hidden treasures early and late, that another order shall enjoin us to know nothing but by statute. When a man hath been labouring the hardest labour in the deep mines of knowledge, hath furnished out his findings in all their equipage, drawn forth his reasons as it were a battle ranged, scattered and defeated all objections in his way, calls out his adversary into the plain, offers him the advantage of wind and sun, if he please; only that he may try the matter by dint of argument, for his opponents then to sulk, to lay ambushments, to keep a narrow bridge of licensing where the challenger should pass, though it be valour enough in soldiership, is but weakness and cowardice in the wars of Truth. For who knows not that Truth is strong next to the Almighty; she need no policies, no stratagems, no licensings to make her victorious, those are the shifts and the defences that error uses against her power.... We do not see that while we still affect by all means a rigid external formality, we may as soon fall again in a gross conforming stupidity, a stark and dead congealment of wood and hay and stubble forced and frozen together, which is more to the sudden degenerating of a Church than many subdichotomies of petty schisms. Not that I can think well of every light separation, or that all in a Church is to be expected gold and silver and precious stones: it is not possible for man to sever the wheat from the tares, the good fish from the other fry; that must be the angels' ministry at the end of mortal things. Yet if all cannot be of one mind, as who looks they should be? this doubtless is more wholesome, more prudent, and more Christian, that many be tolerated, rather than all compelled. I mean not tolerated Popery, and open superstition, which as it extirpates all religions and civil supremacies, so itself should be extirpate provided first that all charitable and compassionate means be used to win and regain the weak and misled: that also which is impious or evil absolutely either against faith or manners no law can possibly permit, that intends not to unlaw itself: but those neighbouring differences, or rather indifferences, are what I speak of, whether in some point of doctrine or of discipline, which though they may be many, yet need not interrupt the unity of Spirit, if we could but find among us the bond of peace. . . .

Chapter 2
Thomas Hobbes
1588-1679

T homas Hobbes, with his gloomy views of humankind and his ominous visions of an all-powerful state, is hardly the most appealing primogenitor of modern democratic theory. It is tempting to ignore Hobbes altogether and look first to the much more cheery John Locke. But it is Hobbes who developed much of the important early work in political philosophy, and to Hobbes we must turn first for the basic thought on the origin and nature of the social contract. The gradual acceptance of Hobbes's principles of the social contract—suggesting that people create government for mutual protection and, in essence, hire the governors to manage it on their behalf—led to an overturning of the then-standard political model of absolute monarchs governing by divine right. It was only under this new model that our more modern ideas of popular sovereignty—of the citizenry ultimately being in charge—is possible.

At the outbreak of the English Civil War in 1642, Hobbes feared that his outspoken preference for an absolute monarchy put him in danger from the rebels in Parliament who were then challenging Charles I for supremacy in England. Therefore, Hobbes, an Oxford-trained scholar, went into self-imposed exile in Paris, where he became a tutor to Charles, Prince of Wales, the son of Charles I and the man who would become, at the restoration of the monarchy in 1660, King Charles II. Hobbes wrote his great political treatise, *Leviathan*, during this self-imposed exile in the 1640s.

As it turned out, Hobbes probably needn't have worried. Once in power, Oliver Cromwell, leader of the Parliamentary rebels, wanted as strong a state as did the Stuart king whom he had deposed. Hobbes became a favorite both with Cromwell and with Charles II for much the same reason: Hobbes was able to take arguments about natural law, which were very much in vogue at the time, and turn them into a defense for an absolutist state.

Hobbes also anticipated by 350 years the post-Freudian argument of psychological egoism when he maintained that all people are inherently and inevitably selfish. Without a created society, he argued, people live in a state of nature, where their natural selfishness and the natural competition among them make life, in his most famous phrase, "solitary, poor, nasty, brutish, and short." The solution is the Leviathan, the ruler of the state, which he argued men would form in their own self-interest. Because of his tepid religious faith, he saw altruism as impossible and thus an all-powerful state as essential, for he believed that the same selfishness that caused people to create the Leviathan would cause them to try to overcome it as well.

Leviathan
1651

Chapter XIII: Of the natural condition of mankind as concerning their felicity, and misery

Nature hath made men so equal, in the faculties of the body, and mind; as that though there be found one man sometimes manifestly stronger in body, or of quicker mind than another; yet when all is reckoned together, the difference between man, and man, is not so considerable, as that one man can thereupon claim to himself any benefit, to which another may not pretend, as well as he. For as to the strength of body, the weakest has strength enough to kill the strongest, either by secret machination, or by confederacy with others, that are in the same danger with himself.

And as to the faculties of the mind . . . I find yet a greater equality amongst men, than that of strength. For prudence is but experience; which equal time, equally bestows on all men, in those things they equally apply themselves unto. . . .

From this equality of ability, ariseth equality of hope in the attaining of our ends. And therefore if any two men desire the same thing, which nevertheless they cannot both enjoy, they become enemies, and . . . endeavour to destroy, or subdue one another. And from hence it comes to pass, that where an invader hath no more to fear, than another man's single power; if one plant, sow, build, or possess a convenient seat, others may probably be expected to come prepared with forces united, to dispossess, and deprive him, not only of fruit of his labour, but also of his life, or liberty. And the invader again is in the like danger of another.

And from this diffidence of one another, there is no way for any man to secure himself, so reasonable, as anticipation; that is, by force, or wiles, to master the persons of all men he can, so long, till he see no other power great enough to endanger him: and this is no more than his own conservation requireth, and is generally allowed. Also because there be some, that taking pleasure in contemplating their own power in the acts of conquest, which they pursue farther than their security requires; if others, that otherwise would be glad to be at ease within modest bounds, should not by invasion increase their power, they would not be able, long time, by standing only on their defence, to subsist. And by consequence, such augmentation of dominion over men being necessary to a man's conservation, it ought to be allowed him.

Again, men have no pleasure, but on the contrary a great deal of grief, in keeping company, where there is no power able to over-awe them all. For every man looketh that his companion should value him, at the same rate he sets upon himself. . . .

So that in the nature of man, we find three principal causes of quarrel. First, competition; secondly, diffidence; thirdly, glory.

The first, maketh men invade for gain; the second, for safety; and the third, for reputation. The first use violence, to make themselves masters of other men's persons, wives, children, and cattle; the second, to defend them; the third, for trifles, as a word, a smile, a different opinion, and any other sign of undervalue, either direct in their persons, or by reflection in their kindred, their friends, their nation, their profession, or their name.

Hereby it is manifest, that during the time men live without a common power to keep them all in awe, they are in that condition which is called war; and such a war, as is of every man, against every man. For war, consisteth not in battle only, or the act of fighting; but in a tract of time, wherein the will to contend by battle is sufficiently known. . . . All other time is peace.

Whatsoever therefore is consequent to a time of war, where every man is enemy to every man; the same is consequent to the time, wherein men live without other security, than what their own strength, and their own invention shall furnish them withal. In such condition, there is no place for industry; because the fruit thereof is uncertain: and consequently no culture of the earth; no navigation, nor use of the commodities that may be imported by sea; no commodious building; no instruments of moving, and removing, such things as require much force; no knowledge of the face of the earth; no account of time; no arts; no letters; no society; and which is worst of all, continual fear, and danger of violent death; and the life of man, solitary, poor, nasty, brutish, and short. . . .

[T]hough there had never been any time, wherein particular men were in a condition of war one against another; yet in all times, kings, and persons of sovereign authority, because of their independency, are in continual jealousies, and in the state and posture of gladiators; having their weapons pointing, and their eyes fixed on one another; that is, their forts, garrisons, and guns upon the frontiers of their kingdoms; and continual spies upon their neighbours; which is a posture of war. . . .

To this war of every man, against every man, this also is consequent; that nothing can be unjust. The notions of right and wrong, justice and injustice have there no place. Where there is no common power, there is no law: where no law, no injustice. Force, and fraud, are in war the two cardinal virtues. Justice, and injustice are none of the faculties neither of the body, nor mind. If they were, they might be in a man that were alone in the world, as well as his senses, and passions. They are qualities, that relate to men in society, not in solitude. It is consequent also to the same condition, that there be no propriety, no dominion, no mine and thine distinct; but only that to be every man's, that he can get; and for so long, as he can keep it. And thus much for the ill condition, which man by mere nature is actually placed in; though with a possibility to come out of it, consisting partly in the passions, partly in his reason.

The passions that incline men to peace, are fear of death; desire of such things as are necessary to commodious living; and a hope by their industry to obtain them. And reason suggesteth convenient articles of peace, upon which men may be drawn to agreement. These articles, are they, which otherwise are called the Laws of Nature: whereof I shall speak more particularly, in the two following chapters.

Chapter XIV: Of the first and second natural laws, and of contracts

The right of nature, which writers commonly call *jus naturale*, is the liberty each man hath, to use his own power, as he will himself, for the preservation of his own nature; that is to say, of his own life; and consequently, of doing anything, which in his own judgment, and reason, he shall conceive to be the aptest means thereunto.

By liberty, is understood, according to the proper signification of the word, the absence of external impediments: which impediments, may oft take away part of a man's power to do what he would; but cannot hinder him from using the power left him, according as his judgment, and reason shall dictate to him.

A law of nature, *lex naturalis*, is a precept or general rule, found out by reason, by which a man is forbidden to do that, which is destructive of his life, or taketh away the means of preserving the same; and to omit that, by which he thinketh it may be best preserved. For though they that speak of this subject, use to confound jus, and lex, right and law: yet they ought to be distinguished; because right, consisteth in liberty to do, or to forbear; whereas law, determineth, and bindeth to one of them: so that law, and right, differ as much, as obligation, and liberty; which in one and the same matter are inconsistent.

And because the condition of man, as hath been declared in the precedent chapter, is a condition of war of every one against every one; in which case every one is governed by his own reason; and there is nothing he can make use of, that may not be a help unto him, in preserving his life against his enemies; it followeth, that in such a condition, every man has a right to every thing; even to one another's body. And therefore, as long as this natural right of every man to every thing endureth, there can be no security to any man, how strong or wise soever he be, of living out the time, which nature ordinarily alloweth men to live. And consequently it is a precept, or general rule of reason, that every man, ought to endeavour peace, as far as he has hope of obtaining it; and when he cannot obtain it, that he may seek, and use, all helps, and advantages of war. The first branch of which rule, containeth the first, and fundamental law of nature; which is, to seek peace, and follow it. The second, the sum of the right of nature; which is, by all means we can, to defend ourselves.

From this fundamental law of nature, by which men are commanded to endeavour peace, is derived this second law; that a man be willing, when others are so too, as far forth, as for peace, and defence of himself he shall think it necessary, to lay down this right to all things; and be contented with so much liberty against other men, as he would allow other men against himself. For as long as every man holdeth this right, of doing any thing he liketh; so long are all men in the condition of war. But if other men will not lay down their right, as well as he; then there is no reason for anyone, to divest himself of his: for that were to expose himself to prey, which no man is bound to, rather than to dipose himself to peace. This is that law of the Gospel; whatsoever you require that others should do to you, that do ye to them. . . .

To lay down a man's right to anything, is to divest himself of the liberty, of hindering another of the benefit of his own right to the same. . . .

Right is laid aside, either by simply renouncing it; or by transferring it to another. By simply renouncing; when he cares not to whom the benefit thereof redoundeth. By transferring; when he intendeth the benefit thereof to some certain person, or persons. And when a man hath in either manner abandoned, or granted away his right; then is he said to be obliged, or bound, not to hinder those, to whom such right is granted, or abandoned, from the benefit of it . . it is called injustice, and injury, voluntarily to undo that, which from the beginning he had voluntarily done. . . .

Whensoever a man transferreth his right, or renounceth it; it is either in consideration of some right reciprocally transferred to himself; or for some other good he hopeth for thereby. For it is a voluntary act: and of the voluntary acts of every man, the object is some good to himself. And therefore there be some rights, which no man can be understood by any words, or other signs, to have abandoned, or transferred. As first a man cannot lay down the right of resisting them, that assault him by force, to take away his life; because he cannot be understood to aim thereby, at any good to himself. . . . [T]he motive, and end for which this renouncing, and transferring of right is introduced, is nothing else but the security of a man's person, in his life, and in the means of so preserving life as not to be weary of it. . . . The mutual transferring of right, is that which men call contract. . . .

[O]ne of the contractors, may deliver the thing contracted for on his part, and leave the other to perform his part at some determinate time after, and in the mean time be trusted; and then the contract on his part, is called pact, or covenant: or both parts may contract now, to perform hereafter: in which cases, he that is to perform in time to come, being trusted, his performance is called keeping of promise, or faith; and the failing of performance, if it be voluntary, violation of faith. . . .

If a convenant be made, wherein neither of the parties perform presently, but trust one another; in the condition of mere nature, which is a condition of war of every man against every man, upon any reasonable suspicion, it is void: but if there be a common power set over them both, with right and force sufficient to compel performance, it is not void. For he that performeth first, has no assurance the other will perform after; because the bonds of words are too weak to bridle men's ambition, avarice, anger, and other passions, without the fear of some coercive power; which in the condition of mere nature, where all men are equal, and judges of the justness of their own fears, cannot possibly be supposed. And therefore he which performeth first, does but betray himself to his enemy; contrary to the right, he can never abandon, of defending his life, and means of living.

But in a civil estate, where there is a power set up to constrain those that would otherwise violate their faith, that fear is no more reasonable; and for that cause, he which by the covenant is to perform first, is obliged so to do. . . .

The force of words, being, as I have formerly noted, too weak to hold men to the performance of their covenants: there are in man's nature, but two imaginable helps to strengthen it. And those are either a fear of the consequence of breaking their word; or a glory, or pride in appearing not to need to break it. This latter is a generosity too rarely found to be presumed on, especially in the pursuers of wealth, command, or sensual pleasure; which are the greatest part of mankind. The passion to be reckoned upon, is fear; whereof there be two very general objects: one, the power of spirits invisible; the other, the power of those men they shall therein offend. Of these two, though the former be the greater power, yet the fear of the latter is commonly the greater fear. The fear of the former is in every man, his own religion: which hath place in the nature of man before civil society. The latter hath not so; at least not place enough, to keep men to their promises; because in the condition of mere nature, the inequality of power is not discerned, but by the event of battle. So that before the time of civil society, or in the interruption thereof by war, there is nothing can strengthen a covenant of peace agreed on, against the temptation of avarice, ambition, lust, or other strong desire, but the fear of that invisible power, which they every one worship as God; and fear as a revenger of their perfidy. . . .

Chapter XV: Of other laws of nature

From that law of nature, by which we are obliged to transfer to another, such rights, as being retained, hinder the peace of mankind, there followeth a third; which is this, that men perform their covenants made: without which covenants are in vain, and but empty words; and the right of all men to all things remaining, we are still in the condition of war.

And in this law of nature, consisteth the fountain and original of justice. For where no covenant hath preceded, there hath no right been transferred, and every man has right to every thing; and consequently, no action can be unjust. But when a covenant is made, then to break it is unjust: and the definition of injustice, is no other than the not performance of covenant. . . .

[B]efore the names of just, and unjust can have place, there must be some coercive power, to compel men equally to performance of their covenants, by the terror of some punishment, greater than the benefit they expect by the breach of their covenant; and to make good that propriety, which by mutual contract men acquire, in recompense of the universal right they abandon: and such power there is none before the erection of a commonwealth. And this is also to be gathered out of the ordinary definition of justice in the Schools: for they say, that justice is the constant will of giving to every man his own. And therefore where there is no own, that is no propriety, there is no injustice; and where is no coercive power erected, that is, where there is no commonwealth, there is no propriety; all men having right to all things: therefore where there is no commonwealth, there nothing is unjust. So that the nature of justice, consisteth in keeping of valid covenants: but the validity of covenants begins not but with the constitution of a civil power, sufficient to compel men to keep them: and then it is also that propriety begins. . . .

Justice therefore, that is to say, keeping of covenant, is a rule of reason, by which we are forbidden to do any thing destructive to our life; and consequently a law of nature. . . .

Chapter XVII: Of the causes, generation, and definition of commonwealth

. . . [T]he laws of nature, as justice, equity, modesty, mercy, and in sum, doing to others, as we would be done to, of themselves, without the terror of some power, to cause them to be observed, are contrary to our natural passions, that carry us to partiality, pride, revenge, and the like. And covenants, without the sword, are but words, and of no strength to secure a man at all. Therefore . . . every man will, and may lawfully rely on his own strength and art, for caution against all other men. And in all places, where men have lived by small families, to rob and spoil one another, has been a trade, and so far from being reputed against the law of nature, that the greater spoils they gained, the greater was their honour; and men observed no other laws therein, but the laws of honour; that is, to abstain from cruelty, leaving to men their lives, and instruments of husbandry. And as small families did then; so now do cities and kingdoms which are but greater families, for their own security, enlarge their dominions, upon all pretences of danger, and fear of invasion, or assistance that may be given to invaders, and endeavour as much as they can, to subdue, or weaken their neighbours, by open force, and secret arts, for want of other caution, justly; and are remembered for it in after ages with honour.

Nor is it the joining together of a small number of men, that gives them this security; because in small numbers, small additions on the one side or the other, make the advantage of strength so great, as is sufficient to carry the victory; and therefore gives encouragement to an invasion. The multitude sufficient to confide in for our security, is not determined by any certain number, but by comparison with the enemy we fear; and is then sufficient, when the odds of the enemy is not of so visible and conspicuous moment, to determine the event of war, as to move him to attempt. . . .

Nor is it enough for the security, which men desire should last all the time of their life, that they be governed, and directed by one judgment, for a limited time; as in one battle, or one war. For though they obtain a victory by their unanimous endeavour against a foreign enemy; yet afterwards, when either they have no common enemy, or he that by one part is held for an enemy, is by another part held for a friend, they must needs by the difference of their interests dissolve, and fall again into a war amongst themselves.

It is true, that certain living creatures, as bees, and ants, live sociably one with another, which are therefore by Aristotle numbered amongst political creatures; and yet have no other direction, than their particular judgments and appetites; nor speech, whereby one of them can signify to another, what he thinks expedient for the common benefit: and therefore some man may perhaps desire to know, why mankind cannot do the same. To which I answer,

First, that men are continually in competition for honour and dignity, which these creatures are not; and consequently amongst men there ariseth on that ground, envy and hatred, and finally war; but amongst these not so.

Secondly, that amongst these creatures, the common good differeth not from the private; and being by nature inclined to their private, they procure thereby the common benefit. But man, whose joy consisteth in comparing himself with other men, can relish nothing but what is eminent.

Thirdly, that these creatures, having not, as man, the use of reason, do not see, nor think they see any fault, in the administration of their common business; whereas amongst men, there are very many, that think themselves wiser, and able to govern the public, better than the rest; and these strive to reform and innovate, one this way, another that way; and thereby bring it into distraction and civil war.

Fourthly, that these creatures, though they have some use of voice, in making known to one another their desires, and other affections; yet they want that art of words, by which some men can represent to others, that which is good, in the likeness of evil; and evil, in the likeness of good; and augment, or diminish the apparent greatness of good and evil; discontenting men, and troubling their peace at their pleasure.

Fifthly, irrational creatures cannot distinguish between injury, and damage; and therefore as long as they be at ease, they are not offended with their fellows: whereas man is then most troublesome, when he is most at ease: for then it is that he loves to shew his wisdom, and control the actions of them that govern the commonwealth.

Lastly, the agreement of these creatures is natural; that of men, is by covenant only, which is artificial: and therefore it is no wonder if there be somewhat else required, besides covenant, to make their agreement constant and lasting; which is a common power, to keep them in awe, and to direct their actions to the common benefit.

The only way to erect such a common power, as may be able to defend them from the invasion of foreigners, and the injuries of one another, and thereby to secure them in such sort, as that by their own industry, and by the fruits of the earth, they may nourish themselves and live contentedly; is, to confer all their power and strength upon one man, or upon one assembly of men, that may reduce all their wills, by plurality of voices, unto one will: which is as much as to say, to appoint one man, or assembly of men, to bear their person; and every one to own, and acknowledge himself to be author of whatsoever he that so beareth their person, shall act, or cause to be acted, in those things which concern the common peace and safety; and therein to submit their wills, every one to his will, and their judgments, to his judgment. This is more than consent, or concord; it is a real unity of them all, in one and the same person, made by covenant of every man with every man, in such manner, as if every man should say to every man, I authorize and give up my right of governing myself, to this man, or to this assembly of men, on this condition, that thou give up thy right to him, and authorize all his actions in like manner. This done, the multitude so united in one person, is called a commonwealth, in Latin *civitas*. This is the generation of that great leviathan, or rather, to speak more reverently, of that mortal god, to which we owe under the immortal God, our peace and defence. For by this authority, given him by every particular man in the commonwealth, he hath the use of so much power and strength conferred on him, that by terror thereof, he is enabled to perform the wills of them all, to peace at home, and mutual aid against their enemies abroad. And in him consisteth the essence of the commonwealth; which, to define it, is one person, of whose acts a great multitude, by mutual covenants one with another, have made themselves every one the author, to the end he may use the strength and means of them all, as he shall think expedient, for their peace and common defence.

And he that carrieth this person, is called sovereign, and said to the sovereign power; and every one besides, his subject.

The attaining to this sovereign power, is by two ways. One, by natural force; as when a man maketh his children, to submit themselves, and their children, to his government, as being able to destroy them if they refuse; or by war subdueth his enemies to his will, giving them their lives on that condition. The other, is when men agree amongst themselves, to submit to some man, or assembly of men, voluntarily, on confidence to be protected by him against all others. This latter, may be called a political commonwealth, or commonwealth by institution; and the former, a commonwealth by acquisition. . . .

Chapter 3
John Locke
1632-1704

I f Thomas Hobbes is properly associated politically with Charles II, the would-be divine-right absolutist, and with Oliver Cromwell, the military dictator, then John Locke is rightly tied to William and Mary, the only British rulers who took the throne by invitation rather than by conquest or by dynastic inheritance. The shift in power away from the crown, inherent in the notion that monarchs can be hired and fired, is central to the difference between Hobbes and Locke. This shift is crucial to the development of modern democratic theory, including the all-important role to be played by a free press.

Locke was an extraordinarily versatile and talented figure—a professor of Greek, a physician, an economist, a popular and venerated philosopher, an education reformer, and a diplomat, among other things. He is widely, though not universally, believed to be the author of the key arguments presented by parliamentary reformers in the 1695 debates that ended the British practice of licensing (what Milton had argued for so forcefully half a century before and what we would call prepublication censorship.)

But it is as a political philosopher that Locke is, for the present purposes, more important still. During most of the short and turbulent reign of James II (1685-88), he lived in self-imposed exile in Holland for fear of arrest and prosecution as a critic of absolutism. Included in his circle of friends and associates was Mary Stuart, a niece of James II and the wife of Prince William of Orange. When William and Mary assumed the throne in 1688, Locke returned to England. Three years later, he published his *Two Treatises of Civil Government*. The first treatise was a rebuttal to a defense of absolutism entitled *Patriarcha* by Sir Robert Filmer, now deservedly obscure except as a Lockean foil. In the second, he laid out the principles of a limited monarchy subject to the will of the subjects. It was essentially a philosophic justification of the Glorious Revolution that had brought William and Mary to the throne. In it, he adopted, in part, Hobbes's idea of governments evolving from humankind's natural state. But while Hobbes argued for an absolute state, Locke argued for a very limited one, leaving to the citizenry the ultimate right to select their rulers, judge their conduct and, if need be, replace them. Thus, Locke defended the ultimate right of revolution, one of many Lockean notions the Colonial revolutionaries cited at the time of the American Revolution.

A critical difference between Hobbes and Locke lies in the two men's religious views. While Hobbes's religious enthusiasm was, by the standards of his own time, so tepid that he was widely denounced as an atheist, Locke was a thoroughgoing Anglican. In Hobbes's social order, religion was relatively unimportant, while Locke saw religious training as essential to the proper moral development needed for a limited state. An extremely limited state was possible in Locke's view because its citizens were moral agents. In Hobbes's much bleaker and more degenerate world, people were not to be trusted with the ultimate power of sovereignty, final control over their lives and destinies. This is a crucial difference in determining the moral right to information—whether government has a right to know about the activities of its citizens or whether the citizens have a right to know about the activities of their government.

On Civil Government: The Second Treatise
1691

Chapter II: Of the state of nature

To understand political power right, and derive it from its original, we must consider what state all men are naturally in, and that is a state of perfect freedom to order their actions and dispose of their possessions and persons as they think fit, within the bounds of the law of nature, without asking leave or depending upon the will of any other man.

A state also of equality, wherein all the power and jurisdiction is reciprocal, no one having more than another; there being nothing more evident than that creatures of the same species and rank, promiscuously born to all the same advantages of nature and the use of the same faculties, should also be equal one amongst another without subordination or subjection; unless the lord and master of them all should, by any manifest declaration of his will, set one above another, and confer on him by an evident and clear appointment an undoubted right to dominion and sovereignty....

But though this be a state of liberty, yet it is not a state of licence; though man in that state have an uncontrollable liberty to dispose of his person or possessions, yet he has not liberty to destroy himself, or so much as any creature in his possession, but where some nobler use than its bare preservation calls for it. The state of nature has a law of nature to govern it which obliges every one; and reason, which is that law, teaches all mankind who will but consult it that, being all equal and independent, no one ought to harm another in his life, health, liberty, or possessions; for men being all the workmanship of one omnipotent and infinitely wise Maker—all the servants of one sovereign master, sent into the world by his order, and about his business—they are his property whose workmanship they are, made to last during his, not one another's, pleasure; and being furnished with like faculties, sharing all in one community of nature, there cannot be supposed any such subordination among us that may authorize us to destroy another, as if we were made for one another's uses as the inferior ranks of creatures are for ours. Every one, as he is bound to preserve himself and not to quit his station wilfully, so by the like reason, when his own preservation comes not in competition, ought he, as much as he can, to preserve the rest of mankind, and may not, unless it be to do justice to an offender, take away or impair the life, or what tends to the preservation of life: the liberty, health, limb, or goods of another.

And that all men may be restrained from invading others' rights and from doing hurt to one another, and the law of nature be observed which willeth the peace and preservation of all mankind, the execution of the law of nature is, in that state, put into every man's hands, whereby everyone has a right to punish the transgressors of that law to such a degree as may hinder its violation; for the law of nature would, as all other laws that concern men in this world, be in vain, if there were nobody that in the state of nature had a power to execute that law and thereby preserve the innocent and restrain offenders. And if any one in the state of nature may punish another for any evil he has done, every one may do so; for in that state of perfect equality where naturally there is no superiority or jurisdiction of one over another, what any may do in prosecution of that law, every one must needs have a right to do.

And thus in the state of nature one man comes by a power over another; but yet no absolute or arbitrary power to use a criminal, when he has got him in his hands, according to the passionate heats or boundless extravagency of his own will; but only to retribute to him, so far as calm reason and conscience dictate, what is proportionate to his transgression, which is so much as may serve for reparation and restraint; for these two are the only reasons why one man may lawfully do harm to another, which is that we call punishment. In transgressing the law of nature, the offender declares himself to live by another rule than that of reason and common equity, which is that measure God has set to the actions of men for their mutual security; and so he becomes dangerous to mankind, the tie which is to secure them from injury and violence being slighted and broken by him. Which being a trespass against the whole species and the peace and safety of it provided for by the law of nature, every man upon this score, by the right he hath to preserve mankind in general, may restrain, or, where it is necessary, destroy things noxious to them, and so may bring such evil on any one who hath transgressed that law, as may make him repent the doing of it and thereby deter him, and by his example others, from doing the like mischief. And in this case, and upon this ground, every man hath a right to punish the offender and be executioner of the law of nature...

Besides the crime which consists in violating the law and varying from the right rule of reason, whereby a man so far becomes degenerate and declares himself to quit the principles of human nature and to be a noxious creature, there is commonly injury done to some person or other, and some other man receives damage by his transgression; in which case he who hath received any damage has, besides the right of punishment common to him with other men, a particular right to seek reparation from him that has done it; and any other person, who finds it just, may also join with him that is injured and assist him in recovering from the offender so much as may make satisfaction for the harm he has suffered.

From these two distinct rights—the one of punishing the crime for restraint and preventing the like offence, which right of punishing is in everybody; the other of taking reparation, which belongs only to the injured party—comes it to pass that the magistrate, who by being magistrate hath the common right of punishing put into his hands, can often, where the public good demands not the execution of the law, remit the punishment of criminal offences by his own authority, but yet cannot remit the satisfaction due to any private man for the damage he has received. That he who has suffered the damage has a right to demand in his own name, and he alone can remit; the damnified person has this power of appropriating to himself the goods or service of the offender by right of self-preservation, as every man has a power to punish the crime to prevent its being committed again, by the right he has of preserving all mankind, and doing all reasonable things he can in order to that end; and thus it is that every man, in the state of nature, has a power to kill a murderer, both to deter others from doing the like injury, which no reparation can compensate, by the example of the punishment that attends it from everybody, and also to secure men from the attempts of a criminal who, having renounced reason—the common rule and measure God hath given to mankind—hath, by the unjust violence and slaughter he hath committed upon one, declared war against all mankind. . . .

Chapter III: Of the state of war

The state of war is a state of enmity and destruction; and, therefore, declaring by word or action, not a passionate and hasty, but a sedate, settled design upon another man's life, puts him in a state of war with him against whom he has declared such an intention, and so has exposed his life to the other's power to be taken away by him, or anyone that joins with him in his defence and espouses his quarrel; it being reasonable and just I should have a right to destroy that which threatens me with destruction; for, by the fundamental law of nature, man being to be preserved as much as possible when all cannot be preserved, the safety of the innocent is to be preferred; and one may destroy a man who makes war upon him, or has discovered an enmity to his being, for the same reason that he may kill a wolf or a lion, because such men are not under the ties of the common law of reason, have no other rule but that of force and violence, and so may be treated as beasts of prey, those dangerous and noxious creatures that will be sure to destroy him whenever he falls into their power.

And hence it is that he who attempts to get another man into his absolute power does thereby put himself into a state of war with him, it being to be understood as a declaration of a design upon his life; for I have reason to conclude that he who would get me into his power without my consent would use me as he pleased when he got me there, and destroy me, too, when he had a fancy to it; for nobody can desire to have me in his absolute power unless it be to compel me by force to that which is against the right of my freedom, *i.e.*, make me a slave. To be free from such force is the only security of my preservation; and reason bids me look on him as an enemy to my preservation who would take away that freedom which is the fence to it; so that he who makes an attempt to enslave me thereby puts himself into a state of war with me. He that, in the state of nature, would take away the freedom that belongs to any one in that state, must necessarily be supposed to have a design to take away everything else, that freedom being the foundation of all the rest; as he that in the state of society, would take away the freedom belonging to those of that society or commonwealth, must be supposed to design to take away from them everything else, and so be looked on as in a state of war.

This makes it lawful for a man to kill a thief who has not in the least hurt him, nor declared any design upon his life any farther than, by the use of force, so to get him in his power as to take away his money, or what he pleases, from him; because, using force where he has no right to get me into his power, let his pretence be what it will, I have no reason to suppose that he who would take away my liberty would not, when he had me in his power, take away everything else. And therefore it is lawful for me to treat him as one who has put himself into a state of war with me, i.e., kill him if I can; for to that hazard does he justly expose himself whoever introduces a state of war and is aggressor in it.

And here we have the plain difference between the state of nature and the state of war which, however some men have confounded, are as far distant as a state of peace, good-will, mutual assistance, and preservation, and a state of enmity, malice, violence, and mutual destruction are one from another. Men living together according to reason, without a common superior on earth with authority to judge between them, is properly the state of nature. But force, or a declared design of force, upon the person of another, where there is no common superior on earth to appeal to for relief, is the state of war; and it is the want of such an appeal gives a man the right of war even against an aggressor, though he be in society and a fellow subject. Thus a thief, whom I cannot harm but by appeal to the law for having stolen all that I am worth, I may kill when he sets on me to rob me but of my horse or coat; because the law, which was made for my preservation, where it cannot interpose to secure my life from present force, which, if lost, is capable of no reparation, permits me my own defence and the right of war, a liberty to kill the aggressor, because the aggressor allows not time to appeal to our common judge, nor the decision of the law, for remedy in a case where the mischief may be irreparable. Want of a common judge with authority puts all men in a state of nature; force without right upon a man's person makes a state of war both where there is, and is not, a common judge. . . .

To avoid this state of war—wherein there is no appeal but to heaven, and wherein every the least difference is apt to end, where there is no authority to decide between the contenders—is one great reason of men's putting themselves into society and quitting the state of nature; for where there is an authority, a power on earth from which relief can be had by appeal, there the continuance of the state of war is excluded, and the controversy is decided by that power. . . .

Chapter V: Of property

Whether we consider natural reason, which tells us that men, being once born, have a right to their preservation, and consequently to meat and drink and such other things as nature affords for their subsistence; or revelation, which gives us an account of those grants God made of the world to Adam, and to Noah and his sons; it is very clear that God, as King David says (Psal. CXV. 16), "has given the earth to the children of men," given it to mankind in common. But this being supposed, it seems to some a very great difficulty how any one should ever come to have a property in anything. . . .

God, who hath given the world to men in common, hath also given them reason to make use of it to the best advantage of life and convenience. The earth and all that is therein is given to men for the support and comfort of their being. And though all the fruits it naturally produces and beasts it feeds belong to mankind in common, as they are produced by the spontaneous hand of nature; and nobody has originally a private dominion exclusive of the rest of mankind in any of them, as they are thus in their natural state; yet, being given for the use of men, there must of necessity be a means to appropriate them some way or other before they can be of any use or at all beneficial to any particular man. The fruit or venison which nourishes the wild Indian, who knows no enclosure and is still a tenant in common, must be his, and so his, i.e., a part of him, that another can no longer have any right to it before it can do him any good for the support of his life.

Though the earth and all inferior creatures be common to all men, yet every man has a property in his own person; this nobody has any right to but himself. The labor of his own body and the work of his hands, we may say, are properly his. Whatsoever then he removes out of the state that nature hath provided and left it in, he hath mixed his labor with, and joined to it something that is his own, and thereby makes it his property. It being by him removed from the common state nature hath placed it in, it hath by this labor something annexed to it that excludes the common right of other men. For this labor being the unquestionable property of the laborer, no man but he can have a right to what that is once joined to, at least where there is enough and as good left in common for others.

He that is nourished by the acorns he picked up under an oak, or the apples he gathered from the trees in the wood, has certainly appropriated them to himself. Nobody can deny but the nourishment is his. I ask, then, when did they begin to be his? when he digested? or when he ate? or when he boiled? or when he brought them home? or when he picked them up? And it is plain, if the first gathering made them not his, nothing else could. That labor put a distinction between them and common; that added something to them more then nature, the common mother of all, had done; and so they became his private right. And will anyone say he had no right to those acorns or apples he thus appropriated, because he had not the consent of all mankind to make them his? Was it a robbery thus to assume to himseif what belonged to all in common? If such a consent as that was necessary, man had starved, notwithstanding the plenty God had given him. We see in commons, which remain so by compact, that it is the taking any part of what is common and removing it out of the state nature leaves it in which begins the property, without which the common is of no use. And the taking of this or that part does not depend on the express consent of all the commoners. Thus the grass my horse has bit, the turfs my servant has cut, and the ore I have digged in any place where I have a right to them in common with others, become my property without the assignation or consent of anybody. The labor that was mine, removing them out of that common state they were in, hath fixed my property in them. . . .

It will perhaps be objected to this that "if gathering the acorns, or other fruits of the earth, etc., makes a right to them, then any one may engross as much as he will." To which I answer: not so. The same law of nature that does by this means give us property does also bound that property, too. "God has given us all things richly" (I Tim. vi. 17), is the voice of reason confirmed by inspiration. But how far has he given it us? To enjoy. As much as any one can make use of to any advantage of life before it spoils, so much he may by his labor fix a property in; whatever is beyond this is more than his share, and belongs to others. Nothing was made by God for man to spoil or destroy. And thus, considering the plenty of natural provisions there was a long time in the world, and the few spenders, and to how small a part of that provision the industry of one man could extend itself and engross it to the prejudice of others, especially keeping within the bounds set by reason of what might serve for his use, there could be then little room for quarrels or contentions about property so established.

But the chief matter of property being now not the fruits of the earth and the beasts that subsist on it, but the earth itself, as that which takes in and carries with it all the rest, I think it is plain that property in that, too, is acquired as the former. As much land as a man tills, plants, improves, cultivates, and can use the product of, so much is his property. He by his labor does, as it were, enclose it from the common. . . .

Nor was this appropriation of any parcel of land by improving it any prejudice to any other man, since there was still enough and as good left, and more than the yet unprovided could use. So that, in effect, there was never the less left for others because of his enclosure for himself; for he that leaves as much as another can make use of does as good as take nothing at all. Nobody could think himself injured by the drinking of another man, through he took a good draught, who had a whole river of the same water left him to quench his thirst; and the case of land and water, where there is enough for both, is perfectly the same.

God gave the world to men in common; but since he gave it them for their benefit and the greatest conveniences of life they were capable to draw from it, it cannot be supposed he meant it should always remain common and uncultivated. He gave it to the use of the industrious and rational—and labor was to be his title to it. . . . Nor is it so strange, as perhaps before consideration it may appear, that the property of labor should be able to overbalance the community of land; for it is labor indeed that put the difference of value on everything; and let any one consider what the difference is between an acre of land planted with tobacco or sugar, sown with wheat or barley, and an acre of the same land lying in common, without any husbandry upon it, and he will find that the improvement of labor makes the far greater part of the value. I think it will be but a very modest computation to say that, of the products of the earth useful to the life of man, nine-tenths are the effects of labor; nay, if we will rightly estimate things as they come to our use and cast up the several expenses about them, what in them is purely owing to nature, and what to labor, we shall find that in most of them ninety-nine hundredths are wholly to be put on the account of labor. . . .

The greatest part of things really useful to the life of man, and such as the necessity of subsisting made the first commoners of the world look after, as it doth the Americans now, are generally things of short duration, such as, if they are not consumed by use, will decay and perish of themselves; gold, silver, and diamonds are things that fancy or agreement hath put the value on, more than real use and the necessary support of life. Now of those good things which nature hath provided in common, every one had a right, as hath been said, to as much as he could use, and property in all that he could effect with his labor; all that his industry could extend to, to alter from the state nature had put it in, was his. He that gathered a hundred bushels of acorns or apples had thereby a property in them; they were his goods as soon as gathered. He was only to look that he used them before they spoiled, else he took more than his share and robbed others. And indeed it was a foolish thing, as well as dishonest, to hoard up more than he could make use of. If he gave away a part to anybody else so that it perished not uselessly in his possession, these he also made use of. And if he also bartered away plums that would have rotted in a week for nuts that would last good for his eating a whole year, he did no injury; he wasted not the common stock, destroyed no part of the portion of the goods that belonged to others, so long as nothing perished uselessly in his hands. Again, if he would give his nuts for a piece of metal, pleased with its colour, or exchange his sheep for shells, or wool for a sparkling pebble or a diamond, and keep those by him all his life, he invaded not the right of others; he might heap as much of these durable things as he pleased; the exceeding of the bounds of his just property not lying in the largeness of his possession, but the perishing of anything uselessly in it.

And thus came in the use of money—some lasting thing that men might keep without spoiling, and that by mutual consent men would take in exchange for the truly useful but perishable supports of life. . . .

Chapter VII: Of political or civil society

. . . Man, being born, as has been proved, with a title to perfect freedom and uncontrolled enjoyment of all the rights and privileges of the law of nature equally with any other man or number of men in the world, hath by nature a power not only to preserve his property—that is, his life, liberty, and estate—against the injuries and attempts of other men, but to judge of and punish the breaches of that law in others as he is persuaded the offence deserves, even with death itself in crimes where the heinousness of the fact in his opinion requires it. But because no political society can be, nor subsist, without having in itself the power to preserve the property and, in order thereunto, punish the offences of all those of that society, there and there only is political society where every one of the members hath quitted his natural power, resigned it up into the hands of the community in all cases that excludes him not from appealing for protection to the law established by it. And thus, all private judgment of every particular member being excluded, the community comes to be umpire by settled standing rules, indifferent and the same to all parties, and by men having authority from the community for the execution of those rules, decides all the differences that may happen between any members of that society concerning any matter of right, and punishes those offences which any member hath committed against the society with such penalties as the law has established; whereby it is easy to discern who are, and who are not, in political society together. Those who are united into one body and have a common established law and judicature to appeal to, with authority to decide controversies between them and punish offenders, are in civil society one with another; but those who have no such common appeal, I mean on earth, are still in the state of nature, each being, where there is no other, judge for himself and executioner, which is, as I have before shown it, the perfect state of nature.

And thus the commonwealth comes by power to set down what punishment shall belong to the several transgressions which they think worthy of it committed amongst the members of that society—which is the power of making laws—as well as it has the power to punish any injury done unto any of its members by any one that is not of it—which is the power of war and peace—and all this for the preservation of the property of all the members of that society as far as is possible. But though every man who has entered into civil society and is become a member of any commonwealth has thereby quitted his power to punish offences against the law of nature in prosecution of his own private judgment, yet, with the judgment of offences which he has given up to the legislative in all cases where he can appeal to the magistrate, he has given a right to the commonwealth to employ his force for the execution of the judgments of the commonwealth, whenever he shall be called to it; which, indeed, are his own judgment, they being made by himself or his representative. And herein we have the origin of the legislative and executive power of civil society which is to judge by standing laws how far offences are to be punished when committed within the commonwealth, and also to determine, by occasional judgments founded on the present circumstances of the fact, how far injuries from without are to be vindicated. . . .

Chapter IX: Of the ends of political society and government

If man in the state of nature be so free, as has been said, if he be absolute lord of his own person and possessions, equal to the greatest, and subject to nobody, why will he part with his freedom, why will he give up his empire and subject himself to the dominion and control of any other power? To which it is obvious to answer that though in the state of nature he hath such a right, yet the enjoyment of it is very uncertain and constantly exposed to the invasion of others; for all being kings as much as he, every man his equal, and the greater part no strict observers of equity and justice, the enjoyment of the property he has in this state is very unsafe, very unsecure. This makes him willing to quit a condition which, however free, is full of fears and continual dangers; and it is not without reason that he seeks out and is willing to join in society with others who are already united, or have a mind to unite, for the mutual preservation of their lives, liberties, and estates, which I call by the general name "property."

The great and chief end, therefore, of men's uniting into commonwealths and putting themselves under government is the preservation of their property. To which in the state of nature there are many things wanting:

First, There wants an established, settled, known law, received and allowed by common consent to be the standard of right and wrong and the common measure to decide all controversies between them; for though the law of nature be plain and intelligible to all rational creatures, yet men, being biased by their interest as well as ignorant for want of studying it, are not apt to allow of it as a law binding to them in the application of it to their particular cases.

Secondly, In the state of nature there wants a known and indifferent judge with authority to determine all difference according to the established law; for every one in that state being both judge and executioner of the law of nature, men being partial to themselves, passion and revenge is very apt to carry them too far and with too much heat in their own cases, as well as negligence and unconcernedness to make them too remiss in other men's.

Thirdly, In the state of nature, there often wants power to back and support the sentence when right, and to give it due execution. They who by any injustice offend will seldom fail, where they are able, by force, to make good their injustice; such resistance many times makes the punishment dangerous and frequently destructive to those who attempt it.

Thus mankind, notwithstanding all the privileges of the state of nature, being but in an ill condition while they remain in it, are quickly driven into society. Hence it comes to pass that we seldom find any number of men live any time together in this state. The inconveniences that they are therein exposed to by the irregular and uncertain exercise of the power every man has of punishing the transgressions of others make them take sanctuary under the established laws of government and therein seek the preservation of their property. It is this makes them so willingly give up every one his single power of punishing, to be exercised by such alone as shall be appointed to it amongst them; and by such rules as the community, or those authorized by them to that purpose, shall agree on. And in this we have the original right of both the legislative and executive power, as well as of the governments and societies themselves. . . .

Chapter XIII: Of the subordination of the powers of the commonwealth

Though in a constituted commonwealth, standing upon its own basis and acting according to its own nature, that is, acting for the preservation of the community, there can be but one supreme power which is the legislative, to which all the rest are and must be subordinate, yet, the legislative being only a fiduciary power to act for certain ends, there remains still in the people a supreme power to remove or alter the legislative when they find the legislative act contrary to the trust reposed in them; for all power given with trust for the attaining an end being limited by that end, whenever that end is manifestly neglected or opposed, the trust must necessarily be forfeited and the power devolve into the hands of those that gave it, who may place it anew where they shall think best for their safety and security. And thus the community perpetually retains a supreme power of saving themselves from the attempts and designs of anybody, even of their legislators, whenever they shall be so foolish or so wicked as to lay and carry on designs against the liberties and properties of the subject; for no man or society of men having a power to deliver up their preservation, or consequently the means of it, to the absolute will and arbitrary dominion of another, whenever any one shall go about to bring them into such a slavish condition, they will always have a right to preserve what they have not a power to part with, and to rid themselves of those who invade this fundamental, sacred, and unalterable law of self-preservation for which they entered into society. And thus the community may be said in this respect to be always the supreme power, but not as considered under any form of government, because this power of the people can never take place till the government be dissolved. . . .

Chapter XIX: Of the dissolution of government

. . . The reason why men enter into society is the preservation of their property; and the end why they choose and authorize a legislative is that there may be laws made and rules set as guards and fences to the properties of all the members of the society, to limit the power and moderate the dominion of every part and member of the society; for since it can never be supposed to be the will of the society that the legislative should have a power to destroy that which every one designs to secure by entering into society, and for which the people submitted themselves to legislators of their own making. Whenever the legislators endeavor to take away and destroy the property of the people, or to reduce them to slavery under arbitrary power, they put themselves into a state of war with the people who are thereupon absolved from any further obedience, and are left to the common refuge which God hath provided for all men against force and violence. Whensoever, therefore, the legislative shall transgress this fundamental rule of society, and either by ambition, fear, folly, or corruption, endeavor to grasp themselves, or put into the hands of any other, an absolute power over the lives, liberties, and estates of the people, by this breach of trust they forfeit the power the people had put into their hands for quite contrary ends, and it devolves to the people who have a right to resume their original liberty, and by the establishment of a new legislative, such as they shall think fit, provide for their own safety and security, which is the end for which they are in society. . . .

[I]t will be said that the people being ignorant and always discontented, to lay the foundation of government in the unsteady opinion and uncertain humour of the people is to expose it to certain ruin; and no government will be able long to subsist, if the people may set up a new legislative whenever they take offence at the old one. To this I answer: Quite the contrary. People are not so easily got out of their old forms as some are apt to suggest. They are hardly to be prevailed with to amend the acknowledged faults in the frame they have been accustomed to. And if there by any original defects, or adventitious one introduced by time or corruption, it is not an easy thing to get them changed, even when all the world sees there is an opportunity for it. This slowness and aversion in the people to quit their old constitutions has in the many revolutions which have been seen in this kingdom, in this and former ages, still kept us to, or after some interval of fruitless attempts still brought us back again to, our old legislative of king, lords, and commons; and whatever provocations have made the crown be taken from some of our princes' heads, they never carried the people so far as to place it in another line.

But it will be said this hypothesis lays a ferment for frequent rebellion. To which I answer:

First, No more than any other hypothesis, for when the people are made miserable, and find themselves exposed to the ill-usage of arbitrary power, cry up their governors as much as you will for sons of Jupiter, let them be sacred or divine, descended, or authorized from heaven, give them out for whom or what you please, the same will happen. The people generally ill-treated, and contrary to right, will be ready upon any occasion to ease themselves of a burden that sits heavy upon them. . . .

Secondly, I answer, such revolutions happen not upon every little mismanagement in public affairs. Great mistakes in the ruling part, many wrong and inconvenient laws, and all the slips of human frailty will be borne by the people without mutiny or murmur. But if a long train of abuses, prevarications, and artifices, all tending the same way, make the design visible to the people, and they cannot but feel what they lie under and see whither they are going, it is not to be wondered that they should then rouse themselves and endeavor to put the rule into such hands which may secure to them the ends for which government was at first erected, and without which ancient names and specious forms are so far from being better that they are much worse than the state of nature or pure anarchy—the inconveniences being all as great and as near, but the remedy farther off and more difficult.

Thirdly, I answer that this doctrine of power in the people of providing for their safety anew by a new legislative, when their legislators have acted contrary to their trust by invading their property, is the best fence against rebellion, and the probablest means to hinder it; for rebellion being an opposition, not to persons, but authority which is founded only in the constitutions and laws of the government, those, whoever they be, who by force break through, and by force justify their violation of them, are truly and properly rebels; for when men, by entering into society and civil government, have excluded force and introduced laws for the preservation of property, peace, and unity amongst themselves, those who set up force again in opposition to the laws do *rebellare*—that is, bring back again the state of war—and are properly rebels. . . .

[W]hen either the legislative is changed or the legislators act contrary to the end for which they were constituted, those who are guilty are guilty of rebellion; for if any one by force takes away the established legislative of any society, and the laws of them made pursuant to their trust, he thereby takes away the umpirage which every one had consented to for a peaceable decision of all their controversies, and a bar to the state of war amongst them. They who remove or change the legislative take away this decisive power which nobody can have but by the appointment and consent of the people, and so destroying the authority which the people did, and nobody else can, set up, and introducing a power which the people hath not authorized, they actually introduce a state of war which is that of force without authority; and thus by removing the legislative established by the society—in whose decisions the people acquiesced and united as to that of their own will—they untie the knot and expose the people anew to the state of war. . . .

But if they who say "it lays a foundation for rebellion" mean that it may occasion civil wars or intestine broils, to tell the people they are absolved from obedience when illegal attempts are made upon their liberties or properties, and may oppose the unlawful violence of those who were their magistrates when they invade their properties contrary to the trust put in them, and that therefore this doctrine is not to be allowed, being so destructive to the peace of the world: they may as well say, upon the same ground, that honest men may not oppose robbers or pirates, because this may occasion disorder or bloodshed. If any mischief come in such cases, it is not to be charged upon him who defends his own right, but on him that invades his neighbour's. If the innocent honest man must quietly quit all he has, for peace's sake, to him who will lay violent hands upon it, I desire it may be considered what a kind of peace there will be in the world, which consists only in violence and rapine, and which is to be maintained only for the benefit of robbers and oppressors. . . .

Here, it is like, the common question will be made: "Who shall be judge whether the prince or legislative act contrary to their trust?" This, perhaps, ill-affected and factious men may spread amongst the people, when the prince only makes use of his due prerogative. To this I reply: The people shall be judge; for who shall be judge whether this trustee or deputy acts well and according to the trust reposed in him but he who deputes him and must, by having deputed him, have still a power to discard him when he fails in his trust? If this be a reasonable in particular cases of private men, why should it be otherwise in that of the greatest moment where the welfare of millions is concerned, and also where the evil, if not prevented, is greater and the redress very difficult, dear, and dangerous?

But further, this question, "Who shall be judge?" cannot mean that there is no judge at all; for where there is no judicature on earth to decide controversies amongst men, God in heaven is Judge. He alone, it is true, is Judge of the right. But every man is judge for himself, as in all other cases, so in this, whether another hath put himself into a state of war with him, and whether he should appeal to the Supreme Judge, as Jephthan did. . . .

To conclude, the power that every individual gave the society when he entered into it can never revert to the individuals again as long as the society lasts, but will always remain in the community, because without this there can be no community, no commonwealth, which is contrary to the original agreement; so also when the society hath placed the legislative in any assembly of men, to continue in them and their successors with direction and authority for providing such successors, the legislative can never revert to the people whilst that government lasts, because having provided a legislative with power to continue for ever, they have given up their political power to the legislative and cannot resume it. But if they have set limits to the duration of their legislative and made this supreme power in any person or assembly only temporary, or else when by the miscarriages of those in authority it is forfeited, upon the forfeiture, or at the determination of the time set, it reverts to the society, and the people have a right to act as supreme and continue the legislative in themselves, or erect a new form, or under the old form place it in new hands, as they think good. . . .

Chapter 4
"Cato" (John Trenchard and Thomas Gordon)
1720-23

Cato's Letters" is the name given a series of political essays appearing in London weekly newspapers, first the *London Journal* and then the *British Journal*, in the 1720s. Each essay was structured as a letter to the editor and was signed "Cato," the Roman statesman noted for his honesty and incorruptibility. The form was common practice in British and Colonial political journalism: think of Jonathan Swift's series of "Drapier's Letters" or the Federalist letters from "Publius," written by Alexander Hamilton and James Madison.

The initial writer of Cato's letters was John Trenchard (1662-1723) a lawyer and minor government official who both inherited and married money, allowing him to enter political journalism full time as a reformer.

Trenchard was soon joined in the Cato venture by Thomas Gordon (1688-1750), a Scot who, like so many of his contemporaries, migrated to London. The pair carried on a running commentary on English political affairs for more than three years and published well over a hundred letters. The columns were collected and published in book form, which went through several editions prior to 1750 and served in large measure as a rough statement of principles of what emerged as the Whig, or liberal, party in Britain.

Several of their letters are of particular interest to journalists. "Cato" was among the first popular writers to examine the role of free speech and free press in the context of the Lockean model of limited government and popular sovereignty. In making this connection, "Cato" made a major contribution to the intellectual movement that burst into full flower during the second half of the eighteenth century, the Enlightenment.

The following two essays were reprinted widely and often in Colonial newspapers, and did much to frame the public debate over what governments should be and do, and how much citizens should know about how those governments operate. Copies of the essays, which were reprinted in John Peter Zenger's *New-York Weekly Journal* newspaper, were important evidence against Zenger in the famous libel trial of 1735.

Cato's Letters
1720

No. 15. Of freedom of speech: that the same is inseparable from publick liberty.

Sir,

Without freedom of thought, there can be no such thing as wisdom; and no such thing as public liberty, without freedom of speech; which is the right of every man, as far as by it he does not hurt or control the right of another; and this is the only check which it ought to suffer, the only bounds which it ought to know.

This sacred privilege is so essential to free governments, that the security of property, and the freedom of speech, always go together; and in those wretched countries where a man cannot call his tongue his own, he can scarce call any thing else his own. Whoever would overthrow the liberty of a nation, must begin by subduing the freedom of speech; a thing terrible to public traitors.

This secret was so well known to the court of King Charles the First, that his wicked ministry procured a proclmation, to forbid the people to talk of Parliaments, which those traitors had laid aside. To assert the undoubted right of the Subject, and defend his Majesty's legal Prerogative, was called Disaffection, and punished as Sedition. Nay, People were forbid to talk of Religion in their Families. For, the Priests had combined with the Ministers to cook up Tyranny, and suppress Truth and the Law. While the late King James, when Duke of York, went avowedly to Mass, Men were fined, imprisoned, and undone, for saying that he was a Papist. And that King Charles the Second might live more securely a Papist, there was an Act of Parliament made, declaring it Treason to say that he was one.

That Men ought to speak well of their Governors, is true, while their Governors deserve to be well spoken of; but to do publick Mischief, without hearing of it, is only the Prerogative and Felicity of Tyranny: A free People will be shewing that they are so, by their Freedom of Speech.

The Administration of Government, is nothing else but the Attendance of the Trustees of the people upon the Interest and Affairs of the People. And as it is the Part and Business of the People, for whose Sake alone all publick Matters are or ought to be transacted, to see whether they be well or ill transacted; so it is the Interest, and ought to be the Ambition, of all honest

Magistrates, to have their Deeds openly examined, and publickly scanned. Only the wicked Governors of Men dread what is said of them.... The publick Censure was true, else he had not felt it bitter.

Freedom of Speech is ever the Symptom, as well as the Effect, of good Government. In old Rome, all was left to the Judgment and Pleasure of the People, who examined the publick Proceedings with such Discretion, and censured those who administered them with such Equity and Mildness, that in the Space of Three Hundred Years, not Five publick Ministers suffered unjustly. Indeed, whenever the Commons proceeded to Violence, the Great Ones had been the Aggressors.

Guilt only dreads Liberty of Speech, which drags it out of its lurking Holes, and exposes its Deformity and Horror to Day-light. Horatius, Valerius, Cincinnatus, and other virtuous and undesigning Magistrates of the Roman Commonwealth, had nothing to fear from Liberty of Speech. Their virtuous Administration, the more it was examined, the more it brightened, and gained by Enquiry. When Valerius, in particular, was accused upon some slight Grounds of affecting the Diadem, he, who was the first Minister of Rome, did not accuse the People for examining his Conduct, but approved his Innocence in a Speech to them, he gave such Satisfaction of them, and gained such Popularity to himself, that they gave him a new Name . . . to denote that he was their Favourite and their Friend....

But Things afterwards took another Turn, Rome, with the Loss of its Liberty, lost also its Freedom of Speech, then Mens Words began to be feared and watched, then first began the poisonous Race of Informers....

The best Princes have ever encouraged and promoted Freedom of Speech, they know that upright measures would defend themselves, and that all upright Men would defend them. Tacitus, speaking of the Reign of some of the Princes above-mentioned says with Extasy ... A blessed Time, when you might think what you would, and speak what you thought.

... Misrepresentation of publick Measures is easily overthrown, by representing publick Measures truly; when they are honest, they ought to be publickly known, that they may be publickly commended; but if they be knavish or pernicious, they ought to be publickly exposed, in order to be publickly detested.

To assert, that King James was a Papist and a Tyrant, was only so far hurtful to him as it was true of him; and if the Earl of Strafford had not deserved to be Impeached, he need not have feared a Bill of Attainder. If our directors and their Confederates be not such Knaves as the World thinks them, let them prove to all the World, that the World thinks wrong, and that they are guilty of none of those Villainies which all the World lays to their Charge. Others too, who would be thought to have no Part of their Guilt, must, before they are thought innocent, shew that they did all that was in their Power to prevent that Guilt, and to check their Proceedings.

Freedom of Speech is the great Bulwark of Liberty; they prosper and die together. And it is the Terror of Traytors and Oppressors, and a Barrier against them. It produces excellent Writers, and encourages Men of fine Genius. Tacitus tells us, That the Roman Commonwealth bred great and numerous Authors, who writ with equal Boldness and Eloquence. But when it was enslaved, those great Wits were no more.... Tyranny has usurped the Place of Equallty, which is the Soul of Liberty, and destroyed publick Courage. The Minds of Men, terrified by unjust Power, degenerates into all the Vileness and Methods of Servitude. Abject Sycophancy and blind Submission grew the only Means of Preferments, and indeed of Safety. Men durst not open their Mouths, but to flatter....

All Ministers . . . who were Oppressors, or intended to be Oppressors; have been loud in their Complaints against Freedom of Speech, and the License of the Press, and always restrained, or endeavoured to restrain Both. In consequence of this, they have brow-beaten Writers, punished them violently, and against Law, and burnt their Works; by all which, they shewed how much truth alarmed them, and how much they were at Enmity with Truth....

Freedom of Speech, therefore, being of such infinite Importance to the Preservation of Liberty; everyone who loves Liberty, ought to encourage Freedom of Speech.

No. 32. Reflections upon Libelling

Sir,

    I design in this letter to lay before the town, some thoughts upon libelling, a sort of writing that hurts particular persons, without doing good to the public; and a sort of writing much complained of amongst us at this time, with great ground, but not more than is pretended.

    A libel is not the less a libel for being true. This may seem a contradiction; but it is neither one in law, or in common sense: There are some truths not fit to be told, where, for example, the discovery of a small fault may do great mischief, or, where the discovery of a great fault can do no good, there ought be no discovery at all. And to make faults where there are none, is still worse.

    But this doctrine only holds truths to private and personal failings, and it is quite otherwise when the crimes of men come to affect the public. Nothing ought to be so dear to us as our country, and nothing ought to come in competition with its interests. Every crime against the public is a great crime, though there be some greater than others. Ignorance and folly may be pleaded in alleviation of private offenses; but when they come to be public offenses, they lose all benefit of such a plea. We are then no longer to consider only to what causes they are owing, but what evils they may produce, and here we shall readily find, that folly has overturned states, and private ignorance been the parent of public confusion.

    The exposing therefore of public wickedness, as it is a duty which every man owes to truth and his country, can never be a libel in the nature of things; and they who call it so, make themselves no compliment. He who is affronted at the reading of the Ten Commandments, would make the decalogue a libel, if he durst, but he tempts us at the same time to form a judgment of his life and morals not at all to his advantage. Whoever calls public and necessary truths libels, does but apprize us of his own character, and arm us with caution against his designs. I doubt not but if the late directors had been above the Parliament, as they once thought themselves, they would have called the votes of the House of Commons against them, false and scandalous libels. . . .

    Slander is certainly a very base and mean thing. But surely it cannot be more pernicious to calumniate even good men, than not to be able to accuse ill ones.

    I have long thought, that the world are very much mistaken in their idea and distinction of libels. It has been hitherto generally understood that there were no other libels but those against magistrates, and those against private men. Now, to me there seems to be a third sort of libels, full as destructive as any of the former can possibly be; I mean, libels against the people. . . . Oppression, they say, will make a wise man mad, and delusion has not less force. But where there are neither oppressors nor impostors, the judgment of the people in the business of property, the preservation of which is the principal business of government, does rarely err. . . . I have indeed often wondered that the inveighing against the interest of the people, and calling their liberties in question, as has been, and is commonly done amongst us by old knaves and young fools, has never been made an express crime.

I must own, I know not what treason is, if sapping and betraying the liberties of a people be not treason, in the eternal and original Nature of Things. Let it be remembered for whose Sake Government is, or could be appointed, then let it be considered, who are more to be regarded, the Governors or the Governed. They indeed owe one another mutual Duties, but if there be any Transgressions committed, the side that is most obliged ought doubtless, to bear the most, and yet it is so far otherwise, that almost all over the Earth, the people, for One Injury that they do their Governors, receive Ten Thousand from them. . . .

But . . . I return more directly to the business of libels. As to libels against government, like all others, they are always base and unlawful, and often mischievous, especially when governments are impudently charged with actions and designs of which they are not guilty. It is certain, that we ought not to enter into the private vices or weaknesses of governors, any further than their private vices enter into their public administration, and when they do, it will be impossible to stop people's mouths. They will be provoked, and show that they are so, in spite of art and threats, if they suffer hardships and woe from the private gratifications of their superiors, from whom they have a right to expect ease and happiness, and if they be disappointed, they will be apt to deal very freely with their characters. . . .

[I]t is as just that reputation should be defended by law, as that property should.

The Praise of Well-doing is the highest Reward that worthy and disinterested Men aim at, and it is villainous and ungrateful to rob them of it, and those that do it, are Libellers and Slanderers. . . .

And yet it is scarce possible in a free Country, to punish by a general Law any Libel so much as it deserves, since such a Law, consisting of so many Branches, and being of such vast Latitude, would make all Writing whatsoever, how innocent soever, and even all Speaking unsafe. Hence it is that in Turkey, though Printing were permitted, it would be of no use, because no body would dare to make any Use of it.

As long as there are such Things as Printing and Writing, there will be Libels. It is an Evil arising out of a much greater good. And as to those who are for locking up the Press, because it produces Monsters, they ought to consider that so do the Sun and the Nile, and that it is something better for the

World to bear some particular Inconveniences arising from general Blessings, than to be wholly deprived of Fire and Water. . . .

Occasion will never be taken from scurrilous and traitorous Writing, to destroy the End of Writing. We know that in all times, there have been Men lying upon the Watch to stifle Liberty, under a Pretence of suppressing Libels, like the late King James, who, having occasion for an Army to suppress Monmouth's Rebellion, would needs keep it up afterwards, because, forsooth, other Rebellions might happen, for which he was resolved to give Cause.

I must own, that I would rather many Libels should escape, than the Liberty of the Press should be infringed, yet no Man in England thinks worse of Libels than I do, especially of such as bid open Defiance to the present Protestant Establishment. . . .

Chapter 5
Tunis Wortman
1773-1822

F rom Cato's time on, writers and political thinkers explored
the implications for journalism of a Lockean form of
government based on popular sovereignty. This was the
period of the Enlightenment, rooted in the optimistic
convictions that the rational mind was capable of vast understanding
and that the power of reason could solve all problems and create
perfect freedom. Knowledge was considered the key, and the
implications for a free press were clear.

The case was made brilliantly by Thomas Erskine, a lawyer who
defended the radical writer Thomas Paine when Paine was charged
in Britain with sedition for *The Rights of Man*, a polemic against the
British monarchy in particular. Erskine argued (unsuccessfully, for
Paine was convicted), "If the people have, without possible recall,
delegated all their authorities, they have no jurisdiction to act, and
therefore none to think or write upon such subjects [as governmental
behavior]; and it would be libel to arraign government or any of its
acts, before those who have no jurisdiction to correct them.
[However] if I am supported in my doctrines concerning the great
unalienable right of the people to reform or change their
governments, no legal argument can shake the freedom of the press.
... It is because the liberty of the press resolved itself into this great
issue, that it has been in every country the last liberty which subjects
have been able to wrest from power. Other liberties are held under
government, but the liberty of opinion keeps governments themselves
in due subjugation to their duties."

Although the historical record is frustratingly incomplete about
exactly what James Madison meant at the time when he wrote the
First Amendment, it seems clear that, in general, Madison intended
to connect the issues of free speech and free press to self-

government. The matter got a full airing a few years later during the debates over the Sedition Act of 1798. The following selection is from *A Treatise Concerning Political Enquiry and the Liberty of the Press*, published in 1801 by a Jeffersonian lawyer named Tunis Wortman. Many writers who shared Jefferson's and Madison's political views wrote on the subject, but Wortman's synthesis, long overlooked by historians, brings together the basic lines of thought that had evolved since the earliest days of the Enlightenment.

A Treatise Concerning Political Enquiry and the Liberty of the Press
1801

T he present subject of discussion, involves a consideration of the following principal questions: Is it the right of society to investigate with freedom into the affairs of government? Is society possessed of abilities competent to the formation of a correct and pertinent opinion upon political measures? Do individuals possess the right of communicating the result of their deliberations upon those topics? And should any, and what restrictions be imposed upon the extent and manner of such communication?

It is an undeniable position, that a continual reciprocity exists between all the human duties. . . . When we say it is the duty of civil government to exercise its powers for the protection of the people, that assertion irresistibly implies a correspondent right of the people to demand such protection from the government.

It has already been perceived, that the source of obligation, is to be traced to the mutual relation subsisting between percipient beings, and that the reciprocal duties between society and government, originate in their social relations. The existence of mutual obligation, presupposes a mutual right of examining into its nature and extent. . . .

The subject is susceptible of further elucidation, from a review of the genuine nature of human society. Whatever disagreement may have existed between the various theories that have obtained with respect to the origin of society, there is an universal coincidence of sentiment concerning the objects it is intended to effect. It is perfectly agreed, that the promotion of general happiness is the only legitimate end of its institution. . . .

It is unnecessary to enter into a detail of the various speculations which fancy has suggested, concerning the original formation of government. The nature of that institution, and its connection with civil society, are sufficiently obvious. Society is not the instrument of government created for the purpose of affording grandeur and consequence to the latter. It was not instituted in order that Leopold might become an Emperor, George a King, or that our present chief magistrate should be inaugurated President.

Government is, strictly speaking, the creature of society originating in its discretion, and dependent upon its will; with whatever awful habiliments the civil magistrate may be invested—whatever imposing appellations he may assume.

With respect to government, therefore, every thing is dependent upon the public will. The powers of society are always adequate to the destruction of its political institutions, whenever such determination is rendered universally prevalent. Unless the public mind becomes enlightened, what principle or what law is possessed of sufficient energy to prevent it from leading to the most violent acts of outrage and desperation? When we examine the records of any age or country, we tremble at the deplorable catastrophes which have ensued from political ignorance and imposture.

What then is the cause of all this complicated calamity? It is ignorance and the imposture which it nourishes. It follows, that the only antidote which can be applied, is the progress of information: in every rational theory of society, it should therefore be established as an essential principle, that freedom of investigation is one of the most important rights of a people. . . . [T]he progress of knowledge must become an effectual preventative of that violent revolution and imposture, which so often marks the person of the magistrate for its death-devoted victim.

Let us for a moment examine into the nature of civil government. What is its genuine province, and from what source does it derive its powers? It is to be observed, that the general superintendence of government, is rather of a negative than a positive kind. Its injunctions are, to abstain from the perpetration of vice, and not to perform particular acts of virtue. On the one side, we are bound to avoid the commission of evil; and it is within the power of government to reach us by a general prohibition. But on the score of virtue, there are degrees of preferableness between one action and another, too subtle to be embraced by any form of civil legislation. Here then we must be left at perfect freedom to decide, independent of the control of human power.

It cannot be denied, that the powers of government are not original, but strictly derivative; that the only fountain from whence its authority proceeds, is public delegation. For whatever may be the particular form of national institution, its existence is equally owing to the general will. It must ever remain in the inherent and incontrovertible right of society, to dissolve its political constitution, whenever the voice of public opinion has declared such dissolution to be essential to the general welfare. Society must, therefore, necessarily possess the unlimited right to examine and investigate. . . . It follows, therefore, as a necessary consequence, that the government which attempts to coerce the progress of opinion, or to abolish the freedom of investigation into political affairs, materially violates the most essential principles of the social state.

Knowledge is the only guardian which can prevent us from becoming the vassals of tyranny and the dupes of imposture. Investigation is dangerous to the systems which are founded in despotism and corruption, but it confers additional energy on those that are established upon the genuine foundation of truth. . . .

[A]s man is the constant object of moral and social duties, and the perpetual subject of political discipline; it is necessary that he should possess and exercise, the means of investigating the nature and extent of such obligation and discipline. From a just and accurate review of the theory of civil society and government, it is apparent, that political institution is but the instrument of society; intended to promote its prosperity and happiness—that the laws of morality are possessed of universal jurisdiction, and are obligatory upon the prince and the magistrate, as well as upon the obscure and private individual—that governments partake of human fallibility and imperfection, and that they are responsible to the people, for the faithful performance of their important trusts—that intelligence is the common property of human beings, and that the progress of knowledge is the only practicable method of diminishing the ascendancy of vice, and destroying the dominion of the passions. From all these considerations it has been maintained, that a liberty of investigation into every subject of thought, is not only the perfect and absolute right of civil society; but that the unrestricted exercise of that right, is indispensable to the progression and happiness of mankind. . . .

Let political institution be confined to its genuine objects of superintendence; let its powers be exclusively directed to the suppression of crime; let us say to government, "You have no legitimate empire over opinion. You have no equitable jurisdiction over the operations of the mind: let science explore the unlimited regions of contemplation. Truth and virtue are the only objects of her pursuit. . . . Improvement is an universal law of human nature. "

In the examination of this question, the first consideration which naturally becomes presented, is the striking uniformity that exists in the human understanding. Intelligence is the common attribute of man. . . . Knowledge is not a rare and uncommon gem which a few are destined to monopolize: on the contrary, its treasures are susceptible of universal communication.

Truth, as an abstract term, is altogether insusceptible of definition. The most sagacious reasoner has hitherto been unable by any circumlocution or form of phraseology, to describe with accuracy in what its essence consists. But whatever may be the abstract nature of truth, its evidences are capable of equal presentation to the percipient powers of all men. It is not a courtier whose residence is confined to palaces, nor is it always to be found in the solemn gravity of a deliberative assembly. Whether it relates to principles or facts, it is to be discovered and ascertained by judgment; and judgment is a faculty possessed in common by mankind. . . .

There is abundant evidence to prove, that all men are possessed of what is termed the moral sense. It matters little in the argument, whether such common property be innate or acquired. Our perceptions concerning the nature of moral and social obligation, are entirely similar, and our decisions with respect to them, will in general be uniform and correspondent.

Even admitting the inequality and extensive variety of human genius, it is nevertheless evident, that the attribute of judgment is more generally and impartially distributed. It is the property of genius to invent and execute; it is the province of judgment to discriminate and decide. The investigation of moral or political subjects, requires not the talent of invention; judgment and not genius is the faculty to be employed. The true merits of the present enquiry will be comprised in the proposition, that the medium of human capacity, is competent to decide upon the ordinary detail of politics. . . .

We might hazard the decision of this subject, upon the solidity of the following propositions: first, that the faculties of all men are susceptible of continual improvement: and secondly, that all men are possessed of the means of distinguishing virtue from vice, benefits from injuries, and justice from its opposite. Unless the human capacity was susceptible of improvement, the arts and the sciences would be useless to the world. . . . Ignorance must have preceded information, and the progress of mind must of necessity have commenced, from the most trivial and imperceptible beginnings. Unless the knowledge of one was communicable to another . . . the discoveries of wisdom unprofitable and nugatory. If education can form the lawyer, mathematician, and divine, why cannot attention and application, render us proficient in political knowledge?

It is the prerogative of justice, to dart its illuminations into every mind. Wherever man exists, the laws of morality will establish their immutable empire. . . .

Justice is a standard of universal authority; it is equally applicable to the conduct of individuals and of nations. Governments as well as men, are the subjects of moral and social obligation: they are equally bound to abstain from oppression and injuries; their acts of injustice and tyranny, are as marked and distinguishable as the vices of private life, and their errors are equally exposed to the light of observation.

He who can form a proper estimate of individual conduct and morality, will be also enabled to form a tolerably correct opinion of the measures and morality of the cabinet. By the frequent habits of discussion, his discriminating powers will be rendered more acute, and his decisions will improve in accuracy . . . the principal requisite will be to furnish him with the necessary means of information, and to present the case with copiousness and perspicuity to his view.

Let us now proceed, and enquire into the nature of that institution, which is generally known by the name of civil government. There is no exercise that can be more important, or more closely connected with the principal subject of discussion, than an examination of the genuine principles, which enter into the foundation of political institution. We have perceived, that man, from the essential constitution of his nature, is a moral and intelligent being: and that a knowledge of the principles of morality, is inseparable from his nature and social existence. If therefore, it should be found on such examination, that political institution, is established upon those universal principles of ethics, which are the common property of mankind, the conclusion will be inevitable, that they are qualified to investigate the nature, and to decide upon the merits of political subjects.

Government, by which is understood the administration of public affairs, is not a mysterious system, involved in impenetrable obscurity, nor is it a science attended with inexplicable difficulty. In theory, it is established upon principles of universal application, and founded in maxims, which are readily embraced, and comprehended by the most common understanding. The laws of morality are open to all men; they are comprised in a volume, which all may read, and all may comprehend. It is undeniable, that the foundation of civil government, is to be discovered in the extensive science of morals.

The practical detail of government, is a series of decisions and measures, in affirmance of the principles established in its theory. To pronounce with accuracy upon any given act of administration—to discover the merits or the impolicy of any particular statute—to perceive its consonancy or disagreement with the general principles of justice . . . requires only the exercise of that judgment, which is the common attribute of humanity, combined with such information, as every intelligent being can with application acquire. . . .

It is evident, that man as a moral being, and the constant object of moral and social discipline, must, from his necessary experience and habits, possess a considerable knowledge of the principles of moral law. It is also sufficiently plain, that the duties attached to the intercourse of nations and individuals, arise from the identical fountain of obligation, and must therefore be in a great measure familiar to every understanding. Without possessing extraordinary depth of intellect, we can readily perceive, whether any given action will be detrimental to our neighbor. We can as readily discern those actions which terminate in public injury: indeed most offenses pronounced of a public nature, consist of injuries primarily inflicted upon individuals, and which considerations of general policy, have rendered a common cause. Without pretensions to superior discernment, every person can as easily perceive what conduct in one nation violates the rights, and operates to the detriment of another; or what acts of a government infallibly terminate in personal injury and oppression. Hence then it is an obvious position, that every intelligent being must necessarily possess a sufficient standard of political discrimination.

Next to the invention of language and of letters, that of printing may justly be considered as the most powerful benefactor of mankind. Before this important and valuable discovery, whatever may have been the attainments of a few distinguished individuals, the great majority of the human race were destined to remain unenlightened and uninformed.

As a vehicle of information the press is possessed of peculiar advantages. The rapidity of oral addresses—the declamatory style, impassioned manner, and intemperate gesture of orator—may arrest the imagination and enlist the passions: but whatever is presented to us in print is less alloyed with any circumstance unconnected with its merits. Reason has time to operate, and truth an opportunity to be enforced. We have leisure to meditate and examine. If our attention has been diverted from the speaker, or we have mistaken his sentiments, our loss in the one case, and our error in the other, is not to be repaired: but the printed volume is ever open to our view; we can ponder upon its contents at leisure, and remove our hasty impressions. The latter, therefore, is more favorable to the propagation of truth, and less liable to become converted into a pernicious engine of design.

The press is undeniably possessed of extensive influence upon government, manners, and morals. Every exertion should, therefore, be employed to render it subservient to liberty, truth, and virtue. While society is furnished with so powerful a vehicle of political information, the conduct of administration will be more cautious and deliberate: it will be inspired with respect towards a censor whose influence is universal. . . .

It cannot be denied that the Press maintains a powerful influence over manners and morals. Argument is the most salutary and rational mean of correcting our prejudices, and establishing the empire of truth. There is no vehicle better adapted for the circulation of reasoning, or the communication of sentiment, than the press.

An instrument which is capable of becoming prostituted to so much mischief, as well as rendering such important and extensive benefits (it will naturally be alleged), "should be carefully confined within the bounds of rectitude and virtue. While we assiduously cultivate and cherish the valuable plant, let us at the same time diligently prune its luxuriant and irregular excrescences." It would, doubtless, be desirable to control the licentiousness of the press, if any means could be pursued for that purpose without endangering its liberty.

There are two opposite extremes of error to which the press is liable to be perverted. The one, an interested partiality towards the government; the other, a wanton or designing misrepresentation of its measures. In each of these cases the press may be considered as licentious: for the evil equally consists in a deviation from truth. Of these evils, the former is incomparably the most formidable; because an administration being an organized, disciplined, and powerful body, is particularly qualified to enlist in its service every instrument that is capable of stamping a forcible impression upon the public mind. Possessed of the gifts of patronage, they have always abundant means to reward the attachment of their favorites. The candidates of preferment, that class of individuals so numerous, and so indefatigable in every community, will be constantly ready to offer the oblations of unmerited panegyric; and there will always be more to apprehend from servility and flattery, than from slander or invective.

Every departure from truth is pernicious. Impartiality should be a perpetual attribute of the press. Neither fear on the one side, nor the hope of reward on the other, should intimidate or influence its enquiries. It should neither be bribed to lavish unmerited applause, nor menaced into silence. The usefulness of periodical publications depends upon their steady and inflexible adherence to rectitude. The moment that corrupt or foreign considerations are suffered to bias, or to stain their pages, they become injurious to the genuine interests of society.

It is essential to examine the prominent principles of the present doctrine of Libels, in order that we may accurately appreciate the grounds upon which it is usually vindicated. Its first proposition is, that in criminal prosecutions the tendency which all Libels have to foment animosities, and to disturb the public peace, is the sole consideration of the law; and that it is, therefore, perfectly immaterial, with respect to the essence of a Libel, whether the matter of it be true or false—since the provocation, and not the falsity, is the thing to be punished criminally.

In the first place, it is to be observed, that agreeably to such doctrine the exclusive consideration of the Law rests upon a circumstance entirely foreign to the intrinsic merits of the subject. Its sole attention is confined to the preservation of the public peace; and its principal pretext is, that the criminal coercion of libels is indispensable to the maintenance of general tranquility. Inasmuch, therefore, as every publication which severely animadverts upon the conduct of any individual, or upon the measures of government, whether it be founded in truth or falsehood, is presumed to have a tendency to disturb the public peace, in the eye of the law it is equally a libel, and its author exposed to punishment.

Truth can never be a libel. The system which maintains so odious a proposition, is founded in the most palpable injustice. Its obvious consequence is to render the political magistrate inviolable, and to protect him from punishment or animadversion, even for the greatest enormities. Wherever such a doctrine obtains, there is an end of freedom and to justice. In the most atrocious oppression that can be exercised by government, according to such theory, there will be the greatest necessity for silence and concealment. As the most aggravated injuries to the community will be the most calculated to kindle popular resentment and indignation, a regard to public tranquility will require that every publication with respect to them should be suppressed. As the well grounded complaint will be more likely to foment disturbances than the unfounded tale of calumny, the greater the truth, the greater will be the libel. If truth is pronounced to be a libel, can it be said that the press possesses freedom, or that it is a check against the encroachments of power? To maintain such doctrine, is to declare open war against political enquiry, entirely destroy the responsibility of the magistrate, and establish the throne of absolute despotism upon the ruins of civil liberty. . . .

Another prominent principle of the present doctrine concerning libels, is, that "the liberty of the press entirely consists in laying no previous restraints upon publications, and not in freedom from censure for criminal matter when published." This definition, of which the principal force consists in its excluding the idea of a previous imprimatur, is true as far as its extends; but it is extremely imperfect. Of what use is the liberty of doing that for which I am punishable afterwards? In the same sense it may be said that I have the liberty to perpetrate felony or murder, if I think proper to expose myself to the penalties annexed to those crimes. In ascertaining the rights I possess, it is not to be enquired what I may do, and be punished; but what I am entitled to perform without being subjected to punishment.... It cannot be said that any liberty of the press is established by law, unless the publication of truth is expressly sanctioned, and it is particularly ascertained what species of writings shall be comprehended under the title of libels.

It is far from being maintained that slander should be suffered to exist with impunity. On the contrary, it is admitted, that rational and judicious measures should be taken to deprive it of its sting. But it is contended, that private prosecutions, at the suit of the injured party, are sufficient to answer every beneficial purpose, and will entirely supersede the necessity of criminal coercion.

To criminal prosecutions for libels there will always exist the most serious objections. They are invariably more formidable than the evil they are intended to prevent. As a security to a virtuous administration, they can never be necessary. In the hands of a vicious minister, they will be prostituted to the most pernicious purposes....

The licentiousness of the press has of late become a theme of fashionable invective: but those who have been most clamorous in their philippics, have in general been most hostile to its liberty. The press is undoubtedly a powerful instrument; and, when left to itself, its natural direction will be towards truth and virtue.... Under arbitrary government it is a practice to prohibit every publication that has not been previously perused and sanctioned by some of its officers. By this means every writing, which is friendly to the spirit of freedom, is suppressed; and nothing can appear but what is on the side of government. By such regulations it is obvious that the press, instead of being a guardian of public liberty, is rendered a dangerous and servile slave to despotism.

Chapter 6
Maximilien Robespierre
1758-1794

A fter the American Revolution, political leadership split in two, into the Federalists, led by Alexander Hamilton and John Adams, and the anti-Federalists, who followed Thomas Jefferson and James Madison. The Federalists generally supported a strong central government (as opposed to greater power to the individual states) and tended to see the French Revolution as inviting anarchy rather than ushering in democracy. The anti-Federalists, also known as Jeffersonians and, later, as Democratic-Republicans, wanted a weak central government and were more eager than anxious about events in France. Fully aware of the important role newspapers had played in the American Revolution, each side founded and supported its own newspapers. The following short defense of free-press principles ran in the Jeffersonian, pro-French paper, the *National Gazette*, in late 1791. It is a translation of a speech given that August to the revolutionary French National Assembly by the radical Jacobin leader Maximilien Robespierre during the height of the revolution.

"Liberty of the Press"
National Gazette, 1791

T he liberty of the press is the only effectual check of arbitrary power. The consequence has been, the uniform endeavor of all such governments so to interpret this liberty, as finally to render it a mere nullity. The moment of a revolution is perhaps a time the least seasonable for discussing the great principles upon which the liberty of the press is founded, because at such a time all parties of men are the subjects of the attacks of the press from one quarter to another, and consequently are too sore to reason deliberately on granting it the full extent of liberty it ought to have. But, let it be the glory of the National Assembly of France to be above prejudice and to disregard all personal considerations—this is the example that has been set before us by the United States of America, of the great question of the liberty of the press. The liberty of publishing our sentiments is the great bulwark of liberty, and can only be limited, even in the smallest degree, by despotic governments. Is the press free when it is prohibited from publishing censure and defamation of characters? I think you will agree with me that it is not. There is no liberty of the press where the author of any piece is liable to arbitrary prosecution—and here I will observe, that there is an essential difference between *criminal acts* and the *offenses of the press*. Criminal actions are of a palpable and sensible nature. They can be proved in conformity to certain established rules and by infallible methods after which the law can take its course without any mixture of arbitrary proceeding. As to mere opinions, published to the world, their merits or their criminality must always depend upon rational principles, justice, and public interest, and often-times upon a multitude of peculiar circumstances which are necessarily productive of great uncertainty. The most particular circumspection, therefore, is necessary in making laws to regulate the liberty of the press. Laws expressly enacted to secure the liberty of the press have always, in the end, proved the infallible means of annihilating it. Recollect, Gentlemen, what has passed under the late French government: under pretense of public good, writers, especially political writers, lived a life of persecution and misery from those whose duty it was to protect them. What were the writings, which, prior to the revolution, were the objects of such marked severity? The very writing which we at this day admire, and whose authors have been thought worthy of the homage of the nation. A proof this, that time and situation alone determine whether an author shall persecuted, or be crowned with honor. Only three years ago the *Social Compact*, was condemned as a treasonable work. John James Rousseau, the man who did the most to bring about the present revolution—that very John James Rousseau, was by a decree of the nation, pronounced a traitor, a man of dangerous principles, a seditious pest—and nothing prevented his neck being brought to the block, but the fears the government began to entertain, in the latter part of his time, of the courage of the patriotic party in France. But even at this late period, if despotism had only known her remaining strength and influence over the nation, existing by the force of long habit—Rousseau's head would have been paid for the services he rendered to mankind, and he would have added one to the number of illustrious victims whom fanaticism, despotism and tyranny have always considered as too dangerous to their cause to be suffered to live. Be assured, then, Gentlemen, that nothing is of more delicate nature, perhaps nothing is more impossible, than to make an equitable law to inflict penalties for the opinions which men may publish, especially on those matters which are the natural objects of human reason, knowledge and enquiry. What you have done is all that can be done in this case; and that is, to consider him a criminal, who plainly and explicitly (not by any kind of implication) offends against the spirit of the law.

Further than this you cannot go without infringing the liberty of the press in its essential properties and principles.

Chapter 7
John Stuart Mill
1802-1873

T o many of us, John Stuart Mill is the most familiar and most accessible of all modern intellectual writers. His moral philosophy of utilitarianism and his political advocacy of maximizing human liberty seem almost axiomatic to many. That this is so is a testament to the widespread adoption by policy makers and by intellectuals of Mill's basic ideas. In the late twentieth century, few contemporary philosophers accept utilitarianism as thoroughly as Mill advocated it, yet many philosophers since Mill have adopted some measure of utilitarianism, and all have had to deal with him in one way or another.

Mill grew up as the product of an educational experiment conducted by his father, James Mill, and his father's close friend, Jeremy Bentham, both of whom believed that the human mind was capable of astonishing accomplishments if it were not exposed to the fripperies and foolishness of contemporary life. Accordingly, young John Stuart was brought up with virtually no childhood companions but had an astonishingly rigorous education, beginning Greek at the age of three, arithmetic and Latin at eight, logic at twelve and political economy at thirteen.

Mill was largely influenced by his father's circle of intellectual friends, most notably Bentham and John Austin. It was Bentham who first promulgated the word "utilitarianism" in the 1780s as the name for "a new religion" more befitting the rationalism and reason of the Enlightenment than older religions with their faiths and their rituals and their inherent ambiguities. Bentham, in turn, said he had found the term that would become the catch-phrase of utilitarianism—"the greatest happiness of the greatest number"—in a treatise by Joseph Priestley, an eminent scientist (he discovered oxygen and did groundbreaking work in electricity) and major contributor to the new religion of Unitarianism.

At one level, Mill pushed Bentham's philosophy into a vastly more complex era. While Bentham's greatest works were written in the late eighteenth century and reflect the Enlightenment's dedication to reason, Mill's work was in the early nineteenth, and was thus much influenced by the Romantic movement and its attendant concerns with individual sensibilities. Bentham, with his emphasis on law, necessarily made little distinction among individuals. However, Mill argued that while the point of government was general happiness, the individual's mental well-being, which he held to be a precursor to happiness, depended upon the freedom of opinion and, of great importance to journalists, the freedom to express that opinion.

There are echoes of Milton in the selection that follows, but note that while both argued for strengthening truth through vigorous battle with falsehood, Mill's argument is almost entirely secular and civic, whereas Milton's is overwhelmingly religious.

On Liberty
1859

Introductory

The sole end for which mankind are warranted, individually or collectively, in interfering with the liberty of action of any of their number is self-protection. That the only purpose for which power can be rightfully exercised over any member of a civilized community, against his will, is to prevent harm to others. His own good, either physical or moral, is not a sufficient warrant. He cannot rightfully be compelled to do or forbear because it will be better for him to do so, because it will make him happier, because, in the opinions of others, to do so would be wise or even right. These are good reasons for remonstrating with him, or reasoning with him, or persuading him, or entreating him, but not for compelling him or visiting him with any evil in case he do otherwise. To justify that, the conduct from which it is desired to deter him must be calculated to produce evil to someone else.... Over himself, over his own body and mind the individual is sovereign.

It is, perhaps, hardly necessary to say that this doctrine is meant to apply only to human beings in the maturity of their faculties.... Liberty, as a principle, has no application to any state of things anterior to the time when mankind have become capable of being improved by free and equal discussion. Until then, there is nothing for them but implicit obedience to an Akbar or a Charlemagne if they are so fortunate as to find one....

It is proper to state that I forego any advantage which could be derived to my argument from the idea of abstract right as a thing independent of utility. I regard utility as the ultimate appeal on all ethical questions: but it must be utility in the largest sense, grounded on the permanent interests of man as a progressive being. Those interests, I contend, authorize the subjection of individual spontaneity to external control only in respect to those actions of each which concern the interest of other people.... There are also many positive acts for the benefit of others which he may rightfully be compelled to perform, such as to give evidence in a court of justice, to bear his fair share in the common defense or in any other joint work necessary to the interest of the society of which he enjoys the protection, and to perform certain acts of individual beneficence, such as saving a fellow creature's life or interposing to protect the defenseless against ill usage—things which whenever it is obviously a man's duty to do he may rightfully be made responsible to society for not doing. . . . To make anyone answerable for doing evil to others is the rule; to make him answerable for not preventing evil is, comparatively speaking, the exception. . . .

But there is a sphere of action in which society, as distinguished from the individual, has, if any, only an indirect interest: comprehending all that portion of a person's life and conduct which affects only himself or, if it also affects others, only with their free, voluntary, and undeceived consent and participation. . . . This, then, is the appropriate region of human liberty. It comprises, first, the inward domain of consciousness, demanding liberty of conscience in the most comprehensive sense, liberty of thought and feeling, absolute freedom of opinion and sentiment on all subjects, practical or speculative, scientific, moral or theological. The liberty of expressing and publishing opinions may seem to fall under a different principle, since it belongs to that part of the conduct of an individual which concerns other people, but, being almost of as much importance as the liberty of thought itself and resting in great part on the same reasons, is practically inseparable from it. Secondly, the principle requires liberty of tastes and pursuits, of framing the plan of our life to suit our own character, of doings as we like, subject to such consequences as may follow, without impediment from our fellow creatures, so long as what we do does not harm them, even though they should think our conduct foolish, perverse, or wrong. Thirdly, from this liberty of each individual follows the liberty, within the same limits, of combination among individuals; freedom to unite for any purpose not involving harm to others: the persons combining being supposed to be of full age and not forced or deceived.

No society in which these liberties are not, on the whole, respected is free, whatever may be its form of government; and none is completely free in which they do not exist absolute and unqualified. The only freedom which deserves the name is that of pursuing our own good in our own way, so long as we do not attempt to deprive others of theirs or impede their efforts to obtain it. Each is the proper guardian of his own health, whether bodily or mental and spiritual. Mankind are greater gainers by suffering each other to live as seems good to themselves than by compelling each to live as seems good to the rest. . . .

Chapter II: Of the liberty of thought and discussion

The time, it is hoped, is gone by when any defense would be necessary of the "liberty of the press" as one of the securities against corrupt or tyrannical government. No argument, we may suppose, can now be needed against permitting a legislature or an executive, not identified in interest with the people, to prescribe opinions to them and determine what doctrines or what arguments they shall be allowed to hear. . . . Let us suppose, therefore, that the government is entirely at one with the people, and never thinks of exerting any power of coercion unless in agreement with what it conceives to be their voice. But I deny the right of the people to exercise such coercion, either by themselves or by their government. The power itself is illegitimate. The best government has no more title to it than the worst. It is as noxious, or more noxious, when exerted in accordance with public opinion than when in opposition to it. If all mankind minus one were of one opinion, mankind would be no more justified in silencing that one person than he, if he had the power, would be justified in silencing mankind. Were an opinion a personal possession of no value except to the owner, if to be obstructed in the enjoyment of it were simply a private injury, it would make some difference whether the injury was inflicted only on a few persons or on many. But the peculiar evil of silencing the expression of an opinion is that it is robbing the human race, posterity as well as the existing generation—those who dissent from the opinion, still more than those who hold it. If the opinion is right, they are deprived of the opportunity of exchanging error for truth; if wrong, they lose, what is almost as great a benefit, the clearer perception and livelier impression of truth produced by its collision with error.

It is necessary to consider separately these two hypotheses, each of which has a distinct branch of the argument corresponding to it. We can never be sure that the opinion we are endeavoring to stifle is a false opinion; and if we were sure, stifling it would be an evil still.

First, the opinion which it is attempted to suppress by authority may possibly be true. Those who desire to suppress it, of course, deny its truth; but they are not infallible. They have no authority to decide the question for all mankind and exclude every other person from the means of judging. To refuse a hearing to an opinion because they are sure that it is false is to assume that their certainty is the same thing as absolute certainty. All silencing of discussion is an assumption of infallibility. Its condemnation may be allowed to rest on this common argument, not the worse for being common.

Unfortunately for the good sense of mankind, the fact of their fallibility is far from carrying the weight in their practical judgment which is always allowed to it in theory; for while everyone well knows himself to be fallible, few think it necessary to take any precautions against their own fallibility, or admit the supposition that any opinion of which they feel very certain may be one of the examples of the error to which they acknowledge themselves to be liable. . . . Nor is his faith in this collective authority at all shaken by his being aware that other ages, countries, sects, churches, classes, and parties have thought, and even now think, the exact reverse. He devolves upon his own world the responsibility of being in the right against the dissentient worlds of other people; and it never troubles him that mere accident has decided which of these numerous worlds is the object of his reliance, and the same causes which make him a churchman in London would have made him a Buddhist or a Confucian in Peking. Yet it is as evident in itself, as any amount of argument can make it, that ages are no more infallible than individuals—every age having held many opinions which subsequent ages have deemed not only false but absurd; and it is as certain that many opinions, now general, will be rejected by future ages, as it is that many, once general, are rejected by the present. . . .

When we consider either the history of opinion or the ordinary conduct of human life, to what is to be ascribed that the one and the other are no worse than they are? Not certainly to the inherent force of the human understanding, for on any matter not self-evident there are ninety-nine persons totally incapable of judging of it for one who is capable; and the capacity of the hundredth person is only comparative, for the majority of the eminent men of every past generation held many opinions now known to be erroneous, and did or approved numerous things which no one will now justify. Why is it then, that there is on the whole a preponderance among mankind of rational opinions and rational conduct? If there really is this preponderance—which there must be unless human affairs are, and have always been, in an almost desperate state—it is owing to a quality of the human mind, the source of everything respectable in man either as an intellectual or as a moral being, namely, that his errors are corrigible. . . . Wrong opinions and practices gradually yield to fact and argument; but . . . [v]ery few facts are able to tell their own story, without comments to bring out their meaning. The whole strength and value, then, of human judgment depending on the one property, that it can be set right when it is wrong, reliance can be placed on it only when the means of setting it right are kept constantly at hand. . . . The steady habit of correcting and completing [one's] own opinion by collating it with those of others, so far from causing doubt and hesitation in carrying it into practice, is the only stable foundation for a just reliance on it. . . .

The most intolerant of churches, the Roman Catholic Church, even at the canonization of a saint admits, and listens patiently to, a "devil's advocate." The holiest of men, it appears, cannot be admitted to posthumous honors until all that the devil could say against him is known and weighed. If even the Newtonian philosophy were not permitted to be questioned, mankind could not feel as complete assurance of its truth as they now do. The beliefs which we have most warrant for have no safeguard to rest on but a standing invitation to the whole world to prove them unfounded. If the challenge is not accepted, or is accepted and the attempt fails, we are far enough from certainty still, but we have done the best that the existing state of human reason admits of. . . .

Strange it is that men should admit the validity of the arguments for free discussion, but object to their being "pushed to an extreme," not seeing that unless the reasons are good for an extreme case, they are not good for any case. Strange they should imagine that they are not assuming infallibility when they acknowledge that there should be free discussion on all subjects which can possibly be doubtful, but think that some particular principle or doctrine should be forbidden to be questioned because it is so certain, that is, because they are certain that it is certain. To call any proposition certain, while there is anyone who would deny its certainty if permitted, but who is not permitted, is to assume that we ourselves, and those who agree with us, are the judges of certainty, and judges without hearing the other side. . . .

Mankind can hardly be too often reminded that there was once a man called Socrates, between whom and the legal authorities and public opinion of his time there took place a memorable collision. Born in an age and country abounding in individual greatness, this man has been handed down to us by those who best knew both him and the age as the most virtuous man in it; while we know him as the head and prototype of all subsequent teachers of virtue, the source equally of the lofty inspiration of Plato and the judicious utilitarianism of Aristotle. . . . This acknowledged master of all the eminent thinkers who have since lived—whose fame, still growing after more than two thousand years, all but outweighs the whole remainder of the names which make his native city illustrious—was put to death by his countrymen, after a judicial conviction, for impiety and immorality. Impiety, in denying the gods recognized by the State; indeed, his accuser asserted . . . that he believed in no gods at all. Immorality, in being, by his doctrines and instructions, a "corruptor of youth." Of these charges the tribunal, there is every ground for believing, honestly found him guilty, and condemned the man who probably of all then born had deserved best of mankind to be put to death as a criminal.

To pass from this to the only other instance of judicial iniquity, the mention of which, after the condemnation of Socrates, would not be an anticlimax: the event which took place on Calvary rather more than eighteen hundred years ago. The man who left on the memory of those who witnessed his life and conversation such an impression of his moral grandeur that eighteen subsequent centuries have done homage to him as the Almighty in person, was ignominiously put to death, as what? As a blasphemer. Men did not merely mistake their benefactor, they mistook him of the exact contrary of what he was and treated him as that prodigy of impiety which they themselves are now held to be for their treatment of him. The feelings with which mankind now regard these lamentable transactions, especially the later of the two, render them extremely unjust in their judgment of the unhappy actors. These were, to all appearance, not bad men—not worse than men commonly are, but rather the contrary; men who possessed in a full, or somewhat more than a full measure, the religious, moral, and patriotic feelings of their time and people; the very kind of men who, in all times, our own included, have every chance of passing through life blameless and respected. The high priest who rent his garments when the words were pronounced, which, according to all the ideas of his country, constituted the blackest guilt, was in all probability quite as sincere in his horror and indignation as the generality of respectable and pious men now are in the religious and moral sentiments they profess; and most of those who now shudder at his conduct, if they had lived in his time, and been born Jews, would have acted precisely as he did. Orthodox Christians who are tempted to think that those who stoned to death the first martyrs must have been worse men than they themselves are ought to remember that one of those persecutors was Saint Paul. . . .

Let us now pass to the second division of the argument, and dismissing the supposition that any of the received opinions may be false, let us assume them to be true and examine into the worth of the manner in which they are likely to be held when their truth is not freely and openly canvassed. However unwillingly a person who has a strong opinion may admit the possibility that his opinion may be false, he ought to be moved by the consideration that, however true it may be, if it is not fully, frequently, and fearlessly discussed, it will be held as a dead dogma, not a living truth.

There is a class of persons (happily not quite so numerous as formerly) who think it enough if a person assents undoubtingly to what they think true, though he has no knowledge whatever of the grounds of the opinion and could not make a tenable defense of it against the most superficial objections. . . . This is not knowing the truth. Truth, thus held, is but one superstition the more, accidentally clinging to the words which enunciate a truth. . . .

Whatever people believe, on subjects on which it is of the first importance to believe rightly, they ought to be able to defend against at least the common objections. . . . [O]n every subject on which difference of opinion is possible, the truth depends on a balance to be struck between two sets of conflicting reasons. Even in natural philosophy, there is always some other explanation possible of the same facts; some geocentric theory instead of heliocentric, some phlogiston instead of oxygen; and it has to be shown why that other theory cannot be the true one; and until this is shown, and until we know how it is shown, we do not understand the grounds of our opinion. But when we turn to subjects infinitely more complicated, to morals, religion, politics, social relations, and the business of life, three-fourths of the arguments for every disputed opinion consist in dispelling the appearances which favor some opinion different from it. The greatest orator, save one, of antiquity, has left it on record that he always studied his adversary's case with as great, if not still greater, intensity than even his own. What Cicero practiced as the means of forensic success requires to be imitated by all who study any subject in order to arrive at the truth. He who knows only his own side of the case knows little of that. His reasons may be good, and no one may have been able to refute them. But if he is equally unable to refute the reasons on the opposite side, if he does not so much as know what they are, he has no ground for preferring either opinion.... Nor is it enough that he should hear the arguments of adversaries from his own teachers, presented as they state them, and accompanied by what they offer as refutations. That is not the way to do justice to the arguments or bring them into real contact with his own mind. He must be able to hear them from persons who actually believe them, who defend them in earnest and do their very utmost for them. He must know them in their most plausible and persuasive form; he must feel the whole force of the difficulty which the true view of the subject has to encounter and dispose of, else he will never really possess himself of the portion of truth which meets and removes that difficulty. Ninety-nine in a hundred of what are called educated men are in this condition even of those who can argue fluently for their opinions. Their conclusion may be true, but it might be false for anything they know; they have never thrown themselves into the mental position of those who think differently from them, and considered what such persons may have to say; and, consequently, they do not, in any proper sense of the word, know the doctrine which they themselves profess.... So essential is this discipline to a real understanding of moral and human subjects that, if opponents of all-important truths do not exist, it is indispensable to imagine them and supply them with the strongest arguments which the most skillful devil's advocate can conjure up.... If the teachers of mankind are to be cognizant of all that they ought to know, everything must be free to be written and published without restraint.

If, however, the mischievous operation of the absence of free discussion, when the received opinions are true, were confined to leaving men ignorant of the grounds of those opinions, it might be thought that this, if an intellectual, is no moral evil and does not affect the worth of the opinions, regarded in their influence on the character. The fact, however, is that not only the grounds of the opinion are forgotten in the absence of discussion, but too often the meaning of the opinion itself. The words which convey it cease to suggest ideas, or suggest only a small portion of those they were originally employed to communicate. Instead of a vivid conception and a living belief, there remain only a few phrases retained by rote; or, if any part, the shell and husk only of the meaning is retained, the finer essence being lost....

It is illustrated in the experience of almost all ethical doctrines and religious creeds. They are all full of meaning and vitality to those who originate them, and to the direct disciples of the originators. Their meaning continues to be felt in undiminished strength, and is perhaps brought out into even fuller consciousness, so long as the struggle lasts to give the doctrine or creed an ascendancy over other creeds. At last it either prevails and becomes the general opinion, or its progress stops; it keeps possession of the ground it has gained, but ceases to spread further. When either of these results has become apparent, controversy on the subject flags, and gradually dies away. The doctrine has taken its place, if not as a received opinion, as one of the admitted sects or divisions of opinion; those who hold it have generally inherited, not adopted it. . . . Instead of being, as at first, constantly on the alert either to defend themselves against the world or to bring the world over to them, they have subsided into acquiescence and neither listen, when they can help it, to arguments against their creed, nor trouble dissentients (if there be such) with arguments in its favor. From this time may usually be dated the decline in the living power of the doctrine. . . . [W]hen the mind is no longer compelled, in the same degree as at first, to exercise its vital powers on the questions which its belief presents to it, there is a progressive tendency to forget all of the belief except the formularies. . . .

To what an extent doctrines intrinsically fitted to make the deepest impression upon the mind may remain as dead beliefs, without being ever realized in the imagination, the feelings, or the understanding, is exemplified by the manner in which the majority of believers hold the doctrines of Christianity. By Christianity, I here mean what is accounted such by all churches and sects—the maxims and precepts contained in the New Testament. These are considered sacred, and accepted as laws, by all professing Christians. Yet it is scarcely too much to say that not one Christian in a thousand guides or tests his individual conduct by reference to those laws. The standard to which he does refer it is the custom of his nation, his class, or his religious profession. He has thus, on the one hand, a collection of ethical maxims which he believes to have been vouchsafed to him by infallible wisdom as rules for his government; and, on the other, a set of everyday judgments and practices which go a certain length with some of those maxims, not so great a length with others, stand in direct opposition to some, and are, on the whole, a compromise between the Christian creed and the interests and suggestions of worldly life. To the first of these standards he gives his homage; to the other his real allegiance. All Christians believe that the blessed are the poor and humble, and those who are ill-used by the world; that it is easier for a camel to pass through the eye of a needle than for a rich man to enter the kingdom of heaven; that they should judge not, lest they be judged; that they should swear not at all; that they should love their neighbor as themselves; that if one take their cloak, they should give him their coat also; that they should take no thought for the morrow; that if they would be perfect they should sell all that they have and give it to the poor. They are not insincere when they say that they believe these things. They do believe them, as people believe what they have always heard lauded and never discussed. But in the sense of that living belief which regulates conduct, they believe these doctrines just up to the point to which it is usual to act upon them. The doctrines in their integrity are serviceable to pelt adversaries with; and it is understood that they are to be put forward (when possible) as the reasons for whatever people do that they think laudable. . . .

Now we may be well assured that the case was not thus, but far otherwise, with the early Christians. Had it been thus, Christianity never would have expanded from an obscure sect of the despised Hebrews into the religion of the Roman empire. When their enemies said, "See how these Christians love one another" (a remark not likely to be made by anybody now), they assuredly had a much livelier feeling of the meaning of their creed than they have ever had since. And to this cause, probably, it is chiefly owing that Christianity now makes so little progress in extending its domain, and after eighteen centuries is still nearly confined to Europeans and the descendants of Europeans. . . . The sayings of Christ coexist passively in their minds, producing hardly any effect beyond what is caused by mere listening to words so amiable and bland. . . .

It still remains to speak of one of the principal causes which make diversity of opinion advantageous, and will continue to do so until mankind shall have entered a stage of intellectual advancement which at present seems at an incalculable distance. We have hitherto considered only two possibilities: that the received opinion may be false, and some other opinion, consequently, true; or that, the received opinion being true, a conflict with the opposite error is essential to a clear apprehension and deep feeling of its truth. But there is a commoner case than either of these: when the conflicting doctrines, instead of being one true and the other false, share the truth between them, and the nonconforming opinion is needed to supply the remainder of the truth of which the received doctrine embodies only a part. Popular opinions, on subjects not palpable to sense, are often true, but seldom or never the whole truth. They are a part of the truth, sometimes a greater, sometimes a smaller part, but exaggerated, distorted, and disjointed from the truths by which they ought to be accompanied and limited. Heretical opinions, on the other hand are generally some of these suppressed and neglected truths, bursting the bonds which kept them down, and either seeking reconciliation with the truth contained in the common opinion, or fronting it as enemies, and setting themselves up, with similar exclusiveness, as the whole truth. . . . Even progress, which ought to superadd, for the most part only substitutes one partial and incomplete truth for another; improvement consisting chiefly in this, that the new fragment of truth is more wanted, more adapted to the needs of the time than that which it displaces. Such being the partial character of prevailing opinions, even when resting on a true foundation, every opinion which embodies somewhat of the portion of truth which the common opinion omits ought to be considered precious, with whatever amount of error and confusion that truth may be blended. . . .

In politics, again, it is almost a commonplace that a party of order or stability and a party of progress or reform are both necessary elements of a healthy state of political life, until the one or the other shall have so enlarged its mental grasp as to be a party equally of order and of progress, knowing and distinguishing what is fit to be preserved from what ought to be swept away.

Each of these modes of thinking derives its utility from the deficiencies of the other; but it is in a great measure the opposition of the other that keeps each within the limits of reason and sanity. Unless opinions favorable to democracy and to aristocracy, to property and to equality, to co-operation and to competition, to luxury and to abstinence, to sociality and individuality, to liberty and discipline, and all the other standing antagonisms of practical life, are expressed with equal freedom and enforced and defended with equal talent and energy, there is no chance of both elements obtaining their due; one scale is sure to go up, and the other down. Truth, in the great practical concerns of life, is so much a question of the reconciling and combining of opposites that very few have minds sufficiently capacious and impartial to make the adjustment with an approach to correctness, and it has to be made by the rough process of a struggle between combatants fighting under hostile banners.... [O]nly through diversity of opinion is there, in the existing state of human intellect, a chance of fair play to all sides of truth. When there are persons to be found who form an exception to the apparent unanimity of the world on any subject, even if the world is in the right, it is always probable that dissentients have something worth hearing to say for themselves, and that truth would lose something by their silence....

The exclusive pretension made by a part of the truth to be the whole must and ought to be protested against; and if a reactionary impulse should make the protestors unjust in their turn, this one-sidedness, like the other, may be lamented but must be tolerated. If Christians would teach infidels to be just to Christianity, they should themselves be just to infidelity. It can do truth no service to blink the fact, known to all who have the most ordinary acquaintance with literary history, that a large portion of the noblest and most valuable moral teaching has been the work, not only of men who did not know, but of men who knew and rejected, the Christian faith.

I do not pretend that the most unlimited use of the freedom of enunciating all possible opinions would put an end to the evils of religious or philosophical sectarianism.... I acknowledge that the tendency of all opinions to become sectarian is not cured by the freest discussion, but is often heightened and exacerbated thereby; the truth which ought to have been, but was not, seen, being rejected all the more violently because proclaimed by persons regarded as opponents. But it is not on the impassioned partisan, it is on the calmer and more disinterested bystander, that this collision of opinions works its salutary effect. Not the violent conflict between parts of the truth, but the quiet suppression of half of it, is the formidable evil; there is always hope when people are forced to listen to both sides; it is when they attend only to one that errors harden into prejudices, and truth itself ceases to have the effect of truth by being exaggerated into falsehood....

We have now recognized the necessity to the mental well-being of mankind (on which all their other well-being depends) of freedom of opinion, and freedom of the expression of opinion, on four distinct grounds, which we will now briefly recapitulate:

First, if any opinion is compelled to silence, that opinion may, for aught we can certainly know, be true. To deny this is to assume our own infallibility.

Secondly, though the silenced opinion be an error, it may, and very commonly does, contain a portion of truth; and since the general or prevailing opinion on any subject is rarely or never the whole truth, it is only by the collision of adverse opinions that the remainder of the truth has any chance of being supplied.

Thirdly, even if the received opinion be not only true, but the whole truth; unless it is suffered to be, and actually is, vigorously and earnestly contested, it will, by most of those who receive it, be held in the manner of a prejudice, with little comprehension or feeling of its rational grounds. And not only this, but fourthly, the meaning of the doctrine itself will be in danger of being lost or enfeebled, and deprived of its vital effect on the character and conduct: the dogma becoming a mere formal profession, inefficacious for good, but cumbering the ground and preventing the growth of any real and heartfelt conviction from reason or personal experience.

Chapter 8
Samuel Warren
and Louis Brandeis
1855-1910 and 1856-1941

I n recent years, the most vexing ethical issue raised by the public, and frequently by new journalists as well, is the question of privacy. While much of the philosophical foundation of journalism consists of arguments for what to publish and why, the privacy argument goes the other way. It tries to justify limiting or preventing the publication of certain kinds of information about certain kinds of people. As has been shown, free press questions date at least to the seventeenth century; privacy is largely a twentieth-century problem. Cato and other eighteenth-century journalists seem to have recognized the right to privacy in a negative sense: they argued for the right and the obligation of open discussion of the affairs of public figures *if they had bearing on matters of public policy.* The corollary is implicit: behavior unrelated to public issues ought to remain a private matter. (Of course, making this distinction hardly fixes the line between the two. If a politician is a chronic philanderer, for example, does this or does this not say important things about that politician's fundamental integrity and judgment? Of course, the sovereign voters may decline to vote on this question of character, or they may decide there are other, more important, dimensions to the election, but are journalists entitled to deny to the voters the information upon which to make that choice?)

The positive argument for a fundamental right to privacy was first made in 1890 by two Boston law partners, Samuel Warren and Louis Brandeis (the same Brandeis who would later, as a Supreme Court justice, make some of the twentieth-century's most important pronouncements defending a free press.) Their privacy argument was essentially a conservative argument. In the Hearst- and Pulitzer-dominated world of both sensationalism and muckraking, the rich, the mighty, and the well-born were subject to scrutiny as never before. High-speed presses allowed newspapers to have circulations of a million and more, and the new half-tone process made photographic reproduction in newspapers possible for the first time. The result was a spate of newspaper articles chronicling, very much unbidden, the lives of the rich and famous. The response from those whose lives were put under the harsh glare of public scrutiny for the first time was outrage at the sense of violation, coupled with the frustrating awareness that the snooping seemed not to be against any laws. The upshot was that Brandeis and Warren went back to the wellhead of modern democratic thought, John Locke, and found in his political philosophy an argument for the right to privacy as a logical extension of Locke's arguments about the inalienable right to property.

"The right to privacy"
Harvard Law Review (4:5), 1890

T hat the individual shall have full protection in person and in property is a principle as old as the common law; but it has been found necessary from time to time to define anew the exact nature and extent of such protection. Political, social, and economic changes entail the recognition of new rights, and the common law, in its eternal youth, grows to meet the demands of society. Thus, in very early times, the law gave a remedy only for physical interference with life and property, for trespasses *vi et armis*. Then the "right to life" served only to protect the subject from battery in its various forms; liberty meant freedom from actual restraint; and the right to property secured to the individual his lands and his cattle. Later, there came a recognition of man's spiritual nature, of his feelings and his intellect. Gradually the scope of these legal rights broadened; and now the right to life has come to mean the right to enjoy life—the right to be let alone; the right to liberty secures the exercise of extensive civil privileges; and the term "property" has grown to comprise every form of possession—intangible, as well as tangible.

Thus, with the recognition of the legal value of sensations, the protection against actual bodily injury was extended to prohibit mere attempts to do such injury; that is, the putting another in fear of such injury. From the action of battery grew that of assault. Much later there came a qualified protection of the individual against offensive noises and odors, against dust and smoke, and excessive vibration. The law of nuisance was developed. So regard for human emotions soon extended the scope of personal immunity beyond the body of the individual. His reputation, the standing among his fellow-men, was considered, and the law of slander and libel arose. Man's family relations became a part of the legal conception of his life, and the alienation of a wife's affections was held remediable. Occasionally the law halted—as in its refusal to recognize the intrusion by seduction upon the honor of the family. But even here the demands of society were met. A mean fiction, the action *per quod servitium amisit*, was resorted to, and by allowing damages for injury to the parents' feelings, an adequate remedy was ordinarily afforded. Similar to the expansion of the right to life was the growth of the legal conception of property. From corporeal property arose the incorporeal rights issuing out of it; and then there opened the wide realm of intangible property, in the products and processes of the mind, as works of literature and art, goodwill, trade secrets, and trademarks.

This development of the law was inevitable. The intense intellectual and emotional life, and the heightening of sensations which came with the advance of civilization, made it clear to men that only a part of the pain, pleasure, and profit of life lay in physical things. Thoughts, emotions, and sensations demanded legal recognition, and the beautiful capacity for growth which characterizes the common law enabled the judges to afford the requisite protection, without the interposition of the legislature.

Recent inventions and business methods call attention to the next step which must be taken for the protection of the person, and for securing to the individual what Judge Cooley calls the right "to be let alone." Instantaneous photographs and newspaper enterprise have invaded the sacred precincts of private and domestic life; and numerous mechanical devices threaten to make good the prediction that "what is whispered in the closet shall be proclaimed from the house-tops." For years there has been a feeling that the law must afford some remedy for the unauthorized circulation of portraits of private persons. . . .

Of the desirability—indeed of the necessity—of some such protection, there can, it is believed, be no doubt. The press is overstepping in every direction the obvious bounds of propriety and of decency. Gossip is no longer the resource of the idle and of the vicious, but has become a trade, which is pursued with industry as well as effrontery. To satisfy a prurient taste the details of sexual relations are spread broadcast in the columns of the daily papers. To occupy the indolent, column upon column is filled with idle gossip, which can only be procured by intrusion upon the domestic circle. The intensity and complexity of life, attendant upon advancing civilization, have rendered necessary some retreat from the wold, and man, under the refining influence of culture, has become more sensitive to publicity, so that solitude and privacy have become more essential to the individual; but modern enterprise and invention have, through invasions upon his privacy, subjected him to mental pain and distress, far greater than could be inflicted by mere bodily injury.

Nor is the harm wrought by such invasions confined to the suffering of those who may be made the subjects of journalistic or other enterprise. . . . Even gossip apparently harmless . . . belittles by inverting the relative importance of things, thus dwarfing the thoughts and aspirations of a people. When personal gossip attains the dignity of print, and crowds the space available for matters of real interest to the community, what wonder that the ignorant and thoughtless mistake its relative importance. Easy of comprehension, appealing to that weak side of human nature which is never wholly cast down by the misfortunes and frailties of our neighbors, no one can be surprised that it usurps the place of interest in brains capable of other things. Triviality destroys at once robustness of thought and delicacy of feeling. No enthusiasm can flourish, no generous impulse can survive under its blighting influence.

It is our purpose to consider whether the existing law affords a principle which can properly be invoked to protect the privacy of the individual; and, if it does, what the nature and extent of such protection is. . . . [T]he legal doctrines relating to infractions of what is ordinarily termed the common-law right to intellectual and artistic property are, it is believed, but instances and applications of a general right to privacy, which properly understood afford a remedy for the evils under consideration.

The common law secures to each individual the right of determining, ordinarily, to what extent his thoughts, sentiments, and emotions shall be communicated to others . . . the protection afforded to thoughts, sentiments, and emotions, expressed through the medium of writing or of the arts, so far as it consists in preventing publication, is merely an instance of the enforcement of the more general right of the individual to be let alone. It is like the right not to be assaulted or beaten, the right not to be imprisoned, the right not to be maliciously prosecuted, the right not to be defamed. In each of these rights, as indeed in all other rights recognized by the law, there inheres the quality of being owned or possessed—and (as that is the distinguishing attribute of property) there may be some propriety in speaking of those rights as property. [E]xisting law affords a principle which may be invoked to protect the privacy of the individual from invasion either by the too enterprising press, the photographer, or the possessor of any other modern device for recording or reproducing scenes or sounds. . . . The principle which protects personal writings and any other productions of the intellect or of the emotions, is the right to privacy, and the law has no new principle to formulate when it extends this protection to the personal appearance, sayings, acts, and to personal relation, domestic or otherwise. . . .

The right to privacy does not prohibit any publication of matter which is of public or general interest.

In determining the scope of this rule, aid would be afforded by the analogy, in the law of libel and slander, of cases which deal with the qualified privilege of comment and criticism on matters of public and general interest.It is the unwarranted invasion of individual privacy which is reprehended, and to be, so far as possible, prevented. . . . There are persons who may reasonably claim as a right, protection from the notoriety entailed by being made the victims of journalistic enterprise. There are others who, in varying degrees, have renounced the right to live their lives screened from public observation. Matters which men of the first class may justly contend, concern themselves alone, may in those of the second be the subject of legitimate interest to their fellow-citizens. Peculiarities of manner and person, which in the ordinary individual should be free from comment, may acquire a public importance, if found in a candidate for political office. Some further discrimination is necessary, therefore, than to class facts or deeds as public or private according to the standard to be applied to the fact or deed per se. To publish of a modest and retiring individual that he suffers from an impediment in his speech or that he cannot spell correctly, is an unwarranted, if not an unexampled, infringement of his rights, while to state and comment on the same characteristics found in a would-be congressman could not be regarded as beyond the pale of propriety.

The general object in view is to protect the privacy of private life, and to whatever degree and in whatever connection a man's life has ceased to be private, before the publication under consideration has been made, to that extent the protection is to be withdrawn. . . .

Part II—Philosophy: The Press and the Search for Truth

I t was largely the result of technological changes, coupled with the economies of cooperation, that led journalism to what has often been seen as a near-sacred demand for truth and objectivity. As an hour with a Revolutionary-era paper will easily attest, the journalism that the founding generation endorsed, supported, and protected was a far cry from the sober, intelligent, balanced, neutral journalism that today is the hallmark of the best of the business. The newspapers the founding generation went to such lengths to protect were shrill, loud, and scurrilous, most making no pretense of being neutral disseminators of factual information. The Revolutionary generation *assumed* partisanship as a natural order of things. The presumption was not so much that any individual journalist would learn and reveal the truth. It was, rather, that truth would gradually emerge from the give-and-take of partisans representing deeply held but widely divergent beliefs. That is why James Madison once argued that newspapers would be better if they could be printed on only one side, allowing someone with an opposing view to write the rebuttal on the blank back side.

While the journalism protected by the First Amendment was essentially a political enterprise, with the coming of the Penny Press in the 1830s, it quickly became a business and a big one. The influence of money on journalism—on the writers and editors, on the readers, and on the content of news itself—will be discussed more fully in Section III. For now, it is enough to observe that by the middle of the nineteenth century, editors realized that huge numbers of ordinary citizens would actually pay money for information, provided it was fresh and interesting. Distant events, such as the war with Mexico in the 1840s, were interesting, and the speed of a new invention, the telegraph, could make them fresh. But the telegraph was also very expensive and editors realized they could split the cost of a single correspondent, but only if the copy was neutral enough to satisfy many masters. The modern idea of the unbiased story was born. For the thoughtful journalist, the loss of a guaranteed voice of opposition, however virulent, implied serious obligations to fairness, to accuracy, and to truth as never before. The essays in this section deal with the questions of truth and objectivity. As the intellectually curious have done for millennia, we turn first to the cradle of Western philosophy, ancient Greece.

Chapter 9
Plato
427?-347 B.C.

T he question of truth—its existence and our ability to grasp it—is as old as the Western tradition itself. Two of the chief themes in this book, truth and democracy, as well as the relationship of the press to both, find their roots in classical Greece.

The issue of how we know reality, and by implication "the truth," constituted one of the more significant debates in early Greek philosophy. Today the term *sophistry* implies elaborate yet empty argumentation. The original Sophists were hired-gun rhetoricians willing to plead, or to teach others to plead, any side of an argument. They could do this without ethical qualms because of their belief in the complete inability of humans to really *know* what constituted truth, or even physical reality. If truth cannot be discerned, and may not even exist, they argued, then all points of view become equally valid and the best one can do is simply to argue well.

Today's journalist may or may not believe in the ability to be truly objective but probably does believe that some objective reality exists. The Sophists were not so sure. The most famous of them, Protagoras, summed it up: "Man," he said, "is the measure of all things." What we take to be real, what we take to be the truth, is simply what we take from a situation, and what we take is heavily influenced, if not wholly determined, by what we bring to it.

It was against this gloomy subjectivity that Plato, through Socrates, and others fought. In the dialogue *Theaetetus*, for example, Plato leads a young man through a detailed criticism of Protagoras. For Plato, there was a substantive and objective reality. Moreover, concepts such as Truth and the Good had their own independent existence, in many ways more real than reality itself in so far as reality, as we typically understand it, constituted only the weak manifestations of the metaphysical world.

Truth, however, is not easily obtained, according to Plato. Most people, in fact, avoid it. What people hold to be true represents only the washed-out shadows of the Truth. They are poorly thought-out opinions and biases. Knowledge, wisdom, and eventually Truth are possible only with considerable effort.

Plato's "Allegory of the Cave" from *The Republic* is the classic illustration of his sense of the relationship between opinion and Truth. It can easily be seen as a metaphor for the illusory nature of mediated reality, wherein Plato's shadows on the wall of the cave are likened to accounts of events, particularly on television. For the journalist, the analogy also suggests several other meanings: a reminder of the early origins of the debate over objectivity; a hope that Truth, the journalist's Holy Grail, does indeed exist, but a caution that it is not easily obtained; and an allegorical tale about the role of mass media as the bonfire that casts the smoky, dancing light of information among the unenlightened.

In the following dialogue Socrates is talking with his companion, Glaucon.

"The Allegory of the Cave"
The Republic, 386?-367? B.C.

P icture men dwelling in a sort of subterranean cavern with a long entrance open to the light on its entire width. Conceive them as having their legs and necks fettered from childhood, so that they remain in the same spot, able to look forward only, and prevented by the fetters from turning their heads. Picture further the light from a fire burning higher up and at a distance behind them, and between the fire and the prisoners and above them a road along which a low wall has been built, as the exhibitors of puppet shows have partitions before the men themselves, above which they show the puppets.

All that I see, he said.

See also, then, men carrying past the wall implements of all kinds that rise above the wall, and human images and shapes of animals as well, wrought in stone and wood and every material, some of these bearers presumably speaking and others silent.

A strange image you speak of, he said, and strange prisoners.

Like to us, I said. For, to begin with, tell me do you think that these men would have seen anything of themselves or of one another except the shadows cast from the fire on the wall of the cave that fronted them?

How could they, he said, if they were compelled to hold their heads unmoved through life?

And again, would not the same be true of the object carried past them? Surely.

If then they were able to talk to one another, do you not think that they would suppose that in naming the things that they saw they were naming the passing objects?

Necessarily.

And if their prison had an echo from the wall opposite them, when one of the passers-by uttered a sound, do you think that they would suppose anything else than the passing shadow to be the speaker?

By Zeus, I do not, said he.

Then in every way such prisoners would deem reality to be nothing else than the shadows of the artificial objects.

Quite inevitabley, he said.

Consider, then, what would be the manner of the release and healing from these bonds and this folly if in the course of nature something of this sort should happen to them. When one was freed from his fetters and compelled to stand up suddenly and turn his head around and walk and to lift up his eyes to the light, and in doing all this felt pain and, because of the dazzle and glitter of the light, was unable to discern the objects whose shadows he formerly saw, what do you suppose would be his answer if someone told him that what he had seen before was all a cheat and an illusion, but that now, being nearer to reality and turned toward more real things, he saw more truly? And if also one should point out to him each of the passing objects and constrain him by questions to say what it is, do you not think that he would be at a loss and that he would regard what he formerly saw as more real than the things now pointed out to him?

Far more real, he said.

And if he were compelled to look at the light itself, would not that pain his eyes, and would he not turn away and flee to those things which he is able to discern and regard them as in very deed more clear and exact than the objects pointed out?

It is so, he said.

And if, said I, someone should drag him thence by force up the ascent which is rough and steep, and not let him go before he had drawn him out into the light of the sun, do you not think that he would find it painful to be so haled along, and would chafe at it, and when he came out into the light, that his eyes would be filled with its beams so that he would not be able to see even one of the things that we call real?

Why, no, not immediately, he said.

Then there would be need of habituation, I take it, to enable him to see the things higher up. And at first he would most easily discern the shadows and, after that, the likenesses or reflections in water of men and other things, and later, the things themselves, and from these he would go on to contemplate the appearances in the heavens and heaven itself, more easily by night, looking at the light of the stars and the moon, than by day the sun and the sun's light.

Of course.

And so, finally, I suppose, he would be able to look upon the sun itself and see its true nature, not by reflections in water or phantasms of it in an alien setting, but in and by itself in its own place.

Necessarily, he said.

And at this point he would infer and conclude that this it is that provides the seasons and the courses of the year and presides over all things in the visible region, and is in some sort the cause of all these things that they had seen.

Obviously, he said, that would be the next step.

Well then, if he recalled to mind his first habitation and what passed for wisdom there, and his fellow bondsmen, do you not think that he would count himself happy in the change and pity them?

He would indeed.

And if there had been honors and commendations among them which they bestowed on one another and prizes for the man who is quickest to make out the shadows as they pass and best able to remember their customary precedences, sequences, and coexistences, and so most successful in guessing at what was to come, do you think he would be very keen about such rewards, and that he would envy and emulate those who were honored by these prisoners and lorded it among them, or that he would feel with Homer and greatly prefer while living on earth to be serf of another, a landless man, and endure anything rather than opine with them and live that life?

Yes, he said, I think that he would choose to endure anything rather than such a life.

And consider this also, said I. If such a one should go down again and take his old place would he not get his eyes full of darkness, thus suddenly coming out of the sunlight?

He would indeed.

Now if he should be required to contend with these perpetual prisoners in evaluating these shadows while his vision was still dim and before his eyes were accustomed to the dark—and this time required for habituation would not be very short—would he not provoke laughter, and would it not be said of him that he had returned from his journey aloft with his eyes ruined and that it was not worthwhile even to attempt the ascent? And if it were possible to lay hands on and to kill the man who tried to release them and lead them up, would they not kill him?

They certainly would, he said.

This image then, dear Glaucon, we must apply as a whole to all that has been said, likening the region revealed through sight to the habitation of the prison, and the light of the fire in it to the power of the sun. And if you assume that the ascent and the contemplation of the things above is the soul's ascension to the intelligible region, you will not miss my surmise, since that is what you desire to hear. But Gods know whether it is true. But, at any rate, my dream as it appears to me is that in the region of the known the last thing to be seen and hardly seen is the idea of good, and that when seen it must needs point us to the conclusion that this is indeed the cause for all things of all that is right and beautiful, giving birth in the visible world to light, and the author of light and itself in the intelligible world being the authentic source of truth and reason, and that anyone who is to act wisely in private or public must have caught sight of this.

Chapter 10
Francis Bacon
1561-1626

F
rancis Bacon, an English lawyer, politician, and philosopher, had in mind a great project, a complete renovation of the sciences and the scientific method. Throughout the Middle Ages the question of how we know about the objective world was answered by our relationship with God. God was the source of the world and the source of all knowledge about the world. As the Church's monopoly on epistemology began to weaken with the Reformation, people began casting about for alternative explanations about the source of knowledge and the existence of the objective world. Questioning whether it was really possible to know anything with certainty was the starting point for the great rationalists such as Descartes—who determined we could, with God's help, know the world—and the ending point for the great skeptic Hume—who nearly demolished all arguments about the certainty of knowledge.

Predating all of them in the quest for objectivity was Francis Bacon. Bacon believed that careful empirical science, the dispassionate observation and reporting of the physical world, was the pathway to knowledge. He was sympathetic to arguments that knowledge that came empirically, through the use of the senses, was fragile and suspect. His famous catalog of how human understanding of the world can be distorted is one of the first and best of many discussions of the topic. The four idols discussed here are the false impressions we have of reality resulting from our common and individual predispositions and selective perceptions. His warning is that only by understanding these vulnerabilities can we overcome them and only through sustained and evenhanded observation and testing can we ultimately add to the progress of knowledge.

Novum Organum
1620

T he doctrine of those who have denied that certainty could be attained at all, has some agreement with my way of proceeding at the first setting out; but they end in being infinitely separated and opposed. For the holders of that doctrine assert simply that nothing can be known; I also assert that not much can be known in nature by the way which is now in use. But then they go on to destroy the authority of the senses and understanding; whereas I proceed to devise and supply helps for the same.

The idols and false notions which are now in possession of the human understanding, and have taken deep root therein, not only so beset men's minds that truth can hardly find entrance, but even after entrance obtained, they will again in the very instauration of the sciences meet and trouble us, unless men being forewarned of the danger fortify themselves as far as may be against their assaults.

There are four classes of idols which beset men's minds. To these for distinction's sake I have assigned names—calling the first class Idols of the Tribe; the second, Idols of the Cave; the third, Idols of the Marketplace; the fourth, Idols of the Theater.

The formation of ideas and axioms by true induction is no doubt the proper remedy to be applied for the keeping off and clearing away of idols. To point them out, however, is of great use, for the doctrine of idols is to the interpretation of nature what the doctrine of the refutation of sophisms is to common logic.

The Idols of the Tribe have their foundation in human nature itself, and in the tribe or race of men. For it is a false assertion that the sense of man is the measure of things. On the contrary, all perceptions, as well of the sense as of the mind, are according to the measure of the individual and not according to the measure of the universe. And the human understanding is like a false mirror, which, receiving rays irregularly, distorts and discolors the nature of things by mingling its own nature with it.

The Idols of the Cave are the idols of the individual man. For everyone (besides the errors common to human nature in general) has a cave or den of his own, which refracts and discolors the light of nature; owing either to his own proper and peculiar nature or to his education and conversation with others; or to the reading of books, and the authority of those whom he esteems and admires; or to the differences of impressions, accordingly as they take place in a mind preoccupied and predisposed or in a mind indifferent and settled; or the like. So that the spirit of man (according as it is meted out to different individuals) is in fact a thing variable and full of perturbation, and governed as it were by chance. Whence it was well observed by Heraclitus that men look for sciences in their own lesser worlds, and not in the greater or common world.

There are also idols formed by the intercourse and association of men with each other, which I call Idols of the Marketplace, on account of the commerce and consort of men there. For it is by discourse that men associate; and words are imposed according to the apprehension of the vulgar. And therefore the ill and unfit choice of words wonderfully obstructs the understanding. Nor do the definitions or explanations wherewith in some things learned men are wont to guard and defend themselves, by any means set the matter right. But words plainly force and overrule the understanding, and throw all into confusion, and lead men away into numberless empty controversies and idle fancies.

Lastly, there are idols which have immigrated into men's minds from the various dogmas of philosophies, and also from wrong laws of demonstration. These I call Idols of the Theater; because in my judgment all the received systems are but so many stage-plays, representing worlds of their own creation after an unreal and scenic fashion. Nor is it only of the systems now in vogue, or only of the ancient sects and philosophies, that I speak: for many more plays of the same kind may yet be composed and in like artificial manner set forth; seeing that errors the most widely different have nevertheless causes for the most part alike. Neither again do I mean this only of entire systems, but also of many principles and axioms in science, which by tradition, credulity, and negligence have come to be received.

But of these several kinds of idols I must speak more largely and exactly, that the understanding may be duly cautioned.

The human understanding is of its own nature prone to suppose the existence of more order and regularity in the world than it finds. And though there be many things in nature which are singular and unmatched, yet it devises for them parallels and conjugates and relatives which do not exist. Hence the fiction that all celestial bodies move in perfect circles; spirals and dragons being (except in name) utterly rejected. Hence too the element of fire with its orb is brought in, to make up the square with the other three which the sense perceives. Hence also the ratio of density of the so-called elements is arbitrarily fixed at ten to one. And so on of other dreams. And these fancies affect not dogmas only, but simple notions also.

The human understanding when it has once adopted an opinion (either as being the received opinion or as being agreeable to itself) draws all things else to support and agree with it. And though there be a greater number and weight of instances to be found on the other side, yet these it either neglects and despises, or else by some distinction sets aside and rejects; in order that by this great and pernicious predetermination that authority of its former conclusions may remain inviolate. And therefore it was a good answer that was made by one who when they showed him hanging in a temple a picture of those who had paid their vows as having escaped shipwreck, and would have him say whether he did not now acknowledge the power of the gods—"Aye," asked he again, "but where are they painted that were drowned after their vows?" And such is the way of all superstition, whether in astrology, dreams, omens, divine judgments, or the like; wherein men, having a delight in such vanities, mark the events where they are fulfilled, but where they fail, though this happen much oftener, neglect and pass them by. But with far more subtlety does this mischief insinuate itself into philosophy and the sciences; in which the first conclusion colors and brings into conformity with itself all that come after, though far sounder and better. Besides, independently of that delight and vanity which I have described, it is the peculiar and perpetual error of the human intellect to be more moved and excited by affirmatives than by negatives; whereas it ought properly to hold itself indifferently disposed towards both alike. Indeed in the establishment of any true axiom, the negative instance is the more forcible of the two.

The human understanding is no dry light, but receives an infusion from the will and affections; whence proceed sciences which may be called "sciences as one would." For what a man had rather were true he more readily believes. Therefore he rejects difficult things from impatience of research; sober things, because they narrow hope; the deeper things of nature, from superstition; the light of experience, from arrogance and pride, lest his mind should seem to be occupied with things mean and transitory; things not commonly believed, out of deference to the opinion of the vulgar. Numberless in short are the ways, and sometimes imperceptible, in which the affections color and infect the understanding.

So much concerning the several classes of idols, and their equipage: all of which must be renounced and put away with a fixed and solemn determination, and the understanding thoroughly freed and cleansed; the entrance into the kingdom of man, founded on the sciences, being not much other than the entrance into the kingdom of heaven, whereinto none may enter except as a little child. . . .

And as men have misplaced the end and goal of the sciences; so again, even if they had placed it right, yet they have chosen a way to it which is altogether erroneous and impassable. And an astonishing thing it is to one who rightly considers the matter, that no mortal should have seriously applied himself to the opening and laying out of a road for the human understanding direct from the sense, by a course of experiment orderly conducted and well built up; but that all has been left either to the mist of tradition, or the whirl and eddy of argument, or the fluctuations and mazes of chance and of vague and ill-digested experience. Now let any man soberly and diligently consider what the way is by which men have been accustomed to proceed in the investigation and discovery of things; and in the first place he will no doubt remark a method of discovery very simple and inartificial; which is the most ordinary method, and is no more than this. When a man addresses himself to discover something, he first seeks out and sets before him all that has been said about it by others; then he begins to meditate for himself; and so by much agitation and working of the wit solicits and as it were evokes his own spirit to give him oracles: which method has no foundation at all, but rests only upon opinions and is carried about with them.

Another may perhaps call in logic to discover it for him; but that has no relation to the matter except in name. For logical invention does not discover principles and chief axioms, of which arts are composed, but only such things as appear to be consistent with them. For if you grow more curious and importunate and busy, and question her of probations and invention of principles or primary axioms, her answer is well known: she refers you to the faith you are bound to give to the principles of each separate art.

There remains simple experience; which, if taken as it comes, is called accident; if sought for, experiment. But this kind of experience is no better than a broom without its band, as the saying is—a mere groping as of men in the dark, that feel all round them for the chance of finding their way; when they had much better wait for daylight, or light a candle, and then go. But the true method of experience on the contrary first lights the candle, and then by means of the candle shows the way; commencing as it does with experience duly ordered and digested, not bungling or erratic, and from it educing axioms, and from established axioms again new experiments; even as it was not without order and method that the divine word operated on the created mass. Let men therefore cease to wonder that the course of science is not yet wholly run, seeing that they have gone altogether astray; either leaving and abandoning experience entirely, or losing their way in it and wandering round and round as in a labyrinth; whereas a method rightly ordered leads by an unbroken route through the woods of experience to the open ground of axioms.

Chapter 11
Walter Lippmann
1889-1974

Walter Lippmann is widely regarded as one of the most profound, yet accessible, of our modern theorists of both the American political system and of journalism's role in helping that system work. Fresh out of Harvard in 1911, he was recruited into the newspaper business by Lincoln Steffens, one of the most famous and best of the muckrakers.

Lippmann worked for Steffens for a couple of years, then went to work for the government, first as an assistant to the secretary of war during World War I and then as secretary to Colonel Edward House's Inquiry Commission, Woodrow Wilson's favorite source of information and advice in trying to design the peace at the end of the war. Lippmann soon became disillusioned with government work and returned to journalism, where he had a long and brilliant career. He was an editorial writer for the New York *World* in the 1920s, then moved to the New York *Herald Tribune*, where for the next thirty years he wrote a column under the standing head, "Today and Tomorrow." In addition to more than four thousand columns, he also wrote ten books of political philosophy, a dozen of contemporary commentary about people and events, and at least another three hundred articles in at least fifty magazines.

Critics have found inconsistencies in his thought and in his writing over the decades, and a familiar drift from radical socialism as a young man to a far more conservative stance in later years. For all that, Lippmann remained wholly consistent in his belief in a liberal democracy, that is, a country of popular rule and a maximum of individual liberty. He also held to a strong belief in the critical role that journalism can and must play in bringing that ideal to fruition. Much of the apparent inconsistency in his writing can be attributed to sharp swings in the prevailing political moods in the country during his career, resulting in swings in Lippmann from cheery optimism to gloomy pessimism about the future.

Lippmann was one of the great champions of journalistic objectivity, by which he meant applying the methods of scientific analysis to social and political questions. Along with Joseph Pulitzer, Lippmann was an enthusiastic proponent of professional journalism schools. At the same time, he was decades ahead of his time in warning that in their striving for objectivity, journalists were too little inclined to put things into any meaningful perspective. Lippmann saw the perils of the then-dominant journalistic ideal of gathering information and then passing it on, largely unsorted, to the reader to figure out. In the simpler world of the nineteenth century, he thought, this might have been enough, but not for the vastly more complex twentieth. Not only had the world been ravaged by an almost unimaginable war, but government was also vastly more active in people's lives than ever before; also, Freud had delivered a fatal blow to the nineteenth century's belief in the rational nature of the human mind. It is to Lippmann we look for important early arguments about providing context and understanding: telling the story behind the breaking news.

This passage, taken from his most famous book, *Public Opinion*, deals with the difficulty of knowing truth and with journalism's role in that pursuit.

Public Opinion
1922

The world outside and the pictures in our heads

There is an island in the ocean where in 1914 a few Englishmen, Frenchmen, and Germans lived. No cable reaches that island, and the British mail steamer comes but once in sixty days. In September it had not yet come, and the islanders were still talking about the latest newspaper which told about the approaching trial of Madame Caillaux for the shooting of Gaston Calmette. It was, therefore, with more than usual eagerness that the whole colony assembled at the quay on a day in mid-September to hear from the captain what the verdict had been. They learned that for over six weeks now those of them who were English and those of them who were French had been fighting in behalf of the sanctity of treaties against those of them who were Germans. For six strange weeks they had acted as if they were friends, when in fact they were enemies.

But their plight was not so different from that of most of the population of Europe. They had been mistaken for six weeks, on the continent the interval may have been only six days or six hours. There was an interval. There was a moment when the picture of Europe on which men were conducting their business as usual, did not in any way correspond to the Europe which was about to make a jumble of their lives. There was a time for each man when he was still adjusted to an environment that no longer existed. All over the world as late as July 25th men were making goods that they would not be able to ship, buying goods they would not be able to import, careers were being planned, enterprises contemplated, hopes and expectations entertained, all in the belief that the world as known was the world as it was. Men were writing books describing that world. They trusted the picture in their heads. And then over four years later, on a Thursday morning, came the news of an armistice, and people gave vent to their unutterable relief that the slaughter was over. Yet in the five days before the real armistice came, though the end of the war had been celebrated, several thousand young men died on the battlefields.

Looking back we can see how indirectly we know the environment in which nevertheless we live. We can see that the news of it comes to us now fast, now slowly; but that whatever we believe to be a true picture, we treat as if it were the environment itself. It is harder to remember that about the beliefs upon which we are now acting, but in respect to other peoples and other ages we flatter ourselves that it is easy to see when they were in deadly earnest about ludicrous pictures of the world. We insist, because of our superior hindsight, that the world as they needed to know it, and the world as they did know it, were often two quite contradictory things. We can see, too, that while they governed and fought, traded and reformed in the world as they imagined it to be, they produced results, or failed to produce any, in the world as it was. They started for the Indies and found America. They diagnosed evil and hanged old women. They thought they could grow rich by always selling and never buying. A caliph, obeying what he conceived to be the Will of Allah, burned the library at Alexandria.

Writing about the year 389, St. Ambrose stated the case for the prisoner in Plato's cave who resolutely declines to turn his head. "To discuss the nature and position of the earth does not help us in our hope to the life to come. It is enough to know what Scripture states. 'That He hung up the earth upon nothing' (Job xxvi. 7). Why then argue whether He hung it up in air or upon the water, and raise a controversy as to how the thin air could sustain the earth; or why, if upon the waters, the earth does not go crashing down to the bottom? . . . Not because the earth is in the middle, as if suspended on even balance, but because the majesty of God constrains it by the law of His will, does it endure stable upon the unstable and the void."

It does not help us in our hope of the life to come. It is enough to know what Scripture states. Why then argue? But a century and a half after St. Ambrose, opinion was still troubled, on this occasion by the problem of the antipodes. A monk named Cosmas, famous for his scientific attainments, was therefore deputed to write a Christian Topography, or "Christian Opinion concerning the World." It is clear that he knew exactly what was expected of him, for he based all his conclusions on the Scriptures as he read them. It appears, then, that the world is a flat parallelogram, twice as broad from east to west as it is long from north to south. In the center is the earth surrounded by ocean, which is in turn surrounded by another earth, where men lived before the deluge. This other earth was Noah's port of embarkation. In the north is a high conical mountain around which revolve the sun and moon. When the sun is behind the mountain it is night. The sky is glued to the edges of the outer earth. It consists of four high walls which meet in a concave roof, so that the earth is the floor of the universe. There is an ocean on the other side of the sky, constituting the "waters that are above the firmament." The space between the celestial ocean and the ultimate roof of the universe belongs to the blest. The space between the earth and sky is inhabited by the angels. Finally, since St. Paul said that all men are made to live upon the "face of the earth" how could they live on the back where the Antipodes are supposed to be? "With such a passage before his eyes, a Christian, we are told, should not 'even speak of the Antipodes.'"

Far less should he go to the Antipodes; nor should any Christian prince give him a ship to try; nor would any pious mariner wish to try. For Cosmas there was nothing in the least absurd about his map. Only by remembering his absolute conviction that this was the map of the universe can we begin to understand how he would have dreaded Magellan or Peary or the aviator who risked a collision with the angels and the vault of heaven by flying seven miles up in the air. In the same way we can best understand the furies of war and politics by remembering that almost the whole of each party believes absolutely in its picture of the opposition, that it takes as fact, not what is, but what it supposes to be the fact. And that therefore, like Hamlet, it will stab Polonius behind the rustling curtain, thinking him the king, and perhaps like Hamlet add:

"Thou wretched, rash, intruding fool, farewell!
I took thee for thy better; take thy fortune." . . .

. . . Our first concern with fictions and symbols is to forget their value to the existing social order, and to think of them simply as an important part of the machinery of human communication. Now in any society that is not completely self-contained in its interests and so small that everyone can know all about everything that happens, ideas deal with events that are out of sight and hard to grasp. Miss Sherwin of Gopher Prairie is aware that a war is raging in France and tries to conceive it. She has never been to France, and certainly she has never been along what is now the battlefront. Pictures of French and German soldiers she has seen, but it is impossible for her to imagine three million men. No one, in fact, can imagine them, and the professionals do not try. They think of them as, say, two hundred divisions. But Miss Sherwin has no access to the order of battle maps, and so if she is to think about the war, she fastens upon Joffre and the Kaiser as if they were engaged in a personal duel. Perhaps if you could see what she sees with her mind's eye, the image in its composition might be not unlike an Eighteenth Century engraving of a great soldier. He stands there boldly unruffled and more than life size, with a shadowy army of tiny little figures winding off into the landscape behind. Nor it seems are great men oblivious to these expectations. M. de Pierrefeu tells of a photographer's visit to Joffre. The General was in his "middle class office, before the worktable without papers, where he sat down to write his signature. Suddenly it was noticed that there were no maps on the walls. But since according to popular ideas it is not possible to think of a general without maps, a few were placed in position for the picture, and removed soon afterwards."

The only feeling that anyone can have about an event he does not experience is the feeling aroused by his mental image of that event. That is why until we know what others think they know, we cannot truly understand their acts. I have seen a young girl, brought up in a Pennsylvania mining town, plunged suddenly from entire cheerfulness into a paroxysm of grief when a gust of wind cracked the kitchen window-pane. For hours she was inconsolable, and to me incomprehensible. But when she was able to talk, it transpired that if a window-pane broke it meant that a close relative had died. She was, therefore, mourning for her father, who had frightened her into running away from home. The father was, of course, quite thoroughly alive as a telegraphic inquiry soon proved. But until the telegram came, the cracked glass was an authentic message to that girl. Why it was authentic only a prolonged investigation by a skilled psychiatrist could show. But even the most casual observer could see that the girl, enormously upset by her family troubles, had hallucinated a complete fiction out of one external fact, a remembered superstition, and a turmoil of remorse, and fear and love for her father.

Abnormality in these instances is only a matter of degree. When an Attorney-General, who has been frightened by a bomb exploded on his doorstep, convinces himself by the reading of revolutionary literature that a revolution is to happen on the first of May 1920, we recognize that much the same mechanism is at work. The war, of course, furnished many examples of this pattern: the casual fact, the creative imagination, the will to believe, and out of these three elements, a counterfeit of reality to which there was a violent instinctive response. For it is clear enough that under certain conditions men respond as powerfully to fictions as they do to realities, and that in many cases they help to create the very fictions to which they respond. Let him cast the first stone who did not believe in the Russian army that passed through England in August, 1914, did not accept any tale of atrocities without direct proof, and never saw a plot, a traitor, or a spy where there was none. Let him cast a stone who never passed on as the real inside truth what he had heard someone say who knew no more than he did.

In all these instances we must note particularly one common factor. It is the insertion between man and his environment of a pseudo-environment. To that pseudo -environment his behavior is a response. But because it is behavior, the consequences, if they are acts, operate not in the pseudo-environment where the behavior is stimulated, but in the real environment where action eventuates. If the behavior is not a practical act, but what we call roughly thought and emotion, it may be a long time before there is any noticeable break in the texture of the fictitious world. But when the stimulus of the pseudo-fact results in action on things or other people, contradiction soon develops. Then comes the sensation of butting one's head against a stone wall, of learning by experience, and witnessing Herbert Spencer's tragedy of the murder of a Beautiful Theory by a Gang of Brutal Facts, the discomfort in short of a maladjustment. For certainly, at the level of social life, what is called the adjustment of man to his environment takes place through the medium of fictions.

By fictions I do not mean lies. I mean a representation of the environment which is in lesser or greater degree made by man himself. The range of fiction extends all the way from complete hallucination to the scientist's perfectly self-conscious use of a schematic model, or his decision that for his particular problem accuracy beyond a certain number of decimal places is not important. A work of fiction may have almost any degree of fidelity, and so long as the degree of fidelity can be taken into account, fiction is not misleading. In fact, human culture is very largely the selection, the rearrangement, the tracing of patterns upon, and the stylizing of, what William James called "the random irradiations and resettlements of our ideas." The alternative to the use of fictions is direct exposure to the ebb and flow of sensation. That is not a real alternative, for however refreshing it is to see at times with a perfectly innocent eye, innocence itself is not wisdom, though a source and corrective of wisdom.

For the real environment is altogether too big, too complex, and too fleeting for direct acquaintance. We are not equipped to deal with so much subtlety, so much variety, so many permutations and combinations. And although we have to act in that environment, we have to reconstruct it on a simpler model before we can manage with it. To traverse the world men must have maps of the world. Their persistent difficulty is to secure maps on which their own need, or someone else's need, has not sketched in the coast of Bohemia. . . .

The world that we have to deal with politically is out of reach, out of sight, out of mind. It has to be explored, reported, and imagined. Man is no Aristotelian god contemplating all existence at one glance. He is the creature of an evolution who can just about span a sufficient portion of reality to manage his survival, and snatch what on the scale of time are but a few moments of insight and happiness. Yet this same creature has invented ways of seeing what no naked eye could see, of hearing what no ear could hear, of weighing immense masses and infinitesimal ones, of counting and separating more items than he can individually remember. He is learning to see with his mind vast portions of the world that he could never see, touch, smell, hear or remember. Gradually he makes for himself a trustworthy picture inside his head of the world beyond his reach.

Those features of the world outside which have to do with the behavior of other human beings, in so far as that behavior crosses ours, is dependent upon us, or is interesting to us, we call roughly public affairs. The pictures inside the heads of these human beings, the pictures of themselves, of others, of their needs, purposes, and relationship, are their public opinions. Those pictures which are acted upon by groups of people, or by individuals acting in the names of groups, are Public Opinion with capital letters. And so in the chapters which follow we shall inquire first into some of the reasons why the picture inside so often misleads men in their dealings with the world outside.

Under this heading we shall consider first the chief factors which limit their access to facts. They are the artificial censorships, the limitations of social contact, the comparatively meager time available in each day for paying attention to public affairs, the distortion arising because events have to be compressed into very short messages, the difficulty of making a small vocabulary express a complicated world, and finally the fear of facing those facts which would seem to threaten the established routine of men's lives.

The analysis then turns from these more or less external limitations to the question of how this trickle of messages from the outside is affected by the stored up images, the preconceptions and prejudices which interpret, fill them out, and in their turn powerfully direct the play of our attention, and our vision itself. From this it proceeds to examine how in the individual person the limited messages from outside, formed into a pattern of stereotypes, are identified with his own interests as he feels and conceives them. In the succeeding sections it examines how opinions are crystallized into what is called Public Opinion, how a National Will, a Group Mind, a Social Purpose, or whatever you chose to call it, is formed.

The first five parts constitute the descriptive section of the book. There follows an analysis of the traditionally democratic theory of public opinion. The substance of the argument is that democracy in its original form never seriously faced the problem which arises because the pictures inside people's heads do not automatically correspond with the world outside. And then, because the democratic theory is under criticism by socialist thinkers, there follows an examination of the most advanced and coherent of these criticisms, as made by the English Guild Socialists. My purpose here is to find out whether these reformers take into account the main difficulties of public opinion. My conclusion is that they ignore the difficulties, as completely as did the original democrats, because they, too, assume, and in a much more complicated civilization, that somehow mysteriously there exists in the hearts of men a knowledge of the world beyond their reach.

I argue that representative government, either in what is ordinarily called politics, or in industry, cannot be worked successfully, no matter what the basis of election, unless there is an independent, expert organization for making the unseen facts intelligible to those who have to make the decisions. I attempt, therefore, to argue that the serious acceptance of the principle that personal representation must be supplemented by representation of the unseen facts would alone permit a satisfactory decentralization, and allow us to escape from the intolerable and unworkable fiction that each of us must acquire a competent opinion about all public affairs. It is argued that the problem of the press is confused because the critics and the apologists expect the press to realize this fiction, expect it to make up for all that was not foreseen in the theory of democracy, and that the readers expect this miracle to be performed at no cost or trouble to themselves. The newspapers are regarded by democrats as a

panacea for their own defects, whereas analysis of the nature of news and of
the economic basis of journalism seems to show that the newspapers
necessarily and inevitably reflect, and therefore, in greater or lesser measure,
intensify, the defective organization of public opinion. My conclusion is that
public opinions must be organized for the press if they are to be sound, not by
the press as is the case today. This organization I conceive to be in the first
instance the task of a political science that has won its proper place as
formulator, in advance of real decision, instead of apologist, critic, or reporter
after the decision has been made. I try to indicate that the perplexities of
government and industry are conspiring to give political science this enormous
opportunity to enrich itself and to serve the public. And, of course, I hope that
these pages will help a few people to realize that opportunity more vividly, and
therefore to pursue it more consciously. . . .

News, truth, and a conclusion

As we begin to make more and more exact studies of the press, much will
depend upon the hypothesis we hold. . . .

The hypothesis, which seems to me the most fertile, is that news and truth
are not the same thing, and must be clearly distinguished. The function of news
is to signalize an event, the function of truth is to bring to light the hidden
facts, to set them into relation with each other, and make a picture of reality
on which men can act. Only at those points, where social conditions take
recognizable and measurable shape, do the body of truth and the body of news
coincide. That is a comparatively small part of the whole field of human
interest. In this sector, and only in this sector, the tests of the news are
sufficiently exact to make the charges of perversion or suppression more than
a partisan judgment. There is no defense, no extenuation, no excuse whatever,
for stating six times that Lenin is dead, when the only information the paper
possesses is a report that he is dead from the source repeatedly shown to be
unreliable. The news, in that instance, is not "Lenin Dead" but "Helsingfors
Says Lenin is Dead." And a newspaper can be asked to take the responsibility
of not making Lenin more dead than the source of the news is reliable; if there
is one subject on which editors are most responsible it is in their judgment of
the reliability of the source. But when it comes to dealing, for example, with
stories of what the Russian people want, no such test exists.

The absence of these exact tests accounts, I think, for the character of the
profession, as no other explanation does. There is a very small body of exact
knowledge, which it requires no outstanding ability or training to deal with.
The rest is in the journalist's own discretion. Once he departs from the region
where it is definitely recorded at the County Clerk's office that John Smith has

gone into bankruptcy, all fixed standards disappear. The story of why John Smith failed, his human frailties, the analysis of the economic conditions on which he was shipwrecked, all of this can be told in a hundred different ways. There is no discipline in applied psychology, as there is a discipline in medicine, engineering, or even law, which has authority to direct the journalist's mind when he passes from the news to the vague realm of truth. There are no canons to direct his own mind, and no canons that coerce the reader's judgment or the publisher's. His version of the truth is only his version. How can he demonstrate the truth as he sees it? He cannot demonstrate it, any more than Mr. Sinclair Lewis can demonstrate that he has told the whole truth about Main Street. And the more he understands his own weaknesses, the more ready he is to admit that where there is no objective test, his own opinion is in some vital measure constructed out of his own stereotypes, according to his own code, and by the urgency of his own interest. He knows that he is seeing the world through subjective lenses. He cannot deny that he too is, as Shelley remarked, a dome of many-colored glass which stains the white radiance of eternity.

And by this knowledge his assurance is tempered. He may have all kinds of moral courage, and sometimes has, but he lacks that sustaining conviction of a certain technic which finally freed the physical sciences from theological control. It was the gradual development of an irrefragable method that gave the physicist his intellectual freedom as against all the powers of the world. His proofs were so clear, his evidence so sharply superior to tradition, that he broke away finally from all control. But the journalist has no such support in his own conscience or in fact. The control exercised over him by the opinions of his employers and his readers, is not the control of truth by prejudice, but of one opinion by another opinion that it is not demonstrably less true. Between Judge Gary's assertion that the unions will destroy American institutions, and Mr. Gomper's assertion that they are agencies of the rights of man, the choice has, in large measure, to be governed by the will to believe.

The task of deflating these controversies, and reducing them to a point where they can be reported as news, is not a task which the reporter can perform. It is possible and necessary for journalists to bring home to people the uncertain character of the truth on which their opinions are founded, and by criticism and agitation to prod social science into making more usable formulations of social facts, and to prod statesmen into establishing more visible institutions. The press, in other words, can fight for the extension of reportable truth. But as social truth is organized to-day, the press is not constituted to furnish from one edition to the next the amount of knowledge which the democratic theory of public opinion demands. This is not due to the Brass Check, as the quality of news in radical papers shows, but to the fact that the press deals with a society in which the governing forces are so imperfectly recorded. The theory that the press can itself record those forces is false. It can normally record only what has been recorded for it by the working of institutions. Everything else is argument and opinion, and fluctuates with the vicissitudes, the self-consciousness, and the courage of the human mind.

If the press is not so universally wicked, nor so deeply conspiring, as Mr. Sinclair would have us believe, it is very much more frail than the democratic theory has as yet admitted. It is too frail to carry the whole burden of popular sovereignty, to supply spontaneously the truth which democrats hoped was inborn. And when we expect it to supply such a body of truth we employ a misleading standard of judgment. We misunderstand the limited nature of news, the illimitable complexity of society; we overestimate our own endurance, public spirit, and all-round competence. We suppose an appetite for uninteresting truths which is not discovered by any honest analysis of our own tastes.

If the newspapers, then, are to be charged with the duty of translating the whole public life of mankind, so that every adult can arrive at an opinion on every moot topic, they fail, they are bound to fail, in any future one can conceive they will continue to fail. It is not possible to assume that a world, carried on by division of labor and distribution of authority, can be governed by universal opinions in the whole population. Unconsciously the theory sets up the single readers as theoretically omnicompetent, and puts upon the press the burden of accomplishing whatever representative government, industrial organization, and diplomacy have failed to accomplish. Acting upon everybody for thirty minutes in twenty-four hours, the press is asked to create a mystical force called Public Opinion that will take up the slack in public institutions. The press has often mistakenly pretended that it could do just that. It has at great moral cost to itself, encouraged a democracy, still bound to its original premises, to expect newspapers to supply spontaneously for every organ of government, for every social problem, the machinery of information which these do not normally supply themselves. Institutions, having failed to furnish themselves with instruments of knowledge, have become a bundle of "problems," which the population as a whole, reading the press as a whole, is supposed to solve.

The press, in other words, has come to be regarded as an organ of direct democracy, charged on a much wider scale, and from day to day, with the function often attributed to the initiative, the referendum, and recall. The Court of Public Opinion, open day and night, is to lay down the law for everything all the time. It is not workable. And when you consider the nature of news, it is not even thinkable. For the news, as we have seen, is precise in proportion to the precision with which the event is recorded. Unless the event is capable of being named, measured, given shape, made specific, it either fails to take on the character of news, or it is subjected to the accidents and prejudices of observation.

Therefore, on the whole, the quality of the news about modern society is an index of its social organization. The better the institutions, the more all interests concerned are formally represented, the more issues are disentangled, the more objective criteria are introduced, the more perfectly an affair can be presented as news. At its best the press is a servant and guardian of institutions; at its worst it is a means by which a few exploit social disorganization to their own ends. In the degree to which institutions fail to function, the unscrupulous journalist can fish in troubled waters, and the conscientious one must gamble with uncertainties.

The press is no substitute for institutions. It is like the beam of a searchlight that moves restlessly about, bringing one episode and then another out of darkness into vision. Men cannot do the work of the world by this light alone. They cannot govern society by episodes, incidents, and eruptions. It is only when they work by a steady light of their own, that the press, when it is turned upon them, reveals a situation intelligible enough for a popular decision. The trouble lies deeper than the press, and so does a remedy. It lies in social organization based on a system of analysis and record, and in all the corollaries of that principle; in the abandonment of the theory of the omnicompetent citizen, in the decentralization of decision, in the coordination of decision by comparable record and analysis. If at the centers of management there is a running audit, which makes work intelligible to those who do it, and those who superintend it, issues when they arise are not the mere collisions of the blind. Then, too, the news is uncovered for the press by a system of intelligence that is also a check upon the press.

That is the radical way. For the troubles of the press, like the troubles of representative government, be it territorial or functional, like the troubles of industry, be it capitalist, cooperative, or communist, go back to a common source; to the failure of self-governing people to transcend their casual experience and their prejudice, by inventing, creating, and organizing a machinery of knowledge. It is because they are compelled to act without a reliable picture of the world, that governments, schools, newspapers and churches make such small headway against the more obvious failings of democracy, against violent prejudice, apathy, preference for the curious trivial as against the dull important, and the hunger for sideshows and three legged calves. This is the primary defect of popular government, a defect inherent in its traditions, and all its other defects can, I believe, be traced to this one.

Chapter 12
Warren Breed
1915-

Warren Breed, a sociologist by training, has had a long-standing interest in the media, including journalism. Since the early 1970s his research interests and publications have been in the area of alcohol, media and social change. He is an Associate with Scientific Analysis Corporation in Berkeley, Calif.

His "Social Control in the Newsroom" is a classic in media sociology. Its inclusion in this section on truth and objectivity is a reminder that journalists are not fully autonomous agents, as much as they might wish to be. They operate in a complex web of interacting social, cultural, economic, and organizational forces. Each strand of that web tugs a bit at the nature of what news is covered, who covers it, what gets written, what gets edited out, and what eventually gets printed.

Reporting is, after all, a social act. It is shaped and fashioned by the values of the culture and the traditions of the profession, by the definitions of what is and what is not news, and by the goals of objectivity and fairness. It is also influenced by the ownership structure of the industry, the demographic composition of the work force, the nature of the local community, and the resources available to and the journalistic philosophy of the news organization itself.

In this essay, which became the jumping-off point for generations of media scholars, Breed addresses himself to the means by which a news organization's philosophy is communicated to young reporters and thereby maintained, as well as ways in which organizational policy is subverted or bypassed. The discussion is important in itself and in its role representing the larger literature of social influence in the covering and reporting of news.

The larger issue is the interplay between these forces and the journalist's struggle for accuracy, objectivity, and the elusive truth. It is part of the journalistic handling of the moral compass to understand and account for the social milieu in which news people must function—to accommodate, as it were, the various magnetic fields, which pull the compass reading away from true north.

"Social Control in the Newsroom"
Social Forces, 33:4 1955

T op leaders in formal organizations are makers of policy, but they must also secure and maintain conformity to that policy at lower levels. The situation of the newspaper publisher is a case in point. As owner or representative of ownership, he has the nominal right to set the paper's policy and see that staff activities are coordinated so that the policy is enforced. In actuality the problem of control is less simple, as the literature of "human relations" and informal group studies and of the professions suggests.

Ideally, there would be no problem of either "control" or "policy" on the newspaper in a full democracy. The only controls would be the nature of the event and the reporter's effective ability to describe it. In practice, we find the publisher does set news policy, and this policy is usually followed by members of his staff. Conformity is not automatic, however, for three reasons: (1) the existence of ethical journalistic norms; (2) the fact that staff subordinates (reporters, etc.) tend to have more "liberal" attitudes (and therefore perceptions) than the publisher and could invoke the norms to justify anti-policy writing; and (3) the ethical taboo preventing the publisher from commanding subordinates to follow policy. How policy comes to be maintained, and where it is bypassed, is the subject of this paper.

Several definitions are required at this point. As to personnel, "newsmen" can be divided into two main categories. "Executives" include the publisher and his editors. "Staffers" are reporters, rewrite men, copyreaders, etc. In between there may be occasional city editors or wire editors who occupy an interstitial status. "Policy" may be defined as the more or less consistent orientation shown by a paper, not only in its editorial but in its news columns and headlines as well, concerning selected issues and events. "Slanting" almost never means prevarication. Rather, it involves omission, differential selection, and preferential placement, such as "featuring" a pro-policy item, "burying" an anti-policy story on an inside page, etc. "Professional norms" are of two types: technical norms deal with the operations of efficient news-gathering, writing, and editing; ethical norms embrace the newsman's obligation to his readers and to his craft and include such ideals as responsibility, impartiality, accuracy, fair play, and objectivity.

Every newspaper has a policy, admitted or not. One paper's policy may be pro-Republican, cool to labor, antagonistic to the school board, etc. The principal areas of policy are politics, business, and labor; much of it stems from considerations of class. Policy is manifested in "slanting." Just what determines any publisher's policy is a large question and will not be discussed here. Certainly, however, the publisher has much say (often in veto form) in both long-term and immediate policy decisions (which party to support, whether to feature or bury a story of imminent labor trouble, how much free space to give "news" of advertisers' doings, etc.). Finally, policy is covert, due to the existence of ethical norms of journalism; policy often contravenes these norms. No executive is willing to risk embarrassment by being accused of open commands to slant a news story.

While policy is set by the executives, it is clear that they cannot personally gather and write the news by themselves. They must delegate these tasks to staffers, and at this point the attitudes or interests of staffers may—and often do—conflict with those of the executives. Of 72 staffers interviewed, 42 showed that they held more liberal views than those contained in their publisher's policy; 27 held similar views, and only 3 were more conservative. It should be noted that data as to intensity of attitudes are lacking. Some staffers may disagree with policy so mildly that they conform and feel no strain. The present essay is pertinent only insofar as dissident newsmen are forced to make decisions from time to time about their relationship to policy.

We will now examine more closely the workings of the newspaper staff. The central question will be: How is policy maintained, despite the fact that it often contravenes journalistic norms, that staffers often personally disagree with it, and that executives cannot legitimately command that it be followed?.

The present data come from the writer's newspaper experience and from intensive interviews with some 120 newsmen, mostly in the northeastern quarter of the country. The sample was not random and no claim is made for representativeness, but on the other hand no paper was selected or omitted purposely and in no case did a newsman refuse the request that he be interviewed. The newspapers were chosen to fit a "middle-sized" group, defined as those with 10,000 to 100,000 daily circulation. Interviews averaged well over an hour in duration.

There is an "action" element inherent in the present subject—the practical democratic need for "a free and responsible press" to inform citizens about current issues. Much of the criticism of the press stems from the slanting induced by the bias of the publisher's policy. This criticism is often directed at flagrant cases such as the Hearst press, the Chicago *Tribune*, and New York tabloids, but also applies, in lesser degree, to the more conventional press. The description of mechanisms of policy maintenance may suggest why this criticism is often fruitless, at least in the short-run sense.

How the staffer learns policy

The first mechanism promoting conformity is the "socialization" of the staffer with regard to the norms of his job. When the new reporter starts work he is not told what policy is. Nor is he ever told. This may appear strange, but interview after interview confirmed the condition. The standard remark was "Never in my '——' years on this paper, have I ever been told how to slant a story." . . . Yet all but the newest staffers know what policy is. . . . Basically, the learning of policy is a process by which the recruit discovers and internalizes the rights and obligations of his status and its norms and values. He learns to anticipate what is expected of him so as to win rewards and avoid punishments. Policy is an important element of the newsroom norms, and he learns it in much the following way.

The staffer reads his own paper every day; some papers require this. It is simple to diagnose the paper's characteristics. Unless the staffer is naive or unusually independent, he tends to fashion his own stories after others he sees in the paper. This is particularly true of the newcomer. The news columns and editorials are a guide to the local norms. . . .

Certain editorial actions taken by editors and older staffers also serve as controlling guides. "If things are blue-penciled consistently," one reporter said, "you learn he [the editor] has a prejudice in that regard." . . .

Note that the boss does not "command"; the direction is more subtle. Also, it seems that most policy indications from executives are negative. . . . It is also to be noted that punishment is implied if policy is not followed.

Staffers also obtain guidance from their knowledge of the characteristics, interests, and affiliations of their executives. This knowlege can be gained in several ways. One is gossip. . . .

Another point of contact with executives is the news conference . . . wherein the staffer outlines his findings and executives discuss how to shape the story. . . . If policy is at stake, the conference may involve several executives and require hours of consideration. From such meetings, the staffer can gain insight through what is said and what is not said by executives. It is important to say here that policy is not stated explicitly in the news conference nor elsewhere, with few exceptions. . . .

Three other channels for learning about executives are house organs . . . observing the executive as he meets various leaders and hearing him voice an opinion. . . .

Reasons for conforming to policy

There is no one factor which creates conformity-mindedness.... Particular factors must be sought in particular cases. The staffer must be seen in terms of his status and aspirations, the structure of the newsroom organization and of the larger society. He also must be viewed with reference to the operations he performs through his workday, and their consequences for him. The following six reasons appear to stay the potentially intransigent staffer from acts of deviance—often, if not always.

1. Institutional Authority and Sanctions.... [S]taffers ... fear punishment ... [but] fear of sanctions, rather than their invocation, is a reason for conformity, but not as potent a one as would seem at first glance.

Editors, for their part, can simply ignore stories which might create deviant actions, and when this is impossible, can assign the story to a "safe" staffer....

2. Feelings of Obligation and Esteem for Superiors. The staffer may feel obliged to the paper for having hired him....

3. Mobility Aspirations.... [T]he younger staffers showed wishes for status achievement. There was agreement that bucking policy constituted a serious bar to this goal....

4. Absence of Conflicting Group Allegiance.... [T]here is no evidence available that a group of staffers has ever "ganged up" on policy.

5. The Pleasant Nature of the Activity. The staffer has a low formal status vis-a-vis executives, but he is not treated as a "worker." Rather, he is a co-worker with executives; the entire staff cooperates congenially on a job they all like and respect: getting the news.... Newsmen like ... the variety of experience, eye-witnessing significant and interesting events, being the first to know, getting "the inside dope" denied laymen, meeting and sometimes befriending notables and celebrities.... Newsmen are close to big decisions without having to make them; they touch power without being responsible for its use.... [T]here is the satisfaction of being a member of a live-wire organization dealing with important matters.

6. News Becomes a Value. Newsmen define their job as producing a certain quantity of what is called "news" every 24 hours.... Newsmen do talk about ethics, objectivity, and the relative worth of various papers, but not when there is news to get. News comes first, and there is always news to get. They are not rewarded for analyzing the social structure, but for getting news....

The staffer, especially the new staffer, identifies himself though the existence of these six factors with the executives and veteran staffers. Although not yet one of them, he shares their norms, and thus his performance comes to resemble theirs.... All six of these factors function to encourage reference group formation. Where the allegiance is directed toward legitimate authority, that authority has only to maintain the equilibrium within limits by the prudent distribution of rewards and punishments. . . .

Situations permitting deviation

. . . The process of learning policy crystallizes into a process of social control, in which deviations are punished (usually gently) by reprimand, cutting one's story, the withholding of friendly comment by an executive, etc. . . .

[However,] now and then cases arise in which a staffer finds his anti-policy stories printed. There seems to be no consistent explanation for this, except to introduce two more specific subjects dealing first, with the staffer's career line, and second, with particular empirical conditions associated with the career line. We can distinguish three stages through which the staffer progresses. First, there is the cub stage, the first few months or years in which the new man learns techniques and policy. He writes short, non-policy stories, such as minor accidents, meeting activity, the weather, etc. The second, or "wiring-in" stage, sees the staffer continuing to assimilate the newsroom values and to cement informal relationships. Finally there is the "star" or "veteran" stage, in which the staffer typically defines himself as a full, responsible member of the group, sees its goals as his, and can be counted on to handle policy sympathetically.

To further specify the conformity-deviation problem, it must be understood that newspapering is a relatively complex activity. The newsman is responsible for a range of skills and judgments which are matched only in the professional and entrepreneurial fields. Oversimplifications about policy rigidity can be avoided if we ask, "Under what conditions can the staffer defy or bypass policy?" . . . Five factors appear significant in the area of the reporter's power to bypass policy.

1. The norms of policy are not always entirely clear, just as many norms are vague and unstructured. . . .

2. Executives may be ignorant of particular facts, and staffers who do the leg (and telephone) work to gather news can use their superior knowledge to subvert policy. On grounds of both personal belief and professional codes, the staffer has the option of selection at many points. . . .

3. Although a paper's policy may proscribe a certain issue from becoming featured, a staffer, on getting a good story about that issue may "plant" it in another paper or wire service through a friendly staffer and submit it to his own editor, pleading the story is now too big to ignore.

4. It is possible to classify news into four types on the basis of source of origination. These are: the policy or campaign story, the assigned story, the

beat story, and the story initiated by the staffer. The staffer's autonomy is larger with the latter than the former types. With the campaign story (build new hospital, throw rascals out, etc.), the staffer is working directly under executives and has little leeway. An assigned story is handed out by the city editor and thus will rarely hit policy head on, although the staffer has some leverage of selection. When we come to the beat story, however, it is clear that the function of the reporter changes. No editor comes between him and his beat (police department, city hall, etc.), thus the reporter gains the "editor" function. It is he who, to a marked degree, can select which stories to pursue, which to ignore.... The fourth type of story is simply one which the staffer originates, independent of assignment or beat.... [T]his area promises much, should staffers pursue their advantage....

5. Staffers with "star" status can transgress policy more easily than cubs.

Consequences of the pattern

To the extent that policy is maintained, the paper keeps publishing smoothly as seen both from the newsroom and from the outside, which is no mean feat if we visualize the country with no press at all. This is the most general consequence. There are several special consequences. For the society as a whole, the existing system of power relationships is maintained. Policy usually protects property and class interests, and thus the strata and groups holding these interests are better able to retain them. For the larger community, much news is printed objectively, allowing for opinion to form openly, but policy news may be slanted or buried so that some important information is denied the citizenry. (This is the dysfunction widely scored by critics.) For the individual readers, the same is true. For the executives, their favorable statuses are maintained, with perhaps occasional touches of guilt over policy. For newsmen, the consequences are the same as for executives. For more independent, critical staffers, there can be several modes of adaptation. At the extremes, the pure conformist can deny the conflict, the confirmed deviate can quit the newspaper business. Otherwise, the adaptations seem to run in this way: (1) Keep on the job but blunt the sharp corners of policy where possible. ("If I wasn't here the next guy would let all that crap go through ... "); (2) Attempt to repress the conflict amorally and anti-intellectually ("What the hell, it's only a job; take your pay and forget it ... "); (3) Attempt to compensate, by "taking it out" in other contexts: drinking, writing "the truth" for liberal publications, working with action programs, the Guild, and otherwise. All of these adjustments were found in the study. As has been suggested, one of the main compensations for all staffers is simply to find justification in adhering to "good news practice."

Possible alternatives and change

A functional analysis, designed to locate sources of persistence of a pattern, can also indicate points of strain at which a structural change may occur. For example, the popular recipe for eliminating bias at one time was to diminish advertisers' power over the news. This theory having proved unfruitful, critics more recently have fastened upon the publisher as the point at which change must be initiated. Our analysis suggests that this is a valid approach, but one requiring that leverage in turn be applied on the publisher from various sources. Perhaps the most significant of these are professional codes. Yet we have seen the weakness of these codes when policy decisions are made. Further leverage is contained in such sources as the professional direction being taken by some journalism schools, in the Guild, and in sincere criticism.

Finally, newspaper readers possess potential power over press performance. Seen as a client of the press, the reader should be entitled to not only an interesting newspaper, but one which furnishes significant news objectively presented. This is the basic problem of democracy: to what extent should the individual be treated as a member of a mass, and to what extent fashioned (through educative measures) as an active participant in public decisions? Readership studies show that readers prefer "interesting" news and "features" over penetrating analyses. It can be concluded that the citizen has not been sufficiently motivated by society (and its press) to demand and apply the information he needs, and to discriminate between worthwhile and spurious information, for the fulfillment of the citizen's role. These other forces—professional codes, journalism schools, the Guild, critics, and readers—could result in changing newspaper performance. It still remains, however, for the publisher to be changed first. . . . Any important change toward a more "free and responsible press" must stem from various possible pressures on the publisher, who epitomizes the policy making and coordinating role.

Chapter 13
Suzanne Pingree
and Robert Hawkins
1945- and 1947-

D
uring the last generation, the definitions of news and
newsworthiness have been challenged as never before.
But while, in times past, individual editors decided on
their own what to include and what to leave out, since the
mid-1950s, huge segments of the population, people historically all
but ignored in the news, have demanded the reporter's attention. The
civil rights movement and then the women's movement argued that
for far too long, what has been considered news is little more than
what white men say and do from their positions of power—the
legislative chamber and the judicial bench, the corporate board room
and the presidential suite, the mayor's office and the police blotter.

These new voices demanding attention, the voices of the
relatively powerless and the disenfranchised, have forced journalists
into a wholesale examination of what they cover and why, of what
is news, and of what is fair and objective coverage of that news. In
one sense, this foreshadows what will be discussed in Part
III—Economics, especially the comments of Upton Sinclair and A.J.
Liebling. But the line of thought that Pingree and Hawkins suggest
in the following passage is far more complex than the observation
that rich people have greater access to sympathetic press coverage
than do poor people. The intellectual argument raised by Pingree and
Hawkins goes all the way back to journalism's most fundamental
definitions—What is news? What is fair? What is balanced?

Some have argued that news must not be a mere record of
specific events, a chronicle of discrete happenings. Rather, the
definition of news must be broadened to explain the social forces and
processes behind and surrounding particular events. In part, this is an
update of the call for context so eloquently issued by Walter

Lippmann early in the century. But this is a very dangerous business. The further one strays from demonstrable, empirical fact, the more one tries to describe social forces, the more difficult it is to be confident in one's own judgment and ability to be fair.

Looking through the other end of the telescope, questions arise over the composition of the professional news staffs. If reporters and editors are predominantly white men, this argument goes, how much real attention will they ever pay to women and people of color, except in terms of how those groups affect white men themselves? This argument often assumes that people of different sexes, races, and ethnic backgrounds inevitably understand truth and reality very differently. But if truth and reality are very different for different people, what does that say about the rational Englightenment principles upon which American society—and American journalism—are based?

The following article focuses on women and the news, but many of the points made could be applied to racial and ethnic minorities as well.

"News Definitions and Their Effects on Women"
Women and the News, 1978

Women are scarce in the first sections of American newspapers; in fact, they are scarce everywhere but in the women's or lifestyle sections of papers. Women's rights as a social issue do not receive much coverage either in absolute terms or in terms of the total newshole devoted to issues, which itself is very small. Finally, much of the information present in newspapers where women figure prominently is in the women's or lifestyle section. Most evidence about the renamed versions of these sections suggests that they remain traditional in their content, emphasizing recipes, advice, and social events and such, and are either shortened or contain more entertainment content. . . .

A number of the factors that would be prominent on many observers' lists probably have a great deal to do with why coverage (or non-coverage) of women is the way it is. For example, despite frequent cries for more issue-oriented news, we already know that 91% of news copy on eight major papers was event-oriented, and this should not surprise us. As Bernard Roshco points out in his cogent book, *Newsmaking*, the basic function of news is to keep us *aware*, not necessarily knowledgeable, of *what is going on* in the world. But starting with this functional premise then requires us to regard reporting that interprets, explains and fosters understanding as secondary or "soft" news—we only need it in order to interpret the event-oriented news, and it is events that are "going on," after all.

Part of the problem women and women's issues have had (a problem shared with minority groups, consumer movements, ecology groups and such) is that much of what we would like to see reported is never event-news at all. The myriad forms of oppression of women did not suddenly begin by Presidential decree last Thursday; they have been around for hundreds of years and have been adapted gradually as changing social and technological circumstances required. The ways in which couples are managing two jobs, children, housekeeping, *and* self-respect and sanity are not events that demand immediate publication because of their recency (and they don't evolve overnight, either!). Regardless of significance, continuing conditions, plans, strategies or potential solutions to problems are not news events, although announcement, confirmation or announced support of them can be.

A simplistic response to the predicament might be to say that it's our own fault if we're caught in this trap. After all, if one wants newspaper and television coverage, and if the press covers events and not issues, aren't we being pig-headed to pin our hopes on coverage of issues and conditions we think important? Shouldn't we be content to be covered when we participate in and shape the events of the day like any other news makers? The problem with this argument is that it ignores the imbalance of power among potentially significant groups and individuals. Often the most significant thing about those in power *is* what they have done, because their actions can affect many other people's lives. Those without power ordinarily cannot, by definition, take such actions. What is significant about them is their powerlessness, their oppression and their struggles to remedy these conditions. But even their struggles, unless they choose to go "outside the system," are a series of small, gradual events with little immediate significance for a wider public. Thus, women as potential news makers are placed in a very difficult position by this aspect of a definition of news: most women are denied the decision-making power that would make their actions news, and without power and the consequent prominence, only their most obtrusive actions are newsworthy.

A related problem for women stems from news-gathering organizations' needs for economic efficiency. Placing reporters on beats where news is deemed most likely to occur (e.g., the White House, police headquarters) produces more stories per person-hour invested than scattering them throughout the city. Quite obviously, this practice is at least partly responsible for the constant stream of stories on essentially trivial Presidential activities (e.g., "the President admitted today that he often has a snack of peanuts before going to bed"). Equally so, the beat structure ensures that we will be informed of all major crimes, fires and accidents. But from the point of view of women and women's issues, generally not on a news beat, the beat structure serves as an additional hurdle. To paraphrase a current saying about women's abilities and job success, a woman has to be twice as newsworthy as a man to get the same coverage.

We mentioned before that reporters and editors probably do not consciously discriminate against women and women's issues in the selection of news, and indeed conscious discrimination is not necessary with the beat structure, power imbalances and an issue-orientation all working against women. But there is at least one further unconscious or incidental way that reporters and editors themselves form a barrier to women in the news, and that is through their perceptions of their audiences. Presidents, movie stars, and beautiful people are not a constant presence in the news simply because of the beat structure or their power to affect others with their actions. They are also there because of their relevance to us (for whatever reason) and what editors believe (and can often demonstrate) to be our interest in them. Thus, out of what has *happened* involving *powerful* people in conventional, *predictable* situations and positions, newspapers are sold and ratings built by trying to give the audience news that is relevant to its needs or, equivalently, of interest to it. . . .

Effects on journalists

One effect of news definitions on journalists is of course obvious—the definitions determine what events the reporter will be sent to cover, define what sorts of information should be obtained and guide the format of presentation. However, a less obvious but no less important effect is on the reporter's own construction of social reality. For one thing, reporters are part of the audience for news, and should be susceptible to the same sorts of effects on their perceptions of the social significance of women and women's issues. In fact, reporters may even be more susceptible than the general public. Since the ability to distinguish significant people and events from the non-significant is an asset in their work, the significance of women is useful in their work instead of being just incidental information.

News definitions themselves work to the same effect, and more directly. The rules and practices of news gathering are not simply an arbitrary system of conventions for a craft to follow, but explicitly purport to locate what is timely and significant. Since we have seen that these conventions systematically exclude women from news pages and broadcasts, it would be surprising if reporters and editors did not quickly form general social attitudes about the insignificance of women that serve as a further bar to women's news and probably to women reporters as well.

News definitions also make it difficult for a feminist reporter (female or male) to personally do anything about the biases against women's news; since the conventions define what is significant, the reporter is restrained seemingly for a good reason from covering what she/he might like to do. To be willing to break the conventions and cover women and women's issues anyway requires some insight into the fact that the conventions act as much to define and confer significance as to simply locate existing significance. Beyond that, such a reporter must *already* have established a reputation for sound news judgment in conventional terms in order for his/her departure to be accepted. Basically, then, the effects of news definitions on reporters derive from the fact that they must learn and operate within the system of conventions that tend to limit coverage of women, and that the conventions provide symbolic messages about women that can easily be incorporated into reporters' own social attitudes.

Strategies for change

We have already implicitly described the effects of news definitions on women news makers; for a variety of reasons, they are systematically excluded from the newspapers and from broadcast news reports. Important but obvious corollary effects probably include doubt in the worthwhileness of what one is doing and/or frustration at one's inability to get news coverage. But potential news makers who are women are also the affected group who probably most want to change things, and we will suggest some ways in which women could get more news coverage.

Before turning to strategies for getting women and women's issues covered as news, we would like to pose a question to be borne in mind. We can demonstrate a lack of coverage and we can suggest some likely effects of this lack, but we need to ask ourselves: "Why do we want to be in the news?" Is it to present our oppression and struggle to a wide audience to gain support and build up our political clout? Or is it that we want confirmation from the prestige-granting media that we are significant? If our reasons are primarily the latter, then it is the *fact* of coverage and where that coverage occurs that concerns us most. But if we want coverage in order to gain support, then we must be concerned with the depth and fullness of stories—*what* is to be covered.

The first and most obvious and least useful way to achieve both goals is by having more women news makers, given conventional definitions of news. If half the Wall Street brokers, half the legislators, half the business executives, and half the Supreme Court and so on were women, then women would begin to be in the news. Women would be on the beat system, making decisions in positions of power so that their actions would meet conventional criteria for news coverage as timely events relevant to the broad public. Or to put it another way, if women weren't discriminated against in society as a whole, we would no longer need to worry about the effects of news definitions on women. Of course, that's not a very satisfying solution, since it so thoroughly puts the cart of our entire society before what we think may be the horse of the news media. Since we wouldn't be focusing on the news media in the first place if we didn't consider them pivotal in social change, we need to find ways to change media coverage *in order to* hasten the changes we want in society.

However, the notion of changing coverage of women by a work force change does make some sense if we limit ourselves to getting more women as reporters and editors. Women journalists probably are less stereotyped in the interests they ascribe to their audience, and also more likely to share interests with the women in their audience, and both these characteristics probably will lead to more coverage of women. Grace Lichtenstein, former head of the *New York Times* Rocky Mountain bureau, reports that she initiated a page-one story on changes in rape laws around the country; the changes met conventional news criteria but male editors hadn't thought of it, and had been closely following capital punishment. Naturally, sheer numbers of women reporters can only solve part of this problem if their stories are always judged for audience interest by editors with stereotyped notions, so we need people who do not share these stereotypes in high-ranking journalism positions as well. However, while this solution is more finite than changing all of society, it too still has two drawbacks. First, it is a relatively long-term solution of little comfort to the feminist with an issue to publicize now. And second, there is relatively little that feminist news makers can hope to do to get non-sexist journalists hired and promoted (although the rare woman news maker whose views are newsworthy because she herself is newsworthy or because her actions will put her in legal jeopardy can demand a non-sexist interviewer).

There are two more direct and immediate options available to the potential news maker who feels ignored by the media, one much used with varying degrees of success, and the other practically unutilized. First, if one is having a hard time getting one's issue-news covered, the widely used tactic is to tie that issue to an event. A march, a noon rally with speakers outside the state legislature, pickets in front of a supermarket, the famous bra-burning that evidently never happened—all of these are more-or-less obtrusive events whose organizers generally do not believe have any direct significance. Its purpose is usually explicitly to call attention to or to symbolize the issue that is the real matter of concern. The hope is that the event will force coverage and that the coverage will present the issue that was the purpose behind the event. Often socially-aware reporters will carefully try to get some statement that sums up the issue behind the event, and then the organizers will probably be at least partially satisfied, although they will probably wish the issue had gotten more air time or column inches and the pseudo-event less.

This tactic contains limitations and pitfalls, however, and its use calls for creativity, realistic expectations and balance. Even though the organizers may be intending to get coverage for an issue, it is their pseudo-event that makes them newsworthy, so there is no guarantee that the issue itself will get more than a mention. Also, the more obtrusive, unusual or outrageous the pseudo-event, the more likely it is to be covered, but also the more likely it is to be ridiculed in the news presentation or seen as over-reacting. Finally, the news maker should know what she expects to achieve. If the goal is to convey information about the issue—why it's important, what the arguments are—then the pseudo-event may have little value, since such statements are likely to get lost in the trivial happenings of the event. However, if her goals have more to do with demonstrating social significance of the issue and its supporting movement, and if she is willing to rely on other channels of communication to provide more substantive information, the pseudo-event may be ideal. For example, when 20,000 supporters of the ERA march on the State Capitol, it is unlikely that their reasons or arguments will get front-page coverage, although they may be described in a feature inside the paper or in a news special. But the fact that 20,000 people marched will be reported on the front page with the clear message that the issue is an important one with substantial support. So, the use of pseudo-events to obtain coverage of one's issues can be effective, if one's goals are the simple signification of importance. However, we reiterate that its use is definitely to be approached as an art form, not a science.

The other strategy available to potential women news makers is to change the journalists' stereotyped perceptions of what the audience wants. One very expensive way to do this is to set up a competing media outlet that provides all the content your nemesis does, plus the issue content you want. As you make some dent in their ratings or circulation, they will probably fight back by copying you to take away your small competitive advantage. Whereupon you will be forced out of business but will have achieved your goal. This sort of Pyrrhic victory could only be indulged in by those with vast personal fortunes, but fortunately there are less expensive ways to make the point.

We suggest telling them what you're interested in and what you aren't; what you find offensive and how they could avoid it. Most editors are aware that they don't get much feedback from their communities and that what they do get is probably not representative. Of course, our potential woman news maker or organization (preferably the organization) isn't representative either, but those who do speak out carry disproportionate weight. And mass media outlets do like to think of themselves as serving their communities, and are even willing to sacrifice small amounts of profitable time and space to make themselves feel good. This is probably especially true of broadcast media, since they have a watchdog (admittedly fairly toothless, but stations often act as if they don't know it) in the FCC seeing to it that they "serve the public interest."

What it comes down to is that the reporters and editors often simply do not know that there are women interested in more than recipes and dirty collars, and if they do know that there are some "libbers" around, they probably don't know what the "libbers" really want—after all, all they know is what they read in the papers. One way to let them know is to simply talk with them, quietly and reasonably.

We have to admit that this notion more or less fell into our laps. The General Manager of one of the Madison, Wisconsin, television stations attended a NOW-sponsored discussion of media stereotypes and said he was willing to talk further about it. Surprised, the NOW chapter formed a Media Task Force with us as co-chairs and we began meeting with the General Manager and various members of his staff. It took some months of sporadic meetings, but gradually they saw that we weren't there simply to attack them (although we did when we thought they deserved it) but to try to find reasonable and inexpensive ways for them to provide better coverage of women and avoid inadvertent sexism. For our part, we came to realize that the things we objected to in their coverage did not stem from intentional sexism, but from some unexamined assumptions about women.

Two of us went to one of the monthly breakfast meetings of the news staff to answer their questions about how we thought they should handle sensitive stories and about which terms we found offensive. We suggested a number of possible women's shows they could produce locally, and they did adopt one and showed it at noon one Tuesday when the network gave them back a half-hour. Finally, in spring 1976 they adopted as station policy a six-page memorandum we prepared outlining guidelines for non-sexist programming and advertising practices (available from Madison NOW), and have sent a one-page summary of these guidelines to all their advertisers. Emboldened by our success, we approached the other two commercial stations in Madison and found that they too were willing to sit down and discuss things—both have since adopted the same guidelines, although our relationships with them have not yet reached the relaxed stage they have with the first station.

Has it made any difference? We think it has. We no longer hear snide anti-feminist comments as small talk between stories—sometimes we even hear the sort of snide comments *we* would make about a story! Recently, coverage of a series of rape-attacks was full, sensitive and responsible (we had just met with "our" station the week before). These may sound like small changes, but we think they are very important ones. And this sort of consciousness-raising activity can be carried out by the relatively small core of active movement members—it doesn't need to turn out masses of people.

In closing, we probably should add that there is one more place to look for changes that might affect women's issues, and that is in the explicit conventions and ideologies of news. In recent years there has been a running debate in journalism between neutral and participant ideologies, with the neutral ideology corresponding to classical objectivity, and the participant ideology arguing for interpretive reporting, background stories, and even advocacy for those without power in society. Obviously, the women's movement has much to gain if the participant position gains further respectability, although the advocacy aspect may now be in some disrepute. But we think that at least part of the participant philosophy is gaining respectability and may be a point one can tap in discussions with reporters and editors.

Still, the position of women and women's issues with respect to the news is not terribly good, even at best. Even if a participant approach to journalism becomes more respectable and flourishes, such writing is likely in the foreseeable future to remain subordinate to "hard" news—a recounting of the day's events. And even with hardworking and clever women trying to put their issues before the public through pseudo-events and through discussions with news editors, one basic fact still leaves women and women's issues at a disadvantage: Until women are no longer discriminated against in society as a whole, they will continue to face an uphill battle to put themselves and their issues before the general public.

Chapter 14
Daniel Boorstin
1914-

I n the following extract, Daniel Boorstin, former librarian of Congress and prolific writer of popular history, deals with two interlocking problems: the development of what he calls "pseudo-events" and the rise of the visual media, especially television.

Boorstin notes that news has become an industry with an insatiable appetite. The public has grown increasingly sophisticated about the nature of that appetite, making the press extremely vulnerable to events manufactured solely for the purposes of getting "on the news." In some ways, he argues, the press has become a knowledgeable participant in the rise of these pseudo-events, much to the detriment of genuinely informed opinion.

Compounding the problem is the technology of television. His cautionary tale is a reminder that all forms of media have their own inherent strengths, weaknesses, and biases. The nature of the medium itself bends and refracts the message, a point made eloquently as early as the mid-eighteenth century by the great Scots political thinker, David Hume. In a 1752 essay, "On the Liberty of the Press," Hume commented on the difference between the excitations of inflamed oratory and the cooler power of print: "We need not dread from this liberty [of the press] any such ill consequences as followed from the harangues of the popular demagogues of Athens and tribunes of Rome," Hume wrote. "A man reads a book or pamphlet alone and coolly. There is none present from whom he can catch the passion by contagion . He is not hurried away by the force and energy of action. And should he be wrought up to never so seditious a humor, there is no violent resolution presented to him by which he can immediately vent his passion. The liberty of the press, therefore,

however abused, can scarce ever excite popular tumults or rebellion."
Samuel Adams and the other journalist-revolutionaries of the 1770s
would argue that Hume seriously underestimated the inflammatory
power of the printed word. However, Hume's point is still well-
taken: print is a more rational and less emotional medium than is
oratory, and, by extension, televison.

For television echoes far more of the orator than of the scribe.
Its power to communicate the emotions or compelling grandeur of an
event is as great as its ability to communicate complex ideas is
limited. So, as the technology itself makes it easier to convey certain
kinds of messages over others, Boorstin draws attention to the
problems that arise when one technology, television, begins to
dominate our political discourse. For the current or future journalist,
the lesson to be learned is a deeper appreciation of the strengths and
weaknesses of the profession, an appreciation that allows one to
exploit a medium's strengths and work to minimize its limitations.

The Image
1964

From News Gathering to News Making:
A Flood of Pseudo-Events

A DMIRING FRIEND: "My, that's a beautiful baby you have there!"
MOTHER: "Oh, that's nothing—you should see his photograph!"

The simplest of our extravagant expectations concerns the amount of novelty in the world. There was a time when the reader of an unexciting newspaper would remark, "How dull is the world today!" Nowadays he says, "What a dull newspaper!" When the first American newspaper, Benjamin Harris' *Publick Occurrences Both Forreign and Domestick*, appeared in Boston on September 25, 1690, it promised to furnish news regularly once a month. But, the editor explained, it might appear oftener "if any Glut of Occurrences happen." The responsibility for making news was entirely God's or the Devil's. The newsman's task was only to give "an Account of such considerable things as have arrived unto our Notice."

Although the theology behind this way of looking at events soon dissolved, this view of the news lasted longer. "The skilled and faithful journalist," James Parton observed in 1866, "recording with exactness and power the thing that has come to pass, is Providence addressing men." The story is told of a Southern Baptist clergyman before the Civil War who used to say, when a newspaper was brought in the room, "Be kind enough to let me have it a few minutes, till I see how the Supreme Being is governing the world." Charles A. Dana, one of the great American editors of the nineteenth century, once defended his extensive reporting of crime in the New York *Sun* by saying, "I have always felt that whatever the Divine Providence permitted to occur I was not too proud to report."

Of course, this is now a very old-fashioned way of thinking. Our current point of view is better expressed in the definition by Arthur MacEwen, whom William Randolph Hearst made his first editor of the San Francisco *Examiner*: "News is anything that makes a reader say, 'Gee whiz!'" Or, put more soberly, "News is whatever a good editor chooses to print."

We need not be theologians to see that we have shifted responsibility for making the world interesting from God to the newspaperman. We used to believe there were only so many "events" in the world. If there were not many intriguing or startling occurrences, it was no fault of the reporter. He could not be expected to report what did not exist.

Within the last hundred years, however, and especially in the twentieth century, all this has changed. We expect the papers to be full of news. If there is no news visible to the naked eye, or to the average citizen, we still expect it to be there for the enterprising newsman. The successful reporter is one who can find a story, even if there is no earthquake or assassination or civil war. If he cannot find a story, then he must make one—by the questions he asks of public figures, by the surprising human interest he unfolds from some commonplace event, or by "the news behind the news." If all this fails, then he must give us a "think piece"—an embroidering of well-known facts, or a speculation about startling things to come.

This change in our attitude toward "news" is not merely a basic fact about the history of American newspapers. It is a symptom of a revolutionary change in our attitude toward what happens in the world, how much of it is new, and surprising, and important. Toward how life can be enlivened, toward our power and the power of those who inform and educate and guide us, to provide synthetic happenings to make up for the lack of spontaneous events. Demanding more than the world can give us, we require that something be fabricated to make up for the world's deficiency. This is only one example of our demand for illusions.

Many historical forces help explain how we have come to our present immoderate hopes. But there can be no doubt about what we now expect, nor that it is immoderate. Every American knows the anticipation with which he picks up his morning newspaper at breakfast or opens his evening paper before dinner, or listens to the newscasts every hour on the hour as he drives across country, or watches his favorite commentator on television interpret the events of the day. Many enterprising Americans are now at work to help us satisfy these expectations. Many might be put out of work if we should suddenly moderate our expectations. But it is we who keep them in business and demand that they fill our consciousness with novelties, that they play God for us.

The new kind of synthetic novelty which has flooded our experience I will call "pseudo-events." The common prefix "pseudo" comes from the Greek word meaning false, or intended to deceive.... A pseudo-event...is a happening that possesses the following characteristics:

(1) It is not spontaneous, but comes about because someone has planned, planted, or incited it. Typically, it is not a train wreck or an earthquake, but an interview.

(2) It is planted primarily (not always exclusively) for the immediate purpose of being reported or reproduced. Therefore, its occurrence is arranged for the convenience of the reporting or reproducing media. Its success is measured by how widely it is reported. Time relations in it are commonly fictitious or factitious; the announcement is given out in

advance "for future release" and written as if the event had occurred in the past. The question, "Is it real?" is less important than, "Is it newsworthy?"

(3) Its relation to the underlying reality of the situation is ambiguous. Its interest arises largely from this very ambiguity. Concerning a pseudo-event the question, "What does it mean?" has a new dimension. While the news interest in a train wreck is in what happened and in the real consequences, the interest in an interview is always, in a sense, in whether it really happened and in what might have been the motives. Did the statement really mean what it said? Without some of this ambiguity a pseudo-event cannot be very interesting.

(4) Usually it is intended to be a self-fulfilling prophecy. . . .

In the last half century a larger and larger proportion of our experience, of what we read and see and hear, has come to consist of pseudo-events. We expect more of them and we are given more of them. They flood our consciousness. Their multiplication has gone on in the United States at a faster rate than elsewhere. Even the rate of increase is increasing every day. This is true of the world of education, of consumption, and of personal relations. It is especially true of the world of public affairs. . . .

A full explanation of the origin and rise of pseudo-events would be nothing less than a history of modern America. For our present purposes it is enough to recall a few of the more revolutionary recent developments.

The great modern increase in the supply and the demand for news began in the early nineteenth century. Until then newspapers tended to fill out their columns with lackadaisical secondhand accounts or stale reprints of items first published elsewhere at home and abroad. The laws of plagiarism and of copyright were undeveloped. Most newspapers were little more than excuses for espousing a political position, for listing the arrival and departure of ships, for familiar essays and useful advice, or for commercial or legal announcements.

Less than a century and a half ago did newspapers begin to disseminate up-to-date reports of matters of public interest written by eyewitnesses or professional reporters near the scene. The telegraph was perfected and applied to news reporting in the 1830's and '40's. Two newspapermen, William M. Swain of the Philadelphia *Public Ledger* and Amos Kendall of Frankfort, Kentucky, were founders of the national telegraphic network. Polk's presidential message in 1846 was the first to be transmitted by wire. When the Associated Press was founded in 1848, news began to be a salable commodity. Then appeared the rotary press, which could print on a continuous sheet and on both sides of the paper at the same time. The New York *Tribune*'s high-speed press, installed in the 1870's, could turn out 18,000 papers per hour. The Civil War, and later the Spanish-American War, offered raw materials and incentive for vivid up-to-the-minute, on-the-spot reporting. The competitive daring of giants like James Gordon Bennett, Joseph Pulitzer, and William Randolph Hearst intensified the race for news and widened newspaper circulation.

These events were part of a great, but little-noticed, revolution—what I would call the Graphic Revolution. Man's ability to make, preserve, transmit, and disseminate precise images—images of print, of men and landscapes and events, of the voices of men and mobs—now grew at a fantastic pace. The increased speed of printing was itself revolutionary. Still more revolutionary were the new techniques for making direct images of nature. Photography was destined soon to give printed matter itself a secondary role. By a giant leap Americans crossed the gulf from the daguerreotype to color television in less than a century. Dry-plate photography came in 1873; Bell patented the telephone in 1876; the phonograph was invented in 1877; the roll film appeared in 1884; Eastman's Kodak No. 1 was produced in 1888; Edison's patent on the radio came in 1891; motion pictures came in and voice was first transmitted by radio around 1900; the first national political convention widely broadcast by radio was that of 1928; television became commercially important in 1941, and color television even more recently.

Verisimilitude took on a new meaning. Not only was it now possible to give the actual voice and gestures of Franklin Delano Roosevelt unprecedented reality and intimacy for a whole nation. Vivid image came to overshadow pale reality. Sound motion pictures in color led a whole generation of pioneering American movie-goers to think of Benjamin Disraeli as an earlier imitation of George Arliss, just as television has led a later generation of television watchers to see the Western cowboy as an inferior replica of John Wayne. The Grand Canyon itself became a disappointing reproduction of the Kodachrome original.

The new power to report and portray what had happened was a new temptation leading newsmen to make probable images or to prepare reports in advance of what was expected to happen. As so often, men came to mistake their power for their necessities. Readers and viewers would soon prefer the vividness of the account, the "candidness" of the photograph, to the spontaneity of what was recounted.

Then came round-the-clock media. The news gap soon became so narrow that in order to have additional "news" for each new edition or each new broadcast it was necessary to plan in advance the stages by which any available news would be unveiled. After the weekly and the daily came the "extras" and the numerous regular editions. The Philadelphia *Evening Bulletin* soon had seven editions a day. No rest for the newsman. With more space to fill, he had to fill it ever more quickly. In order to justify the numerous editions, it was increasingly necessary that the news constantly change or at least seem to change. With radio on the air continuously during waking hours, the reporters' problems became still more acute. News every hour on the hour, and sometimes on the half hour. Programs interrupted any time for special bulletins. How to avoid deadly repetition, the appearance that nothing was happening, that news gatherers were asleep, or that competitors were more alert? As the costs of printing and then of broadcasting increased, it became financially necessary to keep the presses always at work and the TV screen always busy. Pressures toward the making of pseudo-events became ever stronger. News gathering turned into news making. . . .

An innocent observer might have expected that the rise of television and on-the-spot telecasting of the news would produce a pressure to report authentic spontaneous events exactly as they occur. But, ironically, these, like earlier improvements in the techniques of precise representation, have simply created more and better pseudo-events.

When General Douglas MacArthur returned to the United States (after President Truman relieved him of command in the Far East, on April 11, 1951, during the Korean War) he made a "triumphal" journey around the country. He was invited to Chicago to celebrate "MacArthur Day" (April 26, 1951) which had been proclaimed by resolution of the City Council. Elaborate ceremonies were arranged, including a parade. The proceedings were being televised.

A team of thirty-one University of Chicago sociologists, under the imaginative direction of Kurt Lang, took their posts at strategic points along the route of the MacArthur parade. The purpose was to note the reactions of the crowd and to compare what the spectators were seeing (or said they were seeing) with what they might have witnessed on television. This ingenious study confirmed my observation that we tend increasingly to fill our experience with contrived content. The newspapers had, of course, already prepared people for what the Chicago *Tribune* that morning predicted to be "a triumphant hero's welcome—biggest and warmest in the history of the middle west." Many of the actual spectators jammed in the crowd at the scene complained it was hard to see what was going on; in some places they waited for hours and then were lucky to have a fleeting glimpse of the General.

But the television perspective was quite different. The video viewer had the advantage of numerous cameras which were widely dispersed. Television thus ordered the events in its own way, quite different from that of the on-the-spot confusion. The cameras were carefully focused on "significant" happenings—that is, those which emphasized the drama of the occasion. For the television watcher, the General was the continuous center of attraction from his appearance during the parade at 2:21 P.M. until the sudden blackout at 3:00 P.M. Announcers continually reiterated (the scripts showed over fifteen explicit references) the unprecedented drama of the event, or that this was "the greatest ovation this city has ever turned out." On the television screen one received the impression of wildly cheering and enthusiastic crowds before, during, and after the parade. Of course the cameras were specially selecting "action" shots, which showed a noisy, waving audience; yet in many cases the cheering, waving, and shouting were really a response not so much to the General as to the aiming of the camera. Actual spectators, with sore feet, suffered long periods of boredom. Many groups were apathetic. The video viewer, his eyes fixed alternately on the General and on an enthusiastic crowd, his ears filled with a breathless narrative emphasizing the interplay of crowd and celebrity, could not fail to receive an impression of continuous dramatic pageantry.

The most important single conclusion of these sociologists was that the television presentation (as contrasted with the actual witnessing) of the events "remained true to form until the very end, interpreting the entire proceedings according to expectations. . . . The telecast was made to conform to what was interpreted as the pattern of viewers' expectations." Actual spectators at the scene were doubly disappointed, not only because they usually saw very little (and that only briefly) from where they happened to be standing, but also because they knew they were missing a much better performance (with far more of the drama they expected) on the television screen. "I bet my wife saw it much better over television!" and "We should have stayed home and watched it on TV" were the almost universal forms of dissatisfaction. While those at the scene were envying the viewers of the pseudo-event back home, the television viewers were, of course, being told again and again by the network commentators how great was the excitement of being "actually present."

Yet, as the Chicago sociologists noted, for many of those actually present one of the greatest thrills of the day was the opportunity to be on television. Just as everybody likes to see his name in the newspapers, so nearly everybody likes to think that he can be seen (or still better, with the aid of videotape, actually can see himself) on television. Similarly, reporters following candidates Kennedy and Nixon during their tours in the 1960 Presidential campaign noted how many of the "supporters" in the large crowds that were being televised had come out because they wanted to be seen on the television cameras. . . .

On December 2, 1960, during the school integration disorders in New Orleans, Mayor de Lesseps S. Morrison wrote a letter to newsmen proposing a three-day moratorium on news and television coverage of the controversy. He argued that the printed and televised reports were exaggerated and were damaging the city's reputation and its tourist trade. People were given an impression of prevailing violence, when, he said, only one-tenth of 1 per cent of the population had been involved in the demonstration. But he also pointed out that the mere presence of telecasting facilities was breeding disorder. "In many cases," he observed, "these people go to the area to get themselves on television and hurry home for the afternoon and evening telecasts to see the show." At least two television reporters had gone about the crowd interviewing demonstrators with inflammatory questions like "Why are you opposed to intermarriage?" Mayor Morrison said he himself had witnessed a television cameraman "setting up a scene," and then, having persuaded a group of students to respond like a "cheering section," had them yell and demonstrate on cue. The conscientious reporters indignantly rejected the Mayor's proposed moratorium on news. They said that "Freedom of the Press" was at stake. That was once an institution preserved in the interest of the community. Now it is often a euphemism for the prerogative of reporters to produce their synthetic commodity. . . .

Until recently we have been justified in believing Abraham Lincoln's familiar maxim: "You may fool all the people some of the time; you can even fool some of the people all the time; but you can't fool all of the people all the time." This has been the foundation-belief of American democracy. Lincoln's appealing slogan rests on two elementary assumptions. First, that there is a clear and visible distinction between sham and reality, between the lies a demagogue would have us believe and the truths which are there all the time. Second, that the people tend to prefer reality to sham, that if offered a choice between a simple truth and a contrived image, they will prefer the truth.

Neither of these any longer fits the facts. Not because people are less intelligent or more dishonest. Rather because great unforeseen changes—the great forward strides of American civilization—have blurred the edges of reality. The pseudo-events which flood our consciousness are neither true nor false in the old familiar senses. The very same advances which have made them possible have also made the images—however planned, contrived, or distorted—more vivid, more attractive, more impressive, and more persuasive than reality itself.

We cannot say that we are being fooled. It is not entirely inaccurate to say that we are being "informed." This world of ambiguity is created by those who believe they are instructing us, by our best public servants, and with our own collaboration. Our problem is the harder to solve because it is created by people working honestly and industriously at respectable jobs. It is not created by demagogues or crooks, by conspiracy or evil purpose. The efficient mass production of pseudo-events—in all kinds of packages, in black and white, in technicolor, in words, and in a thousand other forms—is the work of the whole machinery of our society. It is the daily product of men of good will. The media must be fed! The people must be informed! Most pleas for "more information" are therefore misguided. So long as we define information as a knowledge of pseudo-events, "more information" will simply multiply the symptoms without curing the disease.

The American citizen thus lives in a world where fantasy is more real than reality, where the image has more dignity than its original. We hardly dare face our bewilderment, because our ambiguous experience is so pleasantly irridescent, and the solace of belief in contrived reality is so thoroughly real. We have become eager accessories to the great hoaxes of the age. These are the hoaxes we play on ourselves.

Pseudo-events from their very nature tend to be more interesting and more attractive than spontaneous events. Therefore in American public life today pseudo-events tend to drive all other kinds of events out of our consciousness, or at least to overshadow them. Earnest, well-informed citizens seldom notice that their experience of spontaneous events is buried by pseudo-events. Yet nowadays, the more industriously they work at "informing" themselves the more this tends to be true.

In his now-classic work, *Public Opinion*, Walter Lippmann in 1922 began by distinguishing between "the world outside and the pictures in our heads." He defined a "stereotype" as an oversimplified pattern that helps us find meaning in the world. As examples he gave the crude "stereotypes we carry about in our heads," of large and varied classes of people like "Germans," "South Europeans," "Negroes," "Harvard men," "agitators," etc. The stereotype, Lippmann explained, satisfies our needs and helps us defend our prejudices by seeming to give definiteness and consistency to our turbulent and disorderly daily experience. In one sense, of course, stereotypes—the excessively simple, but easily grasped images of racial, national, or religious groups—are only another example of pseudo-events. But, generally speaking, they are closer to propaganda. For they simplify rather than complicate. Stereotypes narrow and limit experience in an emotionally satisfying way; but pseudo-events embroider and dramatize experience in an interesting way. This itself makes pseudo-events far more seductive; intellectually they are more defensible, more intricate, and more intriguing. To discover how the stereotype is made—to unmask the sources of propaganda—is to make the stereotype less believable. Information about the staging of a pseudo-event simply adds to its fascination.

Lippmann's description of stereotypes was helpful in its day. But he wrote before pseudo-events had come in full flood. Photographic journalism was then still in its infancy. Wide World Photos had just been organized by the *New York Times* in 1919. The first wirephoto to attract wide attention was in 1924, when the American Telephone and Telegraph Company sent to the *New York Times* pictures of the Republican Convention in Cleveland which nominated Calvin Coolidge. Associated Press Picture Service was established in 1928. *Life*, the first wide-circulating weekly picture news magazine, appeared in 1936; within a year it had a circulation of 1,000,000, and within two years, 2,000,000. *Look* followed, in 1937. The newsreel, originated in France by Pathe, had been introduced to the United States only in 1910. When Lippmann wrote his book in 1922, radio was not yet reporting news to the consumer; television was of course unknown.

Recent improvements in vividness and speed, the enlargement and multiplying of news-reporting media, and the public's increasing news hunger now make Lippmann's brilliant analysis of the stereotype the legacy of a simpler age. For stereotypes made experience handy to grasp. But pseudo-events would make experience newly and satisfyingly elusive. In 1911 Will

Irvin, writing in *Collier's*, described the new era's growing public demand for news as "a crying primal want of the mind, like hunger of the body." The mania for news was a symptom of expectations enlarged far beyond the capacity of the natural world to satisfy. It required a synthetic product. It stirred an irrational and undiscriminating hunger for fancier, more varied items. Stereotypes there had been and always would be; but they only dulled the palate for information. They were an opiate. Pseudo-events whetted the appetite; they aroused news hunger in the very act of satisfying it.

In the age of pseudo-events it is less the artificial simplification than the artificial complication of experience that confuses us. Whenever in the public mind a pseudo-event competes for attention with a spontaneous event in the same field, the pseudo-event will tend to dominate. What happens on television will overshadow what happens off television. Of course I am concerned here not with our private worlds but with our world of public affairs.

Here are some characteristics of pseudo-events which make them overshadow spontaneous events:

(1) Pseudo-events are more dramatic. A television debate between candidates can be planned to be more suspenseful (for example, by reserving questions which are then popped suddenly) than a casual encounter or consecutive formal speeches planned by each separately.

(2) Pseudo-events, being planned for dissemination, are easier to disseminate and to make vivid. Participants are selected for their newsworthy and dramatic interest.

(3) Pseudo-events can be repeated at will, and thus, their impression can be re-enforced.

(4) Pseudo-events cost money to create; hence somebody has an interest in disseminating, magnifying, advertising, and extolling them as events worth watching or worth believing. They are therefore advertised in advance, and rerun in order to get money's worth.

(5) Pseudo-events, being planned for intelligibility, are more intelligible and hence more reassuring. Even if we cannot discuss intelligently the qualifications of the candidates or the complicated issues, we can at least judge the effectiveness of a television performance. How comforting to have some political matter we can grasp!

(6) Pseudo-events are more sociable, more conversable, and more convenient to witness. Their occurrence is planned for our convenience. The Sunday newspaper appears when we have a lazy morning for it. Television programs appear when we are ready with our glass of beer. In the office the next morning, Jack Paar's (or any other star performer's) regular late-night show at the usual hour will overshadow in conversation a casual event that suddenly came up and had to find its way into the news.

(7) Knowledge of pseudo-events—of what has been reported, or what has been staged, and how—becomes the test of being "informed." News magazines provide us regularly with quiz questions concerning not what has happened but concerning "names in the news"—what has been reported in the news magazines. Pseudo-events begin to provide that "common discourse" which some of my old-fashioned friends have hoped to find in the Great Books.

(8) Finally, pseudo-events spawn other pseudo-events in geometric progression. They dominate our consciousness simply because there are more of them, and ever more.

By this new Gresham's law of American public life, counterfeit happenings tend to drive spontaneous happenings out of circulation. The rise in the power and prestige of the Presidency is due not only to the broadening powers of the office and the need for quick decisions, but also to the rise of centralized news gathering and broadcasting, and the increase of the Washington press corps. The President has an ever more ready, more frequent, and more centralized access to the world of pseudo-events. A similar explanation helps account for the rising prominence in recent years of the Congressional investigating committees. In many cases these committees have virtually no legislative impulse, and sometimes no intelligible legislative assignment. But they do have an almost unprecedented power, possessed now by no one else in the Federal government except the President, to make news. Newsmen support the committees because the committees feed the newsmen: they live together in happy symbiosis. The battle for power among Washington agencies becomes a contest to dominate the citizen's information of the government. This can most easily be done by fabricating pseudo-events.

A perfect example of how pseudo-events can dominate is the recent popularity of the quiz show format. Its original appeal came less from the fact that such shows were tests of intelligence (or of dissimulation) than from the fact that the situations were elaborately contrived—with isolation booths, armed bank guards, and all the rest—and they purported to inform the public.

The application of the quiz show format to the so-called "Great Debates" between Presidential candidates in the election of 1960 is only another example. These four campaign programs, pompously and self-righteously advertised by the broadcasting networks, were remarkably successful in reducing great national issues to trivial dimensions. With appropriate vulgarity, they might have been called the $400,000 Question (Prize: a $100,000-a-year job for four years). They were a clinical example of the pseudo-event, of how it is made, why it appeals, and of its consequences for democracy in America.

In origin the Great Debates were confusedly collaborative between politicians and news makers. Public interest centered around the pseudo-event itself: the lighting, make-up, ground rules, whether notes would be allowed, etc. Far more interest was shown in the performance than in what was said. The pseudo-events spawned in turn by the Great Debates were numberless. People who had seen the shows read about them the more avidly, and listened eagerly for interpretations by news commentators. Representatives of both parties made "statements" on the probable effects of the debates. Numerous interviews and discussion programs were broadcast exploring their meaning. Opinion polls kept us informed on the nuances of our own and other people's reactions. Topics of speculation multiplied. Even the question whether there should be a fifth debate became for a while a lively "issue."

The drama of the situation was mostly specious, or at least had an extremely ambiguous relevance to the main (but forgotten) issue: which participant was better qualified for the Presidency. Of course, a man's ability, while standing under klieg lights, without notes, to answer in two and a half minutes a question kept secret until that moment, had only the most dubious relevance—if any at all—to his real qualifications to make deliberate Presidential decisions on long-standing public questions after being instructed by a corps of advisers. The great Presidents in our history (with the possible exception of F.D.R.) would have done miserably; but our most notorious demagogues would have shone. . . .

The television medium shapes this new kind of political quiz-show spectacular in many crucial ways. Theodore H. White has proved this with copious detail in his *The Making of the President 1960* (1961). All the circumstances of this particular competition for votes were far more novel than the old word "debate" and the comparisons with the Lincoln-Douglas Debates suggested. Kennedy's great strength in the critical first debate, according to White, was that he was in fact not "debating" at all, but was seizing the opportunity to address the whole nation; while Nixon stuck close to the issues raised by his opponent, rebutting them one by one.

Nixon, moreover, suffered a handicap that was serious only on television: he has a light, naturally transparent skin. On an ordinary camera that takes pictures by optical projection, this skin photographs well. But a television camera projects electronically, by an "image-orthicon tube" which has an x-ray effect. This camera penetrates Nixon's transparent skin and brings out (even just after a shave) the tiniest hair growing in the follicles beneath the surface. For the decisive first program Nixon wore a make-up called "Lazy Shave" which was ineffective under these conditions. He therefore looked haggard and heavy-bearded by contrast to Kennedy, who looked pert and clean-cut.

This greatest opportunity in American history to educate the voters by debating the large issues of the campaign failed. The main reason, as White points out, was the compulsions of the medium. "The nature of both TV and radio is that they abhor silence and 'dead time.' All TV and radio discussion programs are compelled to snap question and answer back and forth as if the contestants were adversaries in an intellectual tennis match. Although every experienced newspaperman and inquirer knows that the most thoughtful and responsive answers to any difficult question come after long pause, and that the longer the pause the more illuminating the thought that follows it, nonetheless the electronic media cannot bear to suffer a pause of more than five seconds; a pause of thirty seconds of dead time on air seems interminable. Thus, snapping their two-and-a-half-minute answers back and forth, both candidates could only react for the cameras and the people, they could not think." Whenever either candidate found himself touching a thought too large for two-minute exploration, he quickly retreated. Finally the television-watching voter was left to judge, not on issues explored by thoughtful men, but on the relative capacity of the candidates to perform under television stress.

Pseudo-events thus lead to emphasis on pseudo-qualifications. Again the self-fulfilling prophecy. If we test Presidential candidates by their talents on TV quiz performances, we will, of course, choose presidents for precisely these qualifications. In a democracy, reality tends to conform to the pseudo-event. Nature imitates art.

Chapter 15
Sissela Bok
1934-

While it is supposed to be axiomatic, as with the Code of Ethics of the Society of Professional Journalists, that journalists first and foremost serve the truth, this turns out to be not always the surest aim, even when the truth is unavoidably clear. On first inspection it seems obvious that the one thing a journalist should never do is lie. Yet sometimes they do. The infamous Janet Cooke case, in which the reporter fabricated a story about an eight-year-old heroin addict, much to the eventual embarrassment of her paper, the *Washington Post*, is a ready example. In fact, reporters are often confronted with what they feel is the necessity to lie, or at least withhold the truth, from their readers, their sources, or their subjects.

Such lying is typically justified by the worthiest of motives, the greater good to the public. And so a war correspondent is reluctant to report the size or location of troops in a battle zone, even though he has that privileged information. The investigative journalist operates under cover, lying about—or at least withholding—her identity to news subjects in order to get a story of overarching public importance. Or a reporter covering a hostage-taking, in an effort to help free the victims, falsely promises the gunmen that their story will be aired on television. What actually constitutes "a lie"? When is lying justified? What are the ground rules? These are the questions considered at length by ethicist Sissela Bok. Bok earned her Ph.D. in philosophy at Harvard University in 1970 and has been teaching philosophy at Brandeis University since 1985. Her book, *Lying: Moral Choice in Public and Private Life* (New York: Pantheon Books, 1979), has become a touchstone in discussions about professional ethics and directly attacks the problems confronted by journalists around the issue of telling the truth. Some of the principle arguments and guidelines from the 1989 update of the text are excerpted here. She begins one of her chapters with a quote from Carl Bernstein and Bob Woodward's Watergate story, *All the President's Men* (New York: Warner Books, 1974):

> Though it wasn't true, Woodward told Deep Throat that he and Bernstein had a story for the following week saying that Haldeman was the fifth person in control of disbursements from the secret fund.
>
> "You'll have to do it on your own," Deep Throat said. . . . Since he had not cautioned them on Haldeman, he was effectively confirming the story.

Lying
1979

T ruth"—no concept intimidates and yet draws thinkers so powerfully. From the beginnings of human speculation about the world, the questions of what truth is and whether we can attain it have loomed large. Every philosopher has had to grapple with them. Every religion seeks to answer them.

One pre-Socratic Greek tradition saw truth—aletheia—as encompassing all that we remember: singled out through memory from everything that is destined for Lethe, "the river of forgetfulness." The oral tradition required that information be memorized and repeated, often in song, so as not to be forgotten. Everything thus memorized—stories about the creation of the world, genealogies of gods and heroes, advice about health—all partook of truth, even if in another sense completely fabricated or erroneous. In this early tradition, repeating the songs meant keeping the material alive and thus "true," just as creating works of art could be thought of as making an object true, bringing it to life.

Only gradually did the opposition between truth and error come to be thought central to philosophy, and the nature of verification itself spotlighted. The immense preoccupation with epistemology took hold with Plato and has never diminished since. In logic, in epistemology, in theology, and in metaphysics, the topic of "truth" has continued to absorb almost limitless energies. And since the strands from these diverse disciplines are not always disentangled, a great many references to "truth" remain of unsurpassed vagueness.

Truth and Truthfulness

In all such speculation, there is great risk of a conceptual muddle, of not seeing the crucial differences between two domains: the moral domain of intended truthfulness and deception, and the much vaster domain of truth and falsity in general. The moral question of whether you are lying or not is not settled by establishing the truth or falsity of what you say. In order to settle this question, we must know whether you intend your statement to mislead...

Any number of appearances and words can mislead us; but only a fraction of them are intended to do so. A mirage may deceive us, through no one's fault. Our eyes deceive us all the time. We are beset by self-delusion and bias of every kind. Yet we often know when we mean to be honest or dishonest. Whatever the essence of truth and falsity, and whatever the sources of error in our lives, one such source is surely the human agent, receiving and giving out information, intentionally deflecting, withholding, even distorting it at times. Human beings, after all, provide for each other the most ingenious obstacles to what partial knowledge and minimal rationality they can hope to command.

We must single out, therefore, from the countless ways in which we blunder misinformed though life, that which is done with the intention to mislead; and from the countless partial stabs at truth, those which are intended to be truthful. Only if this distinction is clear will it be possible to ask the moral question with rigor. And it is to this question alone—the intentional manipulation of information—that the court addresses itself in its request for "the truth, the whole truth, and nothing but the truth." . . .

Deceit and violence—these are the two forms of deliberate assault on human beings. Both can coerce people into acting against their will. Most harm that can befall victims through violence can come to them also through deceit. But deceit controls more subtly, for it works on belief as well as action. Even Othello, whom few would have dared to try to subdue by force, could be brought to destroy himself and Desdemona through falsehood.

The knowledge of this coercive element in deception, and of our vulnerability to it, underlies our sense of the centrality of truthfulness. Of course, deception—again like violence—can be used also in self-defense, even for sheer survival. Its use can also be quite trivial, as in white lies. Yet its potential for coercion and for destruction is such that society could scarcely function without some degree of truthfulness in speech and action.

Imagine a society, no matter how ideal in other respects, where word and gesture could never be counted upon. Questions asked, answers given, information exchanged—all would be worthless. Were all statements randomly truthful or deceptive, action and choice would be undermined from the outset. There must be a minimal degree of trust in communication for language and action to be more than stabs in the dark. This is why some level of truthfulness has always been seen as essential to human society, no matter how deficient the observance of other moral principles. Even the devils themselves, as Samuel Johnson said, do not lie to one another, since the society of Hell could not subsist without truth any more than others.

A society, then, whose members were unable to distinguish truthful messages from deceptive ones, would collapse. But even before such a general collapse, individual choice and survival would be imperiled. The search for food and shelter could depend on no expectations from others. A warning that a well was poisoned or a plea for help in an accident would come to be ignored unless independent confirmation could be found.

All our choices depend on our estimates of what is the case; these estimates must in turn often rely on information from others. Lies distort this information and therefore our situation as we perceive it, as well as our choices. A lie, in Hartmann's words, "injures the deceived person in his life; it leads him astray."

To the extent that knowledge gives power, to that extent do lies affect the distribution of power; they add to that of the liar, and diminish that of the deceived, altering his choices at different levels. A lie, first, may misinform, so as to obscure some objective, something the deceived person wanted to do or obtain. It may make the objective seem unattainable or no longer desirable. It may even create a new one, as when Iago deceived Othello into wanting to kill Desdemona.

Lies may also eliminate or obscure relevant alternatives, as when a traveler is falsely told a bridge has collapsed. At times, lies foster the belief that there are more alternatives than is really the case; at other times, a lie may lead to the unnecessary loss of confidence in the best alternative. Similarly, the estimates of costs and benefits of any action can be endlessly varied through successful deception. The immense toll of life and human welfare from United States intervention in Vietnam came at least in part from the deception (mingled with self-deception) by those who channeled overly optimistic information to the decision-makers.

Finally, the degree of uncertainty in how we look at our choices can be manipulated through deception. Deception can make a situation falsely uncertain as well as falsely certain. It can affect the objectives seen, the alternatives believed possible, the estimates made of risks and benefits. Such a manipulation of the dimension of certainty is one of the main ways to gain power over the choices of those deceived. And just as deception can initiate actions a person would otherwise never have chosen, so it can prevent action by obscuring the necessity for choice. This is the essence of camouflage and of the cover-up—the creation of apparent normality to avert suspicion.

Everyone depends on deception to get out of a scrape, to save face, to avoid hurting the feelings of others. Some use it much more consciously to manipulate and gain ascendancy. Yet all are intimately aware of the threat lies can pose, the suffering they can bring. This two-sided experience which we all share makes the singleness with which either side is advocated in action all the more puzzling. Why are such radically different evaluations given to the effects of deception, depending on whether the point of view is that of the liar or the one lied to? . . .

The Principle of Veracity

The perspective of the deceived, then, reveals several reasons why lies are undesirable. Those who share it have cause to fear the effects of undiscovered lies on the choices of liars and dupes. They are all too aware of the impact of discovered and suspected lies on trust and social cooperation. And they consider not only the individual lie but the practice of which it forms a part, and the long-term results which it can have.

For these reasons, I believe that we must at the very least accept as an initial premise Aristotle's view that lying is "mean and culpable" and that truthful statements are preferable to lies in the absence of special considerations. This premise gives an initial negative weight to lies. It holds that they are not neutral from the point of view of our choices; that lying requires explanation, whereas truth ordinarily does not. It provides a counterbalance to the crude evaluation by liars of their own motives and of the consequences of their lies. And it places the burden of proof squarely on those who assume the liar's perspective.

This presumption against lying can also be stated so as to stress the positive worth of truthfulness or veracity. I would like, in the chapters to come, to refer to the "principle of veracity" as an expression of this initial imbalance in our weighing of truthfulness and lying.

It is not necessarily a principle that overrides all others, nor even the one most frequently appealed to. Nor is it, obviously, sufficient by itself—witness the brutal but honest regime of the tormentor who prides himself on his frankness. Rather, trust in some degree of veracity functions as a foundation of relations among human beings; when this trust shatters or wears away, institutions collapse.

Such a principle need not indicate that all lies should be ruled out by the initial negative weight given to them, nor does it even suggest what kinds of lies should be prohibited. But it does make at least one immediate limitation in lying: in any situation where a lie is a possible choice, one must first seek truthful alternatives. If lies and truthful statements appear to achieve the same result or appear to be as desirable to the person contemplating lying the lies should be ruled out. And only where a lie is a last resort can one even begin to consider whether or not it is morally justified. Mild as this initial stipulation sounds, it would, if taken seriously, eliminate a great many lies told out of carelessness or habit or unexamined good intentions. . . .

Conflicts of Duty

Although veracity is undoubtedly an important duty, most assume that it leaves room for exceptions. It can clash with other duties, such as that of averting harm to innocent persons. Yet Kant holds that "a conflict of duties and obligations is inconceivable," that if one does one's duty, one will turn out to have had no conflicting obligations. It is this refusal to consider conflicts of duty which drives Kant into such inflexible positions.

Most have held the contrary view—that there are times when truthfulness causes or fails to avert such great harm that a lie is clearly justifiable. One such time is where a life is threatened and where a lie might avert the danger. The traditional testing case advanced against the absolutist position is that discussed by Kant himself, where a would-be murderer inquires whether "our friend who is pursued by him had taken refuge in our house." Should one lie in order to save one's friend? Or should one tell the truth? . . .

Kant's single-minded upholding of truthfulness above all else nullifies the use of falsehoods in self-defense. Can the principle of veracity reasonably be made to carry such a burden?

This burden would clearly create guilt for many: guilt at having allowed the killing of a fellow human rather than lie to a murderer. Kant attempts to assuage this guilt by arguing as follows: If one stays close to the truth, one cannot, strictly speaking, be responsible for the murderous acts another commits. The murderer will have to take the whole blame for his act. In speaking to him truthfully, one has done nothing blameworthy. If, on the other hand, one tells him a lie, Kant argues, one becomes responsible for all the bad consequences which might befall the victim and anyone else. One may, for instance, point the murderer in what one believes to be the wrong direction, only to discover with horror that that is exactly where the victim has gone to hide.

There is much truth in saying that one is responsible for what happens after one has done something wrong or questionable. But it is a very narrow view of responsibility which does not also take some blame for a disaster one could easily have averted, no matter how much others are also to blame. A world where it is improper even to tell a lie to a murderer pursuing an innocent victim is not a world that many would find safe to inhabit.

It may even be that, in less rigorous moments, doubts beset Wesley and Kant and those who hold the most extreme views. A curious form of internal evidence for such a supposition is that they so often preface their most surprisingly intransigent remarks with phrases such as "however strange it may sound." They know that their stance is highly counterintuitive; yet something forces them to adopt it. . . .

Justification and Publicity

How can we single out, then, justifiable lies from all those that their perpetrators regard as so highly excusable? Assume, as before, that we are dealing with clearcut lies, deliberate efforts to mislead. We can examine the alternatives confronting the liar, and the excuses he gives. Which excuses not only mitigate and extenuate, but remove moral blame? And if we accept the excuses for some lies, do we thereby merely remove blame from the liar retroactively? Or are we willing to allow those lies ahead of time under certain circumstances? Could we, finally, recommend a practice of telling such lies whenever those circumstances arise—whenever, for instance, an innocent life is otherwise threatened?

We have already seen how often the liar is caught in a distorting perspective; his efforts to answer questions of justification can then show a systematic bias. His appeals to principle may be hollow, his evaluation flimsy. The result is that he can arrive at diametrically opposed weighings of alternatives and reasons, depending upon what he puts into the weighing process in the first place.

Justification must involve more than such untested personal steps of reasoning. To justify is to defend as just, right, or proper, by providing adequate reasons. It means to hold up to some standard, such as religious or legal or moral standard. Such justification requires an audience: it may be directed to God, or a court of law, or one's peers, or one's own conscience; but in ethics it is most appropriately aimed, not at any one individual or audience, but rather at "reasonable persons" in general. Someone seeking moral justification must, in Hume's words:

> depart from his private and particular situation and must choose a point of view common to him with others; he must move some universal principle of the human frame and touch a string to which all mankind have an accord and symphony.

Moral justification, therefore, cannot be exclusive or hidden; it has to be capable of being made public. In going beyond the purely private, it attempts to transcend also what is merely subjective. Wittgenstein pointed to these elements of justification in observing that "justification consists in appealing to something independent." Many moral philosophers have assumed that such an appeal is of the very essence in reasoning about moral choice. John Rawls has set it forth most explicitly, under the name of publicity, as a formal constraint on any moral principle worth considering. According to such a constraint, a moral principle must be capable of public statement and defense. A secret moral principle, or one which could be disclosed only to a sect or a guild, could not satisfy such a condition.

Such publicity is, I believe, crucial to the justification of all moral choice. But it is, perhaps, particularly indispensable to the justification of lies and other deceptive practices. For publicity is connected more directly to veracity than to other moral principles. In ethics, publicity without truthfulness is misleading and thus worthless. In addition, lies, inherently secretive, may call for submission to public justification more than openly performed problematic acts. Such acts are more likely to arouse controversy eventually, whereas lies, if they succeed, may never do so.

I would like to combine this concept of publicity with the view of justification in ethics as being directed to reasonable persons, in order to formulate a workable test for looking at concrete moral choice. It will be a test to weigh the various excuses advanced for disputed choices, and therefore for lies. Such a test counters the self-deception and bias inherent in the liar's perspective. It challenges privately held assumptions and hasty calculations. It requires clear and understandable formulation of the arguments used to defend the lie—arguments which might otherwise have remained inchoate or seemed intuitively right without ever being questioned. Its advantages, moreover, are cumulative: the objectivity and ability to shift perspectives gained in each appeal to publicity carry over to subsequent ones. Basically, it is through the exercise of such appeals and the debates that they engender that a more finely tuned moral sense will develop.

The test of publicity asks which lies, if any, would survive the appeal for justification to reasonable persons. It requires us to seek concrete and open performance of an exercise crucial to ethics: the Golden Rule, basic to so many religious and moral traditions. We must share the perspective of those affected by our choices, and ask how we would react if the lies we are contemplating were told to us. We must, then, adopt the perspective not only of liars but of those lied to; and not only of particular persons but of all those affected by lies—the collective perspective of reasonable persons seen as potentially deceived. We must formulate the excuses and the moral arguments used to defend the lies and ask how they would stand up under the public scrutiny of these reasonable persons. . . .

Doctors, lawyers, *journalists* [emphasis added], secret-service agents, and military personnel, for example, may find themselves repeatedly in straits where serious consequences seem avoidable only through deception. Their chosen work exposes them frequently to such crises; their professions, moreover, reward competition and unusual achievement. Cutting corners may be one way to such achievements; and if deception is pervasive and rarely punished, then it will be all the more likely to spread. The accepted practices may then grow increasingly insensitive, and abuses and mistakes more common, resulting in harm to self, profession, clients, and society.

There is always an interweaving of self-serving and altruistic motives in such practices. One benefits personally by cutting corners, no one person seems to be too much harmed thereby, and the benefits one can bring about often seem important. But the self-serving motives are not clearly addressed; there is, in fact, rarely a clear professional standard or open discussion of the unspoken standards in professional organizations.

The excerpt from *All the President's Men* at the beginning of this chapter is a good case in point. Certainly, the situation was one of mounting crisis for the nation and of potential danger for investigating journalists who came too close to revealing the facts about Watergate. It is certain, too, that there was great pressure to be first with the revelations; the desire to advance professionally and to gain fame formed no small part of the undertaking. In pursuing their investigation, the two journalists came to tell more than one lie; a whole fabric of deception arose. Persons being interviewed were falsely told that others had already given certain bits of information or had said something about them. One of the reporters tried to impersonate Donald Segretti on the telephone. The other lied to Deep Throat in order to extract corroboration of a fact which this witness would have feared to reveal in other ways. And the newspaper was used to print information for which there was not always adequate evidence.

It is not clear that, beyond the secrecy which had to surround the investigation, deception was actually needed. Yet it is certain that the reporters deserve great credit for exposing the misdeeds of the Watergate scandal. It can be argued that, in order for this exposure to be possible, deception was needed; but what is more troubling in the book than the lies themselves is the absence of any acknowledgment of a moral dilemma. No one seems to have stopped to think that there was a problem in using deceptive means. No one weighed the reasons for and against doing so. There was no reported effort to search for honest alternatives, or to distinguish among different forms and degrees of deception, or to consider whether some circumstances warranted it more than others.

The absence of such reflection may well result in countless young reporters unthinkingly adopting some of these methods. And those who used them successfully at a time of national crisis may do so again with lesser provocation. The impression gained by the reading public is that such standards are taken for granted among journalists. The results, therefore, are severe, both in terms of risks to the personal professional standards of those directly involved, the public view of the profession, and to many within it or about to enter it.

Part III—Economy: The Press and the Marketplace

C apitalism has shaped the modern American press just as it has shaped automobile manufacturing and fast-food chains; whatever journalism's intellectual origins, it is now a creature of commerce as much as it is a creature of politics. The transition from the political press of the early nineteenth century to the commercial press of the twentieth century is the result of many sweeping changes in American life—urbanization, large-scale immigration, industrialization, and many others. The transition is also the result of two important discoveries within the publishing business itself: first, that huge numbers of ordinary citizens would pay for news and entertainment and, second, that advertisers would pay even more for the opportunity to address them. The newspapers that focused on selling news and entertainment came to be called "the penny press" because they were cheap—many of them literally cost only a penny a copy instead of six cents, which was then the standard for the political newspapers. The term has symbolic importance, because it links the gathering and disseminating of news and commentary to the American commitment to capitalism in a very direct way.

With the inauguration of the penny press in the 1830s came one of the great ethical tensions in journalism, that of trying to fulfill the very different and often competing goals of turning a profit and of providing public service. That tension lies at the heart of many of the contemporary ethical dilemmas in journalism—issues of media ownership, "infotainment," sensationalism, conflict of interest, advertiser influence, and even some privacy problems.

In Part I, the logical starting point for an analysis of the proper role of the journalist in a democracy was a discussion of the origins of political power. Similarly, an analysis of the journalist's proper role in a commercial media system should begin with the classic statements on capitalism—on the inherent good or evil of the commercial marketplace. Adam Smith's *Wealth of Nations* and Karl Marx's *Capital* stake out the original and antagonistic positions.

Chapter 16:
Adam Smith
1723-1790

Adam Smith, a Scot, was a professor of logic and of moral philosophy at the very height of the Englightenment, with its beliefs in natural liberty and the power of the rational mind. For all that, he was also an absent-minded genius, who, the story goes, once went down into his garden in his nightclothes and then, seized by a thought, wandered, oblivious to the outside world, for fifteen miles before he realized he had left home.

His *Wealth of Nations*, published in 1776, is the classic exposition of the free-market system. As is almost always the case with great books, not every thought in his magnum opus is original, but in its breadth and detail, *Wealth of Nations* made the case for free-market capitalism better than any other work had done before. Smith's central themes are his faith in self-interested individuals producing the best possible society and his belief in the self-righting mechanism of open competition. When left alone, Smith argued, the free market works to the benefit of all as each looks to her or his own benefit. Contained within the following discussion of foreign and domestic production and trade is Smith's underlying philosophy that self-interest is the "invisible hand" that beneficially governs the operation of the free market system.

Smith's argument for laissez-faire capitalism was a direct challenge to the then-dominant political theory called mercantilism, in which it was argued that governments should control production, erect trade barriers, and in many other ways direct national economic policy toward the goal of amassing the largest possible pile of gold bullion within a nation's borders. Not so, Smith argued. Such governmental interference guarantees inefficiencies and will eventually be self-defeating. Far better, he said, to let supply and demand set "natural" prices, production systems, and trade patterns.

Smith's free-market economic system may be seen as an economic mirror image of the marketplace of ideas that Milton advocated. As such, it fits comfortably within the tradition of liberal pluralism, which both economically and philosphically is the foundation for our modern media system.

An Inquiry into the Nature and Causes of the Wealth of Nations
1776

Of restraints upon the importation from foreign countries of such goods as can be produced at home

By restraining, either by high duties, or by absolute prohibitions, the importation of such goods from foreign countries as can be produced at home, the monopoly of the home market is more or less secured to the domestic industry employed in producing them. Thus the prohibition of importing either live cattle or salt provisions from foreign countries secures to the graziers of Great Britain the monopoly of the home market for butcher's meat. The high duties upon the importation of corn, which in times of modern plenty amount to a prohibition, give a like advantage to the growers of that commodity. The prohibition of the importation of foreign woollens is equally favourable to the woollen manufacturers. The silk manufacture, though altogether employed upon foreign materials, has lately obtained the same advantage. The linen manufacture has not yet obtained it, but is making great strides towards it. Many other sorts of manufacturers have, in the same manner, obtained in Great Britain, either altogether, or very nearly a monopoly against their countrymen. The variety of goods of which the importation into Great Britain is prohibited, either absolutely, or under certain circumstances, greatly exceeds what can easily be suspected by those who are not well acquainted with the laws of the customs.

That this monopoly of the home-market frequently give great encouragement to that particular species of industry which enjoy it, and frequently turns towards that employment a greater share of both the labour and stock of the society than would otherwise have gone to it, cannot be doubted. But whether it tends either to increase the general industry of the society, or to give it the most advantageous direction, is not, perhaps, altogether so evident.

The general industry of the society never can exceed what the capital of the society can employ. As the number of workmen that can be kept in employment by any particular person must bear a certain proportion to his capital, so the number of those that can be continually employed by all the members of a great society, must bear a certain proportion to the whole capital of that society, and never can exceed that proportion. No regulation of commerce can increase the quantity of industry in any society beyond what its capital can maintain. It can only divert a part of it into a direction into which it might not otherwise have gone; and it is by no means certain that this artificial direction is likely to be more advantageous to the society than that into which it would have gone of its own accord.

Every individual is continually exerting himself to find out the most advantageous employment for whatever capital he can command. It is his own advantage, indeed, and not that of the society, which he has in view. But the study of his own advantage naturally, or rather necessarily leads him to prefer that employment which is most advantageous to the society.

First, every individual endeavours to employ his capital as near home as he can, and consequently as much as he can in the support of domestic industry; provided always that he can thereby obtain the ordinary, or not a great deal less than the ordinary profits of stock.

Thus, upon equal or nearly equal profits, every wholesale merchant naturally prefers the home-trade to the foreign trade of consumption, and the foreign trade of consumption to the carrying trade. In the home-trade his capital is never so long out of his sight as it frequently is in the foreign trade of consumption. He can know better the character and situation of the persons whom he trusts, and if he should happen to be deceived, he knows better the laws of the country from which he must seek redress. In the carrying trade, the capital of the merchant is, as it were, divided between two foreign countries, and no part of it is ever necessarily brought home, or placed under his own immediate view and command. The capital which an Amsterdam merchant employs in carrying corn from Konnigsberg to Lisbon, and fruit and wine from Lisbon to Konnigsberg, must generally be the one-half of it at Konnigsberg and the other half at Lisbon. No part of it need ever come to Amsterdam. The natural residence of such a merchant should either be at Konnigsberg or Lisbon, and it can only be some very particular circumstances which can make him prefer the residence of Amsterdam. The uneasiness, however, which he feels at being separate so far from his capital, generally determines him to bring part both of the Konnigsberg goods which he destines for the market in Lisbon, and of the Lisbon goods which he destines for that of Konnigsberg, to Amsterdam: and though this necessarily subjects him to a double charge of loading and unloading, as well as to the payment of some duties and customs, yet for the sake of having some part of his capital always under his own view and command, he willingly submits to this extraordinary charge; and it is in the manner that every country which has any considerable share in the carrying trade, becomes always the emporium, or general market, for the goods of all the different countries whose trade it carries on. The merchant, in order to save a second loading and unloading, endeavours always to sell in the home-market as much of the goods of all those different countries as he can, and thus, so far as he can, to convert his carrying trade into a foreign trade of consumption. A merchant, in the same manner, who is engaged in the foreign trade of consumption, when he collects good for foreign markets, will always be glad, upon equal or nearly equal profits, to sell as great a part of them at home as he can. He saves himself the risk and trouble of exportation, when, so far as he can he thus converts his foreign trade of consumption into a home trade. Home is in this manner the center, if I may say so, round which the capitals of the inhabitants of every country are continually circulating, and towards which they are always tending though by particular causes they may sometimes be driven off as repelled from it towards more distant employments. But a capital employed in the home-trade, it has already been shown, necessarily puts into motion a greater quantity of domestic industry, and gives revenue and employment to a greater number of the inhabitants of the country, than an equal capital employed in the foreign trade of consumption: and one employed in the foreign trade of consumption has the same advantage over an equal capital employed in the carrying trade. Upon equal, or only nearly equal profits, therefore, every individual naturally inclines to employ his capital in the manner in which it is likely to afford the greater support to domestic industry, and to give revenue and employment to the greatest number of people of his own country.

Secondly, every individual who employs his capital in the support of domestic industry, necessarily endeavours so to direct the industry, that its produce may be of the greatest possible value.

The produce of industry is what it adds to the subject or materials upon which it is employed. In proportion as the value of this produce is great or small, so will likewise be the profits of the employer. But it is only for the sake of profit that any man employs capital in the support of industry; and he will always, therefore, endeavour to employ it in the support of that industry of which the produce is likely to be of the greatest value, or to exchange for the greatest quantity either of money or of other goods.

But the annual revenue of every society is always precisely equal to the exchangeable value of the whole annual produce of its industry, or rather is precisely the same thing with that exchangeable value. As every individual, therefore, endeavours as much as he can both to employ his capital in the support of domestic industry, and so to direct that industry that its produce may be of the greatest value; every individual necessarily labours to render the annual revenue of the society as great as he can. He generally, indeed, neither intends to promote the public interest, nor knows how much he is promoting it. By preferring the support of domestic to that of foreign industry, he intends only his own security; and by directing that industry in such a manner as its produce may be of greatest value, he intends only his own gain, and he is in this, as in many other cases, led by an invisible hand to promote an end which was no part of his intention. Nor is it always the worse for the society that it was no part of it. By pursuing his own interest he frequently promotes that of the society more effectually than when he really intends to promote it. I have never known much good done by those who affected to trade for the public good. It is an affectation, indeed, not very common among merchants, and very few words need be employed in dissuading them with it.

What is the species of domestic industry which his capital can employ, and of which the produce is likely to be of the greatest value, every individual, it is evident, can, in his local situation, judge much better than any stateman or lawgiver can do for him. The statesman, who should attempt to direct private people by in what manner they ought to employ their capitals, would not simply load himself with a most unnecessary attention, but assume by authority which could safely be trusted, not only to no single person, but to no council or senate whatever, and which would nowhere be so dangerous as in the hands of a man who had folly and presumption enough to fancy himself fit to exercise it.

To give the monopoly of the home-market to the produce of domestic industry, in any particular art or manufacture, is in some measure to direct private people in what manner they ought to employ their capitals, and must, in almost all cases, be either a useless or a hurtful regulation. If the produce of domestic can be brought there as cheap as that of foreign industry, the regulation is evidently useless. If it cannot, it must generally be hurtful. It is the maxim of every prudent master of a family, never to attempt to make at home what it will cost him more to make than to buy. The taylor does not attempt to make his own shoes, but buys them of the shoemaker. The shoemaker does not attempt to make his own clothes, but employs a taylor. The farmer attempts to make neither the one nor the other, but employs those different artificers. All of them find it for their interest to employ their whole industry in a way in which they have some advantage over their neighbours, and to purchase with a part of its produce, or what is the same thing, with the price of a part of it, whatever else they have occasion for.

What is prudence in that conduct of every private family, can scarce be folly in that of a great kingdom. If a foreign country can supply us with a commodity cheaper than we ourselves can make it, better buy it of them with some part of the produce of our own industry, employed in a way in which we have some advantage. The general industry of the country, being always in proportion to the capital which employs it, will not thereby be diminished, no more than that of the above-mentioned artificers; but only left to find out the way in which it can be employed with the greatest advantage. It is certainly not employed to the greatest advantage when it is thus directed towards an object which it can buy cheaper than it can make. The value of its annual produce is certainly more or less diminished, when it is thus turned away from producing commodities evidently of more value than the commodity which it is directed to produce. According to the supposition, that commodity could be purchased from foreign countries cheaper than it can be made at home. It could, therefore, have been purchased with a part only of the commodities, or, what is the same thing, with a part only of the price of the commodities, which the industry employed by an equal capital would have produced at home, had it been left to follow its natural course. The industry or the country, therefore, is thus turned away from a more, to a less advantageous employment, and the exchangeable value of its annual produce, instead of being increased, according to the intention of the lawgiver, must necessarily be diminished by every such regulation.

By means of such regulations, indeed, a particular manufacture may sometimes be acquired sooner than it could have been otherwise, and after a certain time may be made at home as cheap or cheaper than in the foreign country. But though the industry of the society may be thus carried with advantage into a particular channel sooner than it could have been otherwise, it will by no means follow that the sum total, either of its industry, or of its revenue, can ever be augmented by any such regulation. The industry of the society can augment only in proportion as its capital augments, and its capital can augment only in proportion to what can be gradually saved out of its revenue. But the immediate effect of every such regulation is to diminish its revenue, and what diminishes its revenue is certainly not very likely to augment its capital faster than it would have augmented of its own accord, had both capital and industry been left to find out their natural employments.

Though for want of such regulations the society should never acquire the proposed manufacture, it would not, upon that account, necessarily be the poorer in any one period of its duration. In every period of its duration its whole capital and industry might still have been employed, though upon different objects, in the manner that was most advantageous at the time. In every period its revenue might have been the greatest which its capital could afford, and both capital and revenue might have been augmented with the greatest possible rapidity.

The natural advantages which one country has over another in producing particular commodities are sometimes so great, that it is acknowledged by all the world to be in vain to struggle with them. By means of glasses, hotbeds, and hotwalls, very good grapes can be raised in Scotland, and very good wine too can be made of them at about thirty times the expence for which at least equally good can be brought from foreign countries. Would it be a reasonable law to prohibit the importation of all foreign wines, merely to encourage the making of claret and burgundy in Scotland? But if there would be a manifest absurdity in turning towards any employment, thirty times more of the capital and industry of the country, than would be necessary to purchase from foreign countries an equal quantity of the commodities wanted, there must be an absurdity, though not altogether so glaring, yet exactly of the same kind, in turning towards any such employment a thirtieth, or even a three hundredth part more of either. Whether the advantages which one country has over another, be natural or acquired, is in this respect of no consequence. As long as the one country has those advantages, and the other wants them, it will always be more advantageous for the latter, rather to buy of the former than to make. It is an acquired advantage only, which one artificer has over his neighbour, who exercises another trade; and yet they both find it more advantageous to buy of one another, than to make what does not belong to their particular trades. . . .

Chapter 17
Karl Marx
1818-1883

Adam Smith's "invisible hand" of free market capitalism has been enormously popular for more than two centuries. Yet the examples Smith cited—the tailor trading with the cobbler and the farmer buying the services of both—suggest the most serious flaw in his argument: Smith's economic model was based on the eighteenth-century world of self-employed artisans and hand craftsmen. What Smith did not forsee happening—indeed, what Smith was certain could be prevented—was the development of highly concentrated pockets of massive economic power. Three generations after Smith predicted a bucolic march toward universal happiness, Charles Dickens was describing urban hell, where the air was fetid, the water foul and human life cheap. What happened in between, of course, was the Industrial Revolution and the onset of big factories, big iron and steel, and big capital. The most influential thinker of this new industrial age was Karl Marx. Marx discarded Smith's vision of trading a jacket for boots and replaced it with the far darker picture of the industrial system with its enormous wealth at the top and brutalizing poverty on the bottom. Marx focused on the inhuman treatment of workers, the brutal hours and killing working conditions, the poverty and disease and early death that defined the lives of so many industrial workers. This, he said, is what capitalism did.

This is not to say that Marx did not appreciate the power of industrial capitalism to accomplish great technical feats, the building of cities, bridges, and railroads. He did. But because these gains were purchased at a tremendous cost in human lives, he believed capitalism could not last. He was certain that capitalism's built-in injustices were the seeds of its own destruction, to be replaced—just how he never said—by a new and more equitable economic order.

Beyond Marx's general critique of the profit system, his writing has several direct applications to American journalism. First, Marx observed the tendency for capital to accumulate in fewer and fewer hands. This general tendency for large units to buy out smaller ones has been very evident in the journalism business, with serious implications for the many voices needed to make the marketplace of ideas effective.

Marx also noted the cultural dimension of capitalism's economic inequalities. In a society divided into a ruling class of owners and a subservient class of workers, he argued, the dominant ideas of the culture in any age are the ideas of the ruling class. That is, a society's ideology is grounded in its economic system. All the institutions within that society, especially the vehicles of news and information, inevitably serve to legitimize the aims of the ruling class.

In the following two short pieces, Marx first traces a synopsis of the nature of the workings of the economic system itself and then outlines his thoughts on the relationship of ideology—or values and information—to an individual's lived experience in a particular economic system.

The first extract is from his masterwork, *Capital*, Vol.1; the second is the preface to his book, *Critique of Political Economy*.

Capital
Volume I, 1867

Chapter XXXII: Historical tendency of capitalist accumulation

What does the primitive accumulation of capital, i.e., its historical genesis, resolve itself into? In so far as it is not immediate transformation of slaves and serfs into wage-labourers, and therefore a mere change of form, it only means the expropriation of the immediate producers, i.e., the dissolution of private property based on the labour of its owner. Private property, as the antithesis to social, collective property, exists only where the means of labour and the external conditions of labour belong to private individuals. But according as these private individuals are labourers or not labourers, private property has a different character. The numberless shades, that it at first sight presents, correspond to the intermediate stages lying between these two extremes. The private property of the labourer in his means of production is the foundation of petty industry, whether agricultural, manufacturing, or both; petty industry, again, is an essential condition for the development of social production and of the free individuality of the labourer himself. Of course, this petty mode of production exists also under slavery, serfdom, and other states of dependence. But it flourishes, it lets loose its whole energy, it attains its adequate classical form, only where the labourer is the private owner of his own means of labour set in action by himself: the peasant of the land which he cultivates, the artisan of the tool which he handles as a virtuoso. This mode of production pre-supposes parcelling of the soil, and scattering of the other means of production. As it excludes the concentration of these means of production, so also it excludes co-operation, division of labour within each separate process of production, the control over, and the productive application of the forces of Nature by society, and the free development of the social productive powers. It is compatible only with a system of production, and a society, moving within narrow and more or less primitive bounds. To perpetuate it would be, as Pecqueur rightly says, "to decree universal mediocrity." At a certain stage of development it brings forth the material agencies for its own dissolution. From that moment new forces and new passions spring up in the bosom of society; but the old social organisation fetters them and keeps them down. It must be annihilated; it is annihilated. Its annihilation, the transformation of the individualised and scattered means of production into socially concentrated ones, of the pigmy property of the many into the huge property of the few, the expropriation of the great mass of the people from the soil, from the means of subsistence, and from the means of labour, this fearful and painful expropriation of the mass of the people forms the prelude to the history of capital. It comprises a series of forcible methods, of which we have passed in review only those that have been epoch-making as methods of the primitive accumulation of capital. The expropriation of the immediate producers was accomplished with merciless Vandalism, and under the stimulus of passions the most infamous, the most sordid, the pettiest, the most meanly odious. Self-earned private property, that is based, so to say, on the fusing together of the isolated, independent labouring-individual with the conditions of his labour, is supplanted by capitalistic private property, which rests on exploitation of the nominally free labour of others, i.e., on wage-labour.

As soon as this process of transformation has sufficiently decomposed the old society from top to bottom, as soon as the labourers are turned into proletarians, their means of labour into capital, as soon as the capitalist mode of production stands on its own feet, then the further socialisation of labour and further transformation of the land and other means of production into socially exploited and, therefore, common means of production, as well as the further expropriation of private proprietors, takes a new form. That which is now to be expropriated is no longer the labourer working for himself, but the capitalist exploiting many labourers. This expropriation is accomplished by the action of the immanent laws of capitalistic production itself, by the centralisation of capital. One capitalist always kills many. Hand in hand with this centralisation, or this expropriation of many capitalists by few, develop, on an ever-extending scale, the cooperative form of the labour-process, the conscious technical application of science, the methodical cultivation of the soil, the transformation of the instruments of labour into instruments of labour only usable in common, the economising of all means of production by their use of the means of production of combined, socialised labour, the entanglement of all peoples in the net of the world-market, and with this, the international character of the capitalistic regime. Along with the constantly diminishing number of the magnates of capital, who usurp and monopolise all advantages of this process of transformation, grows the mass of misery, oppression, slavery, degradation, exploitation; but with this too grows the revolt of the working-class, a class always increasing in numbers, and disciplined, united, organised by the very mechanism of the process of capitalist production itself. The monopoly of capital becomes a fetter upon the mode of production, which has sprung up and flourished along with, and under it. Centralisation of the means of production and socialisation of labour at last reach a point where they become incompatible with their capitalist integument.

Thus integument is burst asunder. The knell of capitalist private property sounds. The expropriators are expropriated.

The capitalist mode of appropriation, the result of the capitalist mode of production, produces capitalist private property. This is the first negation of individual private property, as founded on the labour of the proprietor. But capitalist production begets, with the inexorability of a law of Nature, its own negation. It is the negation of negation. This does not re-establish private property for the producer, but gives him individual property based on the acquisitions of the capitalist era: i.e., on co-operation and the possession in common of the land and of the means of production.

The transformation of scattered private property, arising from individual labour, into capitalist private property is, naturally, a process, incomparably more protracted, violent, and difficult, than the transformation of capitalistic private property, already practically resting on socialised production, into socialised property. In the former case, we had the expropriation of the mass of the people by a few usurpers; in the latter, we have the expropriation of a few usurpers by the mass of the people.

A Contribution to the Critique of Political Economy
1859

Author's Preface

I consider the system of bourgeois economy in the following order: Capital, landed property, wage labor; state, foreign trade, world market. Under the first three heads I examine the conditions of the economic existence of the three great classes, which make up modern bourgeois society; the connection of the three remaining heads is self evident. The first part of the first book, treating of capital, consists of the following chapters: 1. Commodity; 2. Money, or simple circulation; 3. Capital in general. The first two chapters form the contents of the present work. The entire material lies before me in the form of monographs, written at long intervals not for publication, but for the purpose of clearing up those questions to myself, and their systematic elaboration on the plan outlined above will depend upon circumstances.

I omit a general introduction which I had prepared, as on second thought any anticipation of results that are still to be proven, seemed to me objectionable, and the reader who wishes to follow me at all, must make up his mind to pass from the special to the general. On the other hand, some remarks as to the course of my own politico-economic studies may be in place here. .

In the social production which men carry on they enter into definite relations that are indispensable and independent of their will; these relations of production correspond to a definite stage of development of their material powers of production. The sum total of these relations of production constitutes the economic structure of society—the real foundation, on which rise legal and political superstructures and to which correspond definite forms of social consciousness. The mode of production in material life determines the general character of the social, political and spiritual processes of life. It is not the consciousness of men that determines their existence, but, on the contrary, their social existence determines their consciousness. At a certain stage of their development, the material forces of production in society come in conflict with the existing relations of production, or—what is but a legal expression for the same thing—with the property relations within which they had been at work before. From forms of development of the forces of production these relations turn into their fetters. Then comes the period of social revolution. With the change of the economic foundation the entire immense superstructure is more or less rapidly transformed. In considering such transformations a distinction should always be made between the material transformation of the economic conditions of production which can be determined with the precision of natural science, and the legal, political, religious, aesthetic or philosophic—in short ideological forms in which men become conscious of this conflict and fight it out. Just as our opinion of an individual is not based on what he thinks of himself, so can we not judge of such a period of transformation by its own consciousness; on the contrary, this consciousness must rather be explained from the contradictions of material life, from the existing conflict between the social forces of production and the relations of production. No social order ever disappears before all the productive forces, for which there is room in it, have been developed; and new higher relations of production never appear before the material conditions of their existence have matured in the womb of the old society. Therefore, mankind always takes up only such problems as it can solve; since, looking at the matter more closely, we will always find that the problem itself arises only when the material conditions necessary for its solution already exist or are at least in the process of formation. In broad outlines we can designate the Asiatic, the ancient, the feudal, and the modern bourgeois methods of production as so many epochs in the progress of the economic formation of society. The bourgeois relations of production are the last antagonistic form of the social process of production—antagonistic not in the sense of individual antagonism, but of one arising from conditions surrounding the life of individuals in society; at the same time the productive forces developing in the womb of bourgeois society create the material conditions for the solution of that antagonism. This social formation constitutes, therefore, the closing chapter of the prehistoric stage of human society.

Chapter 18
James Gordon Bennett
1795-1872

T he arrival of James Gordon Bennett onto the scene represents a sea-change in American journalism. Many of the earliest Colonial papers were advertising sheets largely devoted to commercial news, but the philosophical roots of the political function of the press go back centuries. Recall that in the 1640s, Milton's soaring arguments in the *Areopagitica* came in an address to the British Parliament, as he sought to liberalize the licensing laws. Colonial newspapers became increasingly political during the generation leading up to the American Revolution, and the political parties themselves were largely responsible for most of the newspapers in the new United States.

The new government recognized and endorsed the crucial role it expected newspapers to play in providing the sovereign populace with the information it needed to govern itself. The First Amendment is, of course, the most obvious evidence of the special role the founding generation saw for the press, but the government provided other assistance to the newspapers as well, such as government-subsidized cheap postage (in the form of second-class mailing permits, which exist to this day) and the building of many post offices and roads that population alone could not justify, but which the newspapers could and did put to good use.

But in the 1830s, the Age of Jackson came to America and to the American newspaper. Benjamin Day started the *Sun*, the first penny paper, in 1833, but it was Bennett with his *New York Herald* that truly redefined American journalism and broadened the definition of news far beyond politics. There had been special-interest papers before Bennett's day, but he, for the first time, included in a general-circulation daily paper most of today's familiar elements: sports, financial news, theater reviews and other entertainment, religious news, and personality profiles. Bennett also provided a level of titilating detail that no other "respectable" paper would touch.

When he started, Bennett did not intend to produce a paper for the masses, rather than the political elites. He was effectively forced into it when virtually every major politician and potential backer rebuffed him. Thus his renunciation of politics and politicians smacks more than a little of sour grapes. Brash, arrogant, indefatigable, and infuriating because he was nearly as talented as he claimed to be, Bennett foreshadowed much of what American journalism would become, both for better and for worse. The debate over the *Herald*'s contribution to American journalism is strikingly similar to the contemporary debate over the contributions of *USA Today*. Tne established gray papers sniffed then, as they do now, that the upstarts were pandering to the masses, cheapening the news, ignoring substance for flash. The defenders of the spicy new order maintained the old guard was elitist, arrogant and contemptuous of the great majority of the American public they purported to serve. Bennett, like *USA Today*'s founding editor, Allen Neuharth, argued that his papers were giving readers what they wanted in an attractive package, rather than what the rich and the powerful thought they should have.

Bennett's formula was enormously successful, inviting scores and then hundreds of imitators all across the country. Not all papers abandoned their traditional role of providing the information necessary to make democracy work, of course, but from Bennett's day on, there has been a different and competing driving ideology within American journalism. The harshest critics say Bennett abdicated the near-sacred role of being the informational linchpin of self-government in favor of pandering to the masses for the enormous profits the readers' pennies provided. But defenders argue that Bennett and those who followed him were true libertarians who were entitled, within some bounds of propriety, good taste, and the libel statutes, to print what they chose. A free press meant being able to cover an ax murder or a fire in a brothel instead of city council budget hearings, if that is what the editor thought the readers wanted. To say that the paper was obliged to cover the budget hearings at the expense of the fire, Bennett would argue, implied a very unfree press indeed. Such an arrangement was hardly different than a paper directed by a political party boss, except that a party boss had much clearer lines of communication. This insistence upon the freedom to cover the news as the editor saw fit—the right to be irresponsible, to put it baldly—was and is central to the debate on the proper role of a free press in a free society. Like the best editors of his own time and since, Bennett claimed to have an instinctive sense of the popular mind and the popular will. With that sense, and with a full appreciation of his own considerable talents, Bennett boasted, "My ambition is to make the newspaper Press the great organ and pivot of government, society, commerce, finance, religion and all human civilization." He and those who followed him—Hearst, Pulitzer, Scripps, Ochs, and the rest—very nearly did.

Just a few months after Bennett began the *Herald* in May 1835, fire destroyed the newspaper's office, shutting down the paper for two weeks. But the editor and his paper came back stronger and saucier than ever. The first selection is Bennett's New Year's Day editorial from 1836, when the paper was not yet a year old. In it, he lays out what he sees as his newspaper's rightful place in American society.

A very different observation on Bennett's role in journalism follows from a much harsher source—Bennett's longtime rival, the crusading editor Horace Greeley. While Bennett saw the *Herald* largely as a vehicle for the enrichment and glorification of Bennett, Greeley saw his own paper, the *New York Tribune*, as a noble force for moral change—it was to relieve the cities of their chronic overcrowding and their associated sins and depravity that Greeley issued his famous dictum: "Go west, young man." At Bennett's death in June 1872, Greeley wrote a long, page-one obituary about his most famous rival. In it, Greeley denounced Bennett for bravado, cynicism, intellectual dishonesty, and moral hypocrisy—all of which were doubtless true. Yet he recognized that Bennett had changed the world of journalism with his emphasis on bright writing, local news, and the willingness and abilty to give readers what they wanted.

"To the public—enlargement of the *Herald*"
New York Herald, Jan. 1, 1836

Having determined as soon as arrangements can be made, to enlarge the *Herald* to at least one third over its present size, we shall, with the permissions of our kind and numerous patrons, say a few words on this subject, more interesting to us than to them, and then start afresh on our delightful and pleasant course.

It is yet hardly four months since the *Herald* rose from the Ann street conflagration, with impaired means, but undying energy of mind and spirit. During this brief period, we have struggled with competition as numerous and powerful as the elements themselves. Yet the independent, honorable, and liberal plan on which the *Herald* has been conducted, has attained a complete victory over interested opponents and private foes. The generous public has nobly sustained us.

In the short period of three months and a few days, the *Herald* has reached a circulation among business men, the intelligent public, and families of all classes, four times as large as any small paper ever did in the same period, and already at this day, far beyond the city circulation of any single, six-penny paper now published in Wall street, not even excepting the *Courier and Enquirer*.

Our advertising patronage has even increased beyond this ratio. We appeal to undeniable facts—to the columns of the paper itself for the truth of what we say. On many occasions we have had to leave out advertisers for several days, in order to make room for the crowds asking admission. The enlargement of our paper, as soon as we shall be prepared to carry it into effect, will enable us, we hope, to deal equally and liberally to all our kind advertising customers hereafter.

Meanwhile, we shall endeavor to surpass even our former efforts. The merchants generally are just beginning to find that the small daily press is becoming a much better vehicle for advertising than the large ten dollar papers. One advertisement for a week during the business season is found to be more serviceable in the *Herald* than a dozen hid away in the *Courier and Enquirer* at forty dollars a year. People see, read and remember. This tells at once, on buying and selling. Here, therefore, is the very natural cause of the remarkable revolution now going on in the newspaper press of New York. The *Herald* has probably, as much as any, contributed to elevate the character and purify the morals of the "penny papers," as we are called in contempt. Before we started this journal, the penny papers were generally considered low, vulgar and ignorant. . . .

There is no mistake in our progress—in our character—in our determination—or in the popularity of our course. The first men of the country subscribe to the *Herald*. Not longer ago than Saturday, we had an order to send out paper by mail to Washington, to the Minister of one of the leading powers of Europe—Shoals of members of Congress, diplomatists, &c., have ordered the *Herald*, and we learn that it is a constant companion of the breakfast table of the President and Vice President at Washington. With these remarks—thanking our kind patrons for past favors, and soliciting their continuance only while we deserve it—we briefly wish them, in anticipation, a happy, happy, happy New Year, and many returns of the same. The ladies, a few of them, we shall call on personally, on the day itself, and say the same with all that devotion which ought to be so fervently breathed forth to the Divinities of Earth below.

"A great journalist dead"
New York Tribune, June 3, 1872

T his method of relating in detail and in familiar style, events of purely local interest was a new revelation in journalism, and Bennett found that it repaid him handsomely. . . .

The success which followed in increasing the circulation of the *Herald* . . . established its value as an advertising medium. Dr. Brandreth, the pill-vendor, was then the largest advertiser in the country, and he made a contract with it which is said to have saved the paper from an untimely death, but truth seems to have been that the paper had forced itself upon the public, and, naturally, advertisements came to it. . . .

It was as a collector of news that Bennett shone conspicuous. Editorially he was cynical, inconsistent, reckless, and easily influenced by others' opinions, and by his own prejudices. But he had an unerring judgment of the pecuniary value of news. He knew how to pick out of the events of the day the subjects which engrossed the interest of the greatest number of people, and to give them about that subject all they could read. The quality might be bad, and generally was; but it suited the multitude, and the quanitity at any rate was abundant. He had a method of impressing the importance of news upon others in his employ, which inspired many who served him to energetic act some of them in a remarkable degree, but he inculcated no principle of correctness. The fact is, he was utterly indifferent to the correctness of details or conclusions, provided the principal event of the narrative or argument of the editorial was made clear and published ahead of all competitors. He never tolerated defeat. He once refused to pay the expenses, including one item of a horse killed, for a correspondent who was one day behind the *World* correspondent, and added, in the half humorous, half satirical manner in which he habitually indulged, that "a horse which couldn't beat the *World* wasn't worth paying for." He never questioned or examined the account of reporters who were in advance of their rivals, and frequently paid contributors double rates for welcome news in advance of contemporaries. He once gave a reporter $25 for a news telegram of three words for which a bill of $1 had been rendered. At another time, he ordered $100 to be paid to a contributor for an article of six columns, which had been already contracted for at $8 a column, adding by way of explanation to the editor, "he may have something else as good." In this instance, his judgment was confirmed, and several valuable contributions (relating to the secret history of the Rebellion) followed from the same pen.

He developed the capacities of journalism in a most wonderful manner, but he did it by degrading its character. He made the newspaper powerful, but he made it odious. Those who recognize this, whether claiming it as his admirers or admitting it contemptuously, know that his personal characteristics had everything to do with his forming his paper. He alone made it; it was a personal journalism in all senses of the word. . . .

Chapter 19
Joseph Pulitzer
1847-1911

F or most of its existence, the United States has had an activist, involved central government that clearly believed it proper for government to set social and economic policy, to encourage and regulate industry, and so on. But there was a period in which the United States government took a largely hands-off approach to American business—the generation after the Civil War. There were many reasons for this, including concern with Reconstruction in the South and the explosion of heavy industry after the war.

The upshot was the Gilded Age, that remarkable period in which America industrialized on a scale unprecedented in all of history. Captains of industry—Rockefeller, Fisk, Gould, Morgan, Carnegie and a handful of others—made fabulous fortunes in iron and steel, banking and oil, all largely unregulated. They made their wealth through hard work, good luck and ferocious competition—and through what by contemporary standards would be considered ruthless exploitation of their employees. Social Darwinists came along to explain that the working poor were poor because they deserved it and that to try to alleviate widespread suffering was mere misguided sentiment and in the long run would actually increase misery.

Into this world rode the muckrakers—journalists, mostly magazine writers, who set out to restore the society that the explosion of unfettered capitalism had shattered. They were convinced that once the evils of corruption and graft of the robber barons were exposed, a righteous people would rise up and demand their ouster. It is hard to explain why they emerged just when they did, just after the turn of the century. In part, it was the coming of age of the baby boomer generation after the Civil War, when Billy

Yank (and Johnny Reb, too, although most of the great muckrakers came from the North) came home from the front and began raising a family. In part, the onset of the muckrakers was held up by technology; it took the high-speed rotary presses of the 1880s and beyond to create the mass-circulation magazines in which the social crusaders could raise their cries of injustice. And if one is to put any stock in the venerable "safety valve" theory of Frederick Jackson Turner, it took the closing of the West in the 1890s for Americans to realize that one could no longer just pack up and head west if things got too intolerable in the cities. The very shutting down of the escape route west made the existence of social and economic inequities seem all the worse.

Journalistically, perhaps the muckrakers had to follow the "yellow journalists" with whom they are frequently and mistakenly confused. The muckrakers share a taste for the sensational with the "yellow" newspaper journalists of the 1880s and 1890s and beyond. And to the extent that most people are driven by a complex matrix of motivations, rather than by a single one, there may be some overlap between the "yellows" and the muckrakers. But there is certainly a definable difference. William Randolph Hearst, perhaps the archetypical yellow journalist, saw sensationalism as a circulation-booster and, thus, a money-maker for his newspaper empire. Since the 1830s, that is, for roughly half a century since Bennett and Day showed the way, selling a mass public what it wanted had been a publisher's way to riches. Along the way, Hearst and his competitors championed many a little guy and exposed many a villainy, but for the most part the "yellow journalists" were out for details of vice and crime, the sexier and more lurid the better.

The muckrakers were different. They typically worked for magazines, not newspapers, and they were writers and editors, not publishers. More important, they were focused on exposing graft and corruption, not on laying bare the graphic details of a sex crime. Some made a pretty good living at their craft for a number of years, but none amassed the fortune that a Hearst or a Scripps did. Indeed, such wealth was anathema to most of the muckrakers. Many learned to write on the yellow newspapers of the 1880s and 1890s and by the turn of the century were able and ready to move onto to magazine work, which afforded both the time and the national scope necessary for taking on the robber barons and the politicians whom they had corrupted.

One of the earliest of the muckrakers was Joseph Pulitzer, the Hungarian immigrant who, in the last quarter of the nineteenth century, built first the *St. Louis Post-Dispatch* and then the New York *World* into two of the most influential newspapers in the country. Along the way, Pulitzer became enormously rich and powerful himself, and, indeed, during the sordid era surrounding the Spanish-American War, engaged in the most tawdry circulation war in American newspaper history with his archrival, Hearst. Yet, fundamentally, Pulitzer was different. Before and after his dishonorable contest with Hearst, Pulitzer championed the loftiest goals of journalism. He realized early on that it was no longer enough to fight corrupt politicians, the traditional foe of democratic self-government. With the arrival of the Gilded Age, Pulitzer argued, it was now money, not politics, that threatened to doom the country's noblest goals. Barely a year into a brilliant publishing career, Pulitzer began to sound the alarm that is still rung today. The occasion was the U.S. Senate candidacy of a railroad magnate, Tom Allen. In a long editorial decrying Allen's candidacy, Pulitzer laid out what would become the heart of the muckrakers' case.

"The Great Issue"
St. Louis Post and Dispatch, Jan. 10, 1879

W hat is the great demoralizer of our public life? Of course, corruption. And what causes corruption? Of course, the greed for money. And who offers the greatest temptations to that greed? Corporations. And what are corporations? All monopolies, all special privileges, all classes favored by law.

Democracy means opposition to all special privileges. Republicanism means favoritism to corporations. The Jay Goulds and Tom Scotts and Vanderbilts are all Republicans. So are ninety-nine out of a hundred bank presidents. So are nearly all railroad presidents and millionaires generally.

Money is the great power of today. Men sell their souls for it. Women sell their bodies for it. Many who seem to be better prostrate themselves before it. Others worship it. And few, very few indeed, are entirely free from its influence and power. It is the great power of today. It is the great danger of tomorrow. It is the growing dark cloud of our free institutions. It is the natural great enemy of the Democracy. It is the irresistible conflict of the future.

The money power has grown so great that the issue of all issues, after all, is whether the corporations shall rule this country or the country shall again rule the corporations.

We say again, because he must be deaf and blind indeed who does not see and hear everywhere the signs of the growing and corrupting power of corporations. Their influence reaches almost into every County Court and City Council, extends to every State Legislature, every Congress, every Senate, nay reaches the Supreme Court—and the White House itself! . . .

Yet is seriously proposed by purchased papers and political prostitutes to send, in the language of Senator Thurman, the most conspicuous creature of "capital and privilege" in this State to the Senate of the United States to sit beside Allen G. Thurman, Lucius Lamar and Wade Hampton as the representatives of Missouri Democracy! What would be said of the Republicans if they elected Tom Scott Senator from Pennsylvania or Vanderbilt from New York! And is there, relatively and comparatively speaking, any differences between Tom Scott and Tom Allen?

Yes, there is. Tom Scott owes his fortune and his railroad to his brains. Tom Allen owes it all to his marriage. The one made and created. The other married and inherited. No one outside of the lunatic asylum believes that Tom Allen's name would be even mentioned if, instead of having riches and railroads, he were poor and penniless. And if credit is due for his fortune it should be given to old man Russell, who made and left it, not him who married it.

But it is said that, no matter how he got his fortune, he used it to the interest of this city and State, and is entitled to credit for it. Very well. Give him credit, but not the Senatorship. This is an entirely different thing. We admit unhesitatingly that Mr. Allen's enterprise in extending a railroad which he originally got by most questionable means and methods, benefitted, greatly benefitted the State. But while we give him credit, great credit, for this, none but idiots or paid penny-a-liners and purchased mercenaries will seriously claim that he built his railroad as a matter of pure benevolence. He did whatever he did for gain and business. He began his career that way. He will end it that way. We do not blame him for that. Only we do not wish to see him get a seat in the Senate for it.

But it is said that Mr. Allen as Senator could not benefit his railroad interests nor influence legislation in this State. How absurd! He is one of the most influential men in the State today on account of his railroad and his money and their manifold ramifications. Add to this influence the great power and prestige of a seat in the United States Senate for six years at least, and Tom Allen would be, politically, the most powerful man in the State. His influence in the Democratic party would at once become commanding. His power would be felt in every Legislature, every Democratic convention, every election. The ordinary, vulgar breed of politicians, and very many of a higher stamp, would be completely subservient to his interests and do his bidding. No Democratic platform would contain a word against his wishes, no Legislature would ever think of passing a law that the great "Senator-President" opposed; no Board of Equalization would press the "President-Senator" for the large amount of taxes out of which the State is swindled; no railroad commission would push him and his road to obey the laws that are now violated. The Democratic party would be simply paralyzed. It could neither nor act freely. It would lose the confidence of the people. And in the great struggle of 1880, instead of raising its voice and rallying under Senator Thurman's banner of hostility to "capital and privilege," it would be pointed at with scorn and ridicule by other States as the decayed and demoralized Democracy that surrendered all principles to "capital and privilege." . . .

Chapter 20
Upton Sinclair
1878-1968

U pton Sinclair was perhaps the most ideologically committed of all the muckrakers. He was passionate in his devotion to economic and social reform and, as is so often the case with true believers, bitterly unforgiving of those who compromised their principles or otherwise appeared to abandon the good fight. His series of articles on municipal corruption, which appeared in *McClure's Magazine* in 1903 under the headline "Shame of the Cities," remains a virtual textbook of muckraking journalism. It is detailed, thorough, scrupulously accurate, and burning with outrage at the injustice of police graft, of political malfeasance, of entire institutions bought and sold by monied interests.

Probably his most famous and influential work was *The Jungle*, a grisly exposé of the meat-packing industry in Chicago. The national outrage the novel produced led to the passage of the Pure Food and Drug Act and the Meat Inspection Act, both passed in 1906. But Sinclair wrote the book not so much to detail the nauseating impurities of packaged meat as to expose the horrific conditions under which meat packers and their families were forced to live and work.

By 1920, most of Sinclair's old comrades had left muckraking, and Sinclair turned his jaundiced eye on journalism itself. Newspapers, he concluded, had been corrupted by the same money-lust that he and the other muckrakers had exposed in government and in private industry. The result was *The Brass Check*, a searing indictment of the newspaper industry. Many who came after Sinclair have made similar charges, but none with more fervor than this disillusioned and angry journalist.

The Brass Check
1920

Chapter XXXV: The causes of things

I studied Latin for five years in college, and from this study brought away a dozen Latin verses. One of them is from Virgil: "Happy he who has learned to know the causes of things." The words have stayed in my mind, summing up the purpose of my intellectual life: Not to rest content with observing phenomena, but to know what they mean, how they have come to be, how they may be guided and developed, or, if evil, may be counteracted. I would not have taken the trouble to write a book to say to the reader: I have been persecuted for twenty years by prostitute Journalism. The thing I am interested in saying is: The prostitution of Journalism is due to such and such factors, and may be remedied by such and such changes.

Here is one of the five continents of the world, perhaps the richest of the five in natural resources. As far back as history, anthropology, and even zoology can trace, these natural resources have been the object of competitive struggle. For the past four hundred years this struggle has been ordained by the laws and sanctified by the religions of man. "Each for himself," we say, and "the devil take the hindmost." "Dog eat dog," we say. "Do others or they will do you," we say. "Business is business," we say. "Get the stuff," we say. "Money talks," we say. "The Almighty Dollar," we say. So, by a thousand native witticisms, we Americans make clear our attitude toward the natural resources of our continent.

As a result of four centuries of this attitude, ordained by law and sanctified by religion, it has come about that at this beginning of the twentieth century the massed control of the wealth of America lies in the hands of perhaps a score of powerful individuals. We in America speak of steel kings and coal barons, of lords of wheat and lumber and oil and railroads, and think perhaps that we are using metaphors; but the simple fact is that the men to whom we refer occupy in the world of industry precisely the same position and fill precisely the same roles as were filled in the political world by King Louis, who said, "I am the State."

This power of concentrated wealth which rules America is known by many names. It is "Wall Street," it is "Big Business," it is "the Trusts." It is the "System" of Lincoln Steffens, the "Invisible Government" of Woodrow Wilson, the "Empire of Business" of Andrew Carnegie, the "Plutocracy" of the populists. It has been made the theme of so much stump-oratory that in cultured circles it is considered good form to speak of it in quotation marks, with a playful and skeptical implication; but the simple fact is that this power has controlled American public life since the Civil War, and is greater at this hour than ever before in our history.

The one difference between the Empire of Business and the Empire of Louis is that the former exists side by side with a political democracy. To keep this political democracy subservient to its ends, the industrial autocracy maintains and subsidizes two rival political machines, and every now and then stages an elaborate sham-battle, contributing millions of dollars to the campaign funds of both sides, burning thousands of tons of red fire, pouring out millions of reams of paper propaganda and billions of words of speeches. The people take interest in this sham-battle—but all sensible men understand that whichever way the contest is decided, business will continue to be business, and money will continue to talk.

So we are in position to understand the facts presented in this book. Journalism is one of the devices whereby industrial autocracy keeps its control over political democracy; it is the day-by-day, between-elections propaganda, whereby the minds of the people are kept in a state of acquiescence, so that when the crisis of an election comes, they go to the polls and cast their ballots for either one of the two candidates of their exploiters. Not hyperbolically and contemptuously, but literally and with scientific precision, we define Journalism in America as the business and practice of presenting the news of the day in the interest of economic privilege.

A modern newspaper is an enormously expensive institution. The day is past when a country printer could set up a hand-press and print news about the wedding of the village blacksmith's daughter and the lawn-party of the Christian Endeavor Society, and so make his way as a journalist. Now-a-days people want the last hour's news from the battle-field or the council-hall. If they do not get it in the local paper, they get it in the "extras" from the big cities, which are thrown off the fast express-trains. The franchise which entitles a paper to this news from all over the world is very costly; in most cities and towns it is an iron-clad monopoly. You cannot afford to pay for this service, and to print this news, unless you have a large circulation, and for that you need complicated and costly presses, a big building, a highly trained staff. Incidentally, you will find yourself running an advertising agency and a public employment service; you will find yourself giving picnics for news-boys, investigating conditions in the county-hospital, raising subscription funds for a monument to Our Heroes in France. In other words, you will be an enormous and complex institution, fighting day and night for the attention of the public, pitting your composite brain against other composite brains in the struggle to draw in the pennies of the populace.

Incidentally, of course, you are an institution running under the capitalist system. You are employing hundreds, perhaps thousands of men, women and children. You are paying them under the iron law of wages, working them under the rule of "the devil take the hindmost." You have foremen and managers and directors, precisely as if you were a steel-mill or a coal-mine; also you have policemen and detectives, judges and courts and jailers, soldiers with machine-guns and sailors with battleships to protect you and your interests—precisely as does the rest of the predatory system of which you are a part.

And, of course, you have the capitalist psychology; you have it complete and vivid—you being the liveliest part of that system. You know what is going on hour by hour; you are more class-conscious, more alert to the meaning of events than anyone else in the capitalist community. You know what you want from your wage-slaves, and you see that they "deliver the goods." You know what you are furnishing to your advertisers, and your terms are "net cash." You know where you get your money, your "credit"; so you know "Who's Who" in America, you know whom to praise and whom to hate and fear.

There are perhaps a dozen newspapers in America which have been built up by slow stages out of the pennies of workingmen, and which exist to assert the rights of workingmen. The ones I happen to know are the *New York Call*, the *Jewish Daily Forward*, the *Milwaukee Leader*, the *Seattle Union Record*, the *Butte Daily Bulletin*. It should be understood that in future discussions I except such newspapers from what I say about American Journalism. This reservation being made, I assert there is no daily newspaper in America which does not represent and serve vested wealth, and which has not for its ultimate aim the protection of economic privilege.

I am trying in this book to state the exact facts. I do not expect to please contemporary Journalism, but I expect to produce a book which the student of the future will recognize as just. So let me explain that I realize fully the differences between newspapers. Some are dishonest, and some are more dishonest; some are capitalistic, and some are more capitalistic. But great as are the differences between them, and clever as are the pretenses of some of them, there is not one which does not serve vested wealth, which has not for its ultimate aim the protection of economic privilege. The great stream of capitalist prosperity may flow irregularly, it may have eddies and counter-currents, stagnant places which deceive you for a while; but if you study this great stream long enough, you find that it all moves in one direction, and that everything upon its surface moves with it. A capitalist newspaper may espouse this cause or that, it may make this pretense or that, but sooner or later you realize that a capitalist newspaper lives by the capitalist system, it fights for that system, and in the nature of the case cannot do otherwise. Some one has said that to talk of regulating capital is to talk of moralizing a tiger; I would say that to expect justice and truth-telling of a capitalist newspaper is to expect asceticism at a cannibal feast.

It would be instructive to take the leading newspapers of America and classify them according to the nature of their financial control, showing precisely how and where this control shapes the policy of the paper. There will be certain immediate financial interests—the great family which owns the paper, the great bank which holds its bonds, the important local trade which furnishes its advertising. Concerning these people you observe that no impolite word is ever spoken, and the debut parties given to the young ladies of these families are reported in detail. On the other hand, if there are interests aggressively hostile to the great family, the great bank, the important local trade, you observe that here the newspaper becomes suddenly and unexpectedly altruistic. It will be in favor of more rigid control of state banks; whatever its policy may be, you will, if you sit at the dinner-tables of the rich in that city, have revealed to you the financial interests which lie behind that unexpected altruism.

In the days of the ancient regime, nations went to war because someone made a slighting remark about the king's mistress; and in our present Empire of Business you find exactly the same thing happening. I know of a newspaper which is still living upon the reputation it made by defending the strikers in a great labor struggle. The paper had never defended strikers before, it has never defended strikers since; but on this occasion it happened that the president of the corporation involved in the strike had remarked at a dinner-party that the owner of the newspaper was living with an opera-singer.

Some ten years ago I remember that the city of Chicago was torn wide open by a teamster's strike. Brickbats were flying, mobs were swarming in the streets, militiamen were stabbing people with bayonets. Some time afterwards there was an investigation, and it transpired that a certain laborleader, Sam Parks by name, had been paid five or ten thousand dollars by a great mail-order house to call a strike on a rival mail-order house. And in precisely this way great newspapers quarrel, and the public has no idea what it means. I have heard a leading Hearst editor tell, quite simply and as a matter of course, how Mr. Hearst would come into the office at twelve o'clock at night and turn the batteries of the *New York American* and *Journal* upon the business and politics of August Belmont, because Mr. Belmont had slighted Mr. Hearst, or Mr. Hearst's wife—I forget which—at a dinner party. One year you would see Mr. Hearst printing a cartoon every day, showing "Charlie" Murphy, boss of Tammany Hall, in convict's stripes; next year Mr. Hearst would make a deal with Tammany—and the other newspapers of New York would be showing Mr. Hearst in convict's stripes!

Or come to the other side of the continent, and consider the *San Francisco Chronicle*, owned by "Mike" de Young. Here is a picture of Mr. de Young, drawn by one of his wageslaves, a man who for many years has helped to run his profit-machine:

He uses much perfume, and is extremely conceited. He is author of the remark that no reporter is worth more than twenty dollars a week, or ever will be. He is a secret laugh-producer because of his inordinate love for the camera spotlight. Strangely enough, his likeness is seldom to be found in any paper except his own; the *Chronicle*'s camera men have standing instructions at public gatherings to pay as little attention to other men as possible and to concentrate on de Young. On his own paper everybody is Jones or Smith except himself. He must always be referred to as Mr. de Young. Owner of much valuable real estate near Golden Gate park, he made a vigorous fight to have the Panama-Pacific Exposition located in the park, hoping thereby to increase the value of his holdings. Defeated, he turned his wrath on the exposition officials, and denounces them at every opportunity. Mention of President C.C. Moore of the Exposition Company is forbidden in the columns of the *Chronicle*.

There are differences, of course, in the moral character of men. There are some men who do not take part in large-scale real-estate intrigues, and some who do not live with opera-singers; there are capitalists who pay their debts, and regard their word of honor at their bond. And there have been newspapers owned by such men, and conducted according to such principles. You could not buy the editorial support of the *Springfield Republican* or the *Baltimore Sun*; you could not buy the advertising space of these papers for the cheaper and more obvious kinds of fraud. But ask yourself this question: Is there a newspaper in America which will print news unfavorable to department-stores? If the girl-slaves of the local department-store go on strike, will the newspaper maintain their right to picket? Will it even print the truth about what they do and say?

Some years ago a one-time teacher of mine was killed by falling down the elevator-shaft of a New York department-store. I noted that my newspaper did not give the name of the department-store. As a matter of curiosity, I bought all the newspapers, and discovered that none of them gave the name of the department-store. It was not absolutely essential, of course; my one-time teacher was just as dead as if the name of the store had been given. But suppose the accident had taken place at the People's House, owned by the Socialists—would all the newspapers of New York have withheld the name of the place?

In New York City one of the Gambel brothers, owners of a Philadelphia department store, was arrested, charged with sodomy, and he cut his throat. Not a single newspaper in Philadelphia gave this news! This was in the days before Gambel Brothers had a store in New York, therefore it occurred to the *New York Evening Journal* that here was an opportunity to build up circulation in a new field. Large quantities of the paper were shipped to Philadelphia, and the police of Philadelphia stopped the newsboys on the street and took away the papers, and the Philadelphia papers said nothing about it!

And this department-store interest supervises not only the news columns, but the editorial columns. Some years ago one of the girl-slaves of a New York department-store committed suicide, leaving behind her a note to the effect that she could not stand twenty-cent dinners any longer. The *New York World*, which collects several thousand dollars every day from department-stores, judged it necessary to deal with this incident. The *World*, you understand, is a "democratic" paper, a "liberal" paper, an "independent" paper, a paper of "the people." Said the *World*:

There are some people who make too large a demand upon fortune. Fixing their eyes upon the standards of living flaunted by the rich, they measure their requirements by their desires. Such persons are easily affected by outside influences, and perhaps in this case the recent discussions, more often silly than wise, concerning the relation of wages to vice, may have made the girl more susceptible than usual to the depressing effects of cheap dinners.

And do you think that is a solitary instance, the result of a temporary editorial aberration? No, it is typical of the capitalistic mind, which is so frugal that it extracts profit even from the suicide of its victims. Some years ago an old man committed suicide because his few shares of express-stock lost their value. The *New York Times* was opposing parcel-post, because the big express-companies were a prominent part of the city's political and financial machine; the *New York Times* presented this item of news as a suicide caused by the parcel-post! . . .

Chapter 21
A. J. Liebling
1904-1963

A. J. Liebling is a true journalistic hero. His vision is easily comparable to that of Lippmann's, and his acerbic wit is a legitimate rival to that of the Baltimore Curmudgeon, H. L. Mencken. His ear for dialect is reminiscent of Twain's, and his war reporting was as good as Ernie Pyle's. His passion for New York's poor evokes Jacob Riis and the other turn-of-the-century muckrakers. His experimentation with first-person narrative and innovative, syncopated writing techniques inspired a whole school of writers who make up the New Journalism of the 1960s and beyond.

Like many a great journalist, Liebling cared passionately about the craft and its mission of public service. Arguably his best work was his *Wayward Press* column of press criticism he wrote for the *New Yorker*. The piece that follows is part of the forward to a collection of those *New Yorker* columns published in 1961 as *The Press*. Since this piece was written, several things have happened to the newspaper industry that would not brighten Liebling's mood, were he still here to complain. The consolidation of which he spoke so darkly has continued apace, and the number of big-city papers with genuine competition is now down to a handful. Television-inspired changes to the printed press have produced shorter, brighter, snappier, and more colorful stories, but not more reflective or profound ones. But the principles he held dear are certainly as current—indeed as timeless—as ever.

"Prologue: The End of the Free Lunch"
The Press, 1961

I n Great Britain, the Government, whether of Right or Left, considers the state of the press a matter of public concern. When, early this past winter, Lord Rothermere, owner of the morning *Daily Mail* and the *Evening News* in London, bought the *News-Chronicle* (morning) and the *Star* (evening) and scuttled them, thus making life easier for his own papers, there were questions in Parliament. When, a month or two later, Cecil King and Roy Thomson, each the proprietor of a press empire, made rival bids for Odhams Press, which publishes the *Daily Herald* and the Sunday newspaper *People*, a storm broke that compelled the Prime Minister to appoint a Royal Commission to investigate the state of the press. Doing so, he said, in part: "The recent developments are widely taken to suggest that conditions . . . are such as to lead inevitably toward concentration of ownership and a reduction in—to quote the words of the Royal Commission of 1949—the number and variety of the voices speaking to the public through the press." The 1949 Royal Commission was appointed by a Labor Government. Here the Tory Prime Minister, like his predecessors, acknowledged that the more voices, and the more various they that spoke, the better for the public.

In the United States, the American Newspaper Publishers' Association would treat such a pronouncement as heresy and interference in their own damned business, not to mention an infringement of the freedom of the press and a partisan pronouncement—since the press being almost exclusively Republican, any criticism is implicitly Democratic.

Yet the United States is much farther advanced toward a monovocal, monopolistic, monocular press than Britain. With the decline in the "number and variety" of voices there is a decline in the number and variety of reporting eyes, which is at least as malign.

Editor & Publisher, a trade publication, recently stated that of 1,461 American cities with daily newspapers, all but 61 were one-ownership towns—that is, monopolies. In Great Britain, where the London papers circulate everywhere, the regional journals cannot dent the London hold on news and opinion. The typical American monopoly is local rather than national. The big-city papers, since they do not arrive, cannot dent the local monopoly. Sixty or seventy years ago, the founders of great newspaper chains, like E.W. Scripps and William (the Real Article) Randolph Hearst, would fight for 20 cities simultaneously with 20 newspapers, taking on three or four enemy newspapers in each city. They would win in one place, lose in another, struggle on without profit for anybody in a third. It was a costly and wasteful process.

The industry's ideal now is absolute control in a moderate number of cities, or even one. These become one-ownership towns, and as the publisher turns monopolist, his troubles end. He is in the position of a feudal lord after the period of wars in the Middle Ages ended. He has his goods, but he need no longer fight for it. He is a rentier.

Such properties fall into only three classes: good, better, and bestest. There are no poor ones, since the proprietor can impose his own terms; he gets all the advertising, all the circulation, and he can give, in return, exactly as much or little newspaper as his heart tells him. Newspaper proprietors are not distinguished as a class for large or talkative hearts.

As the number of cities in the United States with only a single newspaper ownership increases, news becomes increasingly nonessential to the newspaper. In the mind of the average publisher, it is a costly and uneconomic frill, like the free lunch that saloons used to furnish to induce customers to buy beer. If the quality of the free lunch fell off, the customers would go next door.

When New York State created its Alcohol Board of Control after the repeal of the prohibition amendment, the A.B.C. abolished the handout. With no free lunch to be had anywhere, the customers continued to buy beer, and the saloonkeepers raised the price and pocketed the difference. In a monopoly situation, the paper can cut out news as the saloons cut out free lunch. There is no longer a place next door for the customers to go to. They will continue to buy the paper to read the advertisements. The advertisers will continue to buy space in order that they be read.

Under present conditions, frightened still by old superstitions about what newspapers are for, the publisher, out of force of habit and because he does not wish to be called a piker, usually provides for the customer a smattering of press association scraps and syndicated features. The saloonkeeper, in the same moral position, puts out a few stale pretzels and moldy salted peanuts.

Each publicly blames his own soft heart for his display of generosity. It comes under the head of public service, and the newspaper owner probably will make a speech about it at the next convention of the American Newspaper Publishers' Association. He will then suggest that the Associated Press, a burden on all of them, ought to cut down on excessive foreign coverage; he often sees a dispatch almost a hundred words long. But such vestigia offer little to rely on the future. Like the immigrant orthodox Jew, who learns to dispense first with his sidecurls, then his beard, and at length his skullcap, the publisher will progressively shed his scruples.

With the years, the quantity of news in newspapers is bound to diminish from its present low. The proprietor, as Chairman of the Board, will increasingly often say that he would like to spend 75 cents now and then on news coverage but that he must be fair to his shareholders.

This, of course, is the current excuse for every instance of ignobility. A drug company, controlling 95 percent of its own shares, says it would like to hold the profit on its pet pill down to 1,500 percent, but it has to protect the minority shareholders, all widows of F.B.I. men strangled by juvenile delinquents. The president of a motor company says he would like to build cars that would last at least a year, but he could do it only at the expense of his shareowners, who are entitled to maximum profit and are without exception paraplegics. He then whips around backstage and exercises his option on the three shares that he has let his uncle hold during the annual meeting. And so it goes, even in novels. The popular hero-victim is the thief-in-spite-of-himself, the fundamentally decent corporation executive who has to steal for the stockholders. He is a Robin Hood misunderstood, since the stockholders are a cross-section of the American Public, and the American Public is not rich. There will, almost inevitably, be proxy fights within newspaper corporations, as there are within railroads, in which potty widows with two shares will arise to denounce management for extravagance. They will say that a telephone-answering service for murderers who want to turn themselves in and a subscription to *Time* should be enough of a news side.

Many proprietors, moreover, have a prejudice against news—they never feel at home with it. In this they resemble racing owners who are nervous around horses.

The corrective for the deterioration of a newspaper is provided, in nineteenth-century theory, by competition, which is governed equally by nature's abhorrence of a vacuum and Heaven will protect the working girl. Theoretically, a newspaper that does not give news, or is corrupt, or fails to stand up for the underdog attracts the attention of a virtuous newspaper looking for a home, just as the tarantula, in the Caribbees, attracts the blue hornet. Good and bad paper will wrestle, to continue our insect parallel. Virtue will triumph, and the good paper will place its sting in the bad paper's belly and yell, "Sic semper Newhouse management!" or something of the sort. Then it will eat the advertising content of the bad paper's breadbasket.

This no longer occurs. Money is not made by competition among newspapers, but by avoiding it. The wars are over, and newspaper owners are content to buy their enemies off, or just to buy them. The object of diplomacy is to obtain an unassailable local position, like a robber-castle, in New Orleans or Elizabeth or Des Moines, and then levy tribute on the helpless peasantry, who will have no other means of discovering what is playing at the Nugget.

To cite an example of the new strategy of noncombat: the Hearst people, who have a paper in Albany, buy the second paper and thus make a monopoly. They sell the Detroit Times and skedaddle from that city, leaving the purchaser, the Detroit News, with an evening monopoly there. This substitutes two monopolies for two competitive situations. All the respective owners need by way of a staff is a cash register.

The old system was abandoned even before the historically recent deaths of the last specimens of the Giant Primordial Gobblers. William (the Genuine)

Randolph Hearst, Joseph Medill Patterson and Col. Robert Rutherford McCormick, when they went into a city, tried to make its inhabitants obey them as well as pay tribute. Their personalities howled, and they displayed their photographs constantly on their mealtickets. The men of the new order do not meddle with the locals as long as they come up with the tithe. They are, for the public, faceless, and their coups are often inside jobs. Hearst tried to take cities by storm, but the new men prefer a rendezvous at the back gate.

Mr. Samuel I. Newhouse, the archetype, specializes in disgruntling heritors, or profiting by their disgruntlement. A family feud is grist to his mill, but if he can't get a paper that way he will talk beautifully of the satisfactions of cash, rapidly quoting sections of the capital-gains law as he accepts his hat. If the owner shows him the door, he exhibits no resentment.

"I regret that you do not feel you can sell me the overcoat now, Madame," he says as he backs down the porch steps, "but if your husband dies and you should reconsider, I do hope you'll give me the first chance to make you an offer." (Mr. Roy Thomson, the Canadian who has taken to buying newspapers in Britain, is the same sort.) Newhouse and Thomson, quizzed about their politics, are evasive. They have no political ideas; just economic convictions.

The function of the press in society is to inform, but its role is to make money. The monopoly publisher's reaction, on being told that he ought to spend money on reporting distant events, is therefore exactly that of the proprietor of a large, fat cow, who is told that he ought to enter her in a horse race.

To concretize the dichotomy, as I might write if I were a popular sociologist, last summer I made a talk before a small group of fellowship winners that got reported in *Newsweek*. In it I said that the *Washington Star*, a disgustingly rich newspaper with an unassailable position, spent millions on promotional activities while it maintained only one foreign correspondent. In the *Star*'s opinion this ill-merited a reproach, because there are even richer, if that is remotely conceivable, papers, that have no foreign correspondents at all. I got an indignant letter, day and date with the magazine, from a Mr. Newbold Noyes, Jr., vice-president of the *Star*, saying it spent only $375,000 a year on promotion. This of course would run into millions pretty fast, but I accept the correction, if it is one. He did not say that the *Star* had more than one foreign correspondent, though, so I assume it hasn't. They may, indeed, have fired that one. . . .

Chapter 22
Ben H. Bagdikian
1920-

Ben Bagdikian has had a distinguished career as a journalist, press critic and professor of journalism at the University of California at Berkeley. Throughout his career, one of Bagdikian's enduring concerns has been the concentration of ownership in the newspaper industry. One of his major works, *The Media Monopoly* (1983), details the development of chain ownership, one-newspaper towns, corporate control, and the interlocking boards of directors that have come to characterize much of the industrial structure of modern American media. Like Sinclair and Liebling before him, Bagdikian worries about the concentration of ownership, the concentration of media power, and the potential threat it may pose to the diversity of viewpoints and voices that comprise the democratic dialogue. In the following article, from the *Nation*, Bagdikian extends his argument from the home soil of the newspaper industry to the foreign shores of the developing multinational corporate world of the 1990s. He argues that the issue of the industrial control of information has jumped national borders and bridged media forms. Corporate ownership of newspaper chains has expanded to corporate ownership of movie studios, cable television networks, magazines, record companies, and even telephone and computer companies. Bagdikian considers the rise of these transnational media conglomerates and what they portend for Milton's marketplace of ideas and Englightenment notions of information as a linchpin of popular sovereignty. In the high-speed world of global communications, events move so swiftly that any chronicle is destined to be outdated almost as soon as it is printed, but the trends Bagdikian noted are, if anything, even more true than just a few years ago when he wrote them.

"The Lords of the Global Village"
The Nation, 1989

I n the 1960s, Marshall McLuhan promulgated the idea of a new "global village," a world knit together and transformed by television and other marvels of the electronic age. His popular book, *Understanding Media*, predicted that an information network would envelop the planet, spreading democracy and leading to "a Pentecostal condition of universal understanding and unity . . . a general cosmic consciousness." The global village is growing. Glasnost in the Soviet Union, stirrings in Eastern Europe and demands for openness in China all respond in real measure to images of freedom and dignity transmitted by the penetrating networks foreseen by McLuhan.

But in recent years there have grown other networks designed to penetrate the world with messages far from the enlightenment and openness of "a general cosmic consciousness." A handful of mammoth private organizations have begun to dominate the world's mass media. Most of them confidently announce that by the 1990s they—five to ten corporate giants—will control most of the world's important newspapers, magazines, books, broadcast stations, movies, recordings and videocassettes. Moreover, each of these planetary corporations plans to gather under its control every step in the information process, from creation of "the product" to all the various means by which modern technology delivers media messages to the public. "The product" is news, information, ideas, entertainment and popular culture; the public is the whole world.

The driving force for all this is simple: these closed corporate circuits are worth staggering sums. In 1979 the largest media merger in history was the Gannett newspaper chain's purchase of a billboard and television company for $362 million. Nine years later, Rupert Murdoch bought *TV Guide* and other magazines from Walter Annenberg's Triangle Publications for $3 billion. Only seven months later, the merger of Time Inc. and Warner Communications Inc. created the world's largest media firm, worth $18 billion. On April 9, Gulf + Western (Simon & Schuster books and Paramount Pictures), once the country's most diversified conglomerate, announced that it was entering the global race by selling all its non-media industries in order to concentrate on the new gold mine of planetary media, and after nearly half a century was changing its name to Paramount Communications Inc.

The men who run these empires are lords of the global village. Some, like Rupert Murdoch and Robert Maxwell, are flamboyant figures known to much of the literate world. Some are so obscure that most Americans would be astonished to learn that much of what they read is published by a quiet figure from Gutersloh, West Germany. Others come and go in impersonal empires, in the gray anonymity that marks most large bureaucracies. But whatever the style, this new media royalty is bent on capitalizing on global technological and political trends.

New developments like fiber optics and satellites make it possible to publish and broadcast across the world's surface at ever greater speeds and lower costs. National boundaries grow increasingly meaningless: Already, the *Encyclopedia Americana* is published by the French, New American Library books by the British and the *Encyclopedia Britannica* by Americans. In many countries, particularly those in Western Europe, government broadcasting monopolies are giving way to commercial operations with advertising increasingly aimed at mega-markets that stretch across continents. It is no accident that media consolidation has paralleled a like trend among advertising agencies. The world's largest agency, Saatchi & Saatchi of London, has offices in eighty countries and buys 20 percent of the world's broadcast commercials, for clients like Procter & Gamble. Recently, the stock of the ad agency Ogilvy Group, one of the world's largest, rose 53 percent after a hostile takeover bid from the WPP Group of London. With the deal complete, WPP would be the world's second largest agency, with billings of $13.5 billion and operations in fifty-three countries.

Combining the thrust of all these corporate forces produces economic power that dwarfs that of many nations. The newly wed Time Warner, for example, has a total value of $18 billion, more than the combined gross domestic products of Jordan, Bolivia, Nicaragua, Albania, Laos, Liberia and Mali. . . .

The global media oligopoly is not visible to the eye of the consumer. Newsstands still display rows of newspapers and magazines in a dazzling variety of colors and subjects. Bookstores and libraries still offer miles of shelves stocked with individual volumes. Throughout the world, broadcast and cable channels continue to multiply, as do videocassettes and music recordings in dozens of languages. But if this bright kaleidoscope suddenly disappeared and was replaced by the corporate colophons of those who own this output, the collage would go gray with the names of the few media multinationals that now command the field.

This does not bode well for McLuhan's "universal understanding." The lords of the global village have their own political agenda. All resist economic changes that do not support their own financial interests. Together, they exert a homogenizing power over ideas, culture and commerce that affects populations larger than any in history. Neither Caesar nor Hitler, Franklin Roosevelt nor any Pope, has commanded as much power to shape the information on which so many people depend to make decision about everything from whom to vote for to what to eat.

As the world heads into the last decade of the twentieth century, five media corporations dominate the fight for the hundreds of millions of minds in the global village. The rankings of the giants change, sometimes week by week, as they compete to take over more smaller companies. The Big Five are:

Time Warner Inc. This merger would have seemed unimaginable to its forebears: Henry Luce, the Presbyterian missionary's son who built the Time Inc. magazine empire, and Harry and Jack Warner, sons of a Jewish peasant from Poland and creators of the Warner Brothers dream factory in Hollywood. Nor does the consolidation support Luce's oft-pronounced dictum that the twentieth was "the American century." One reason Time and Warner have merged is fear of the economic power of Europe and Japan.

The merged company has subsidiaries in Australia, Asia, Europe and Latin America and modestly insists it is "the world's leading direct marketer of information and entertainment." It is the largest magazine publisher in the United States, with the greatest single share of all magazine revenues—flowing from *Time, Life, Sports Illustrated, Fortune, People* and other periodicals—and a worldwide readership estimated at 120 million. The new corporation embraces Warner mass market paperbacks, Scott Foresman, Little Brown, Time-Life Books and the Book-of-the-Month Club, making it one of the world's largest dealers in books. It runs the world's second largest record company (WCI) and second largest cable TV operation, which includes American Television and Communications Corporation, Home Box Office and Cinemax pay television, which collectively have 23 million subscribers. And, of course, there is Warner Brothers.

Time and Warner have a total of 35,460 employees, with few vestiges of the idiosyncratic nature and personal touch of their founders. Thousands of shareholders now have to be satisfied, the largest being a number of banks, institutions not widely known for their interest in magazines, movies or television programming that push beyond the safe perimeters of conventional wisdom and popular entertainment.

Bertelsmann AG. This German firm, founded in the mid-nineteenth century, is owned by Reinhard Mohn, who, given the magnitude of his international operations, is remarkably little-known. Indeed, until the Time-Warner merger, Bertelsmann may have been the worlds' largest media corporation. Some time ago the company reached the limit of market share permitted in the West German print media by that country's tough Federal Cartel Office. The firm now concentrates on making acquisitions in the rest of the world, though it recently outbid two governmental public systems for a new TV satellite channel that will cover Germany. Bertlesmann's specialties are book clubs and book publishing. In the United States it owns Doubleday, Bantam Books, Dell and the Literary Guild book club, as well as RCA and Arista records. Its subsidiary, Gruner & Jahr, publishes some forty magazines, including *Parents* and *Young Miss* in the United States. Bertelsmann's reach extends to fifteen countries on four continents.

News Corporation Ltd. This bland name denotes the domain of the global village's most compulsive empire-builder, Rupert Murdoch. His Australia-based company claims more newspaper circulation than any other publisher in the world, about 14 million in that country, Great Britain and the United States. In Australia, Murdoch controls two-thirds of all newspaper circulation; in New Zealand he has a stake in almost a half. He owns 40 percent of the Australian Associated Press. In Britain he owns the biggest Sunday newspaper in the West, *News of the World* (circulation 5 million); the country's largest daily, *The Sun* (circulation 4 million); and the papers of the English upper class, the London daily and Sunday *Times*. His papers account for a third of all newspaper circulation in the nation. He also controls William Collins books, and owns 7 percent of the news service Reuters and 20 percent of Pearsons PLC (*Financial Times, The Economist* and Viking Penguin books). Murdoch's satellite channels blanket the continent, the largest satellite television system in Europe. In Asia, he owns the *South China Morning Post*.

Murdoch publishes daily papers in Boston and San Antonio, controls Fox Broadcasting, the fourth largest U.S. television network, and the 20th Century-Fox movie studio. He bought Harper & Row books in 1987. Just one of his magazines, *TV Guide*, has a circulation of 17 million. Besides that weekly, he owns *Seventeen, New York* and nine other periodicals, making him one of the largest publishers of magazines in the United States. He is also the largest publisher of evangelical Christian books in this country; presumably, most of his fundamentalist readers are unaware that he is also the world's principal purveyor of blood-and-breasts journalism.

Hachette SA is the world's largest producer of magazines—seventy-four in ten countries, including *Elle* and *Paris-Match*. And it is the world's largest publisher of reference books, among them the *Encyclopedia Americana*, which the firm acquired in 1988 when it purchased the Grolier publishing house in the United States. Hachette, a French company, sells more than 30 percent of all books bought in that country and recently acquired Salvat of Spain, which offers the largest distribution network for printed works in the Spanish-speaking world. Jean-Luc Lagardere, the arms manufacturer who purchased Hachette in 1980, hopes soon to combine a major television operation with the company's Europe 1, the biggest radio network in France.

Capital Cities/ABC Inc. has less global reach than its Big Five competitors, but through its ABC television network is a force to be reckoned with. Cap Cities, as it is known, owns eight local television and twenty-one radio stations around the United States, including outlets in most major cities. It also owns a chain of nine daily newspapers, including the *Fort Worth Star-Telegram* and the *Kansas City Star and Times*; Hollywood studios; Word Inc., the country's largest publisher of religious material; the ESPN cable sports channel; 38 percent of the Arts and Entertainment cable channel; and 33 percent of the Lifetime cable channel. Through Fairchild Publications, Cap

Cities publishes *Women's Wear Daily* and twenty-nine other trade and specialized consumer magazines. While the company is not driven by a commanding personality, its largest single stockholder is Warren Buffett, whose holdings provide a glimpse of the kind of interlock that increasingly characterizes media ownership in much of the global village. With his family, Buffett controls Berkshire Hathaway, through which he owns the *Buffalo News*; is the second largest stockholder in The Washington Post Company; and has a 6 percent interest in Coca-Cola and therefore in Columbia Pictures, which the soft-drink company owns.

Inevitably, a number of midsize giants are pushing hard to displace one of the Big Five, or if that proves impossible, to grow big enough to expand the charmed inner circle. Coming on hardest may be Robert Maxwell, whose firm controls hundreds of publications in England alone, including the Mirror Group newspapers, with an estimated circulation of 10 million. The International Thomson Organization of Canada is another contender, a conglomerate with subsidiaries in travel and business services as well as in the media. Like Gulf + Western, International Thomson is in the process of shucking off some non-media properties to concentrate on newspaper and other publishing ventures, and is planning a family merger with Thomson Newspapers Ltd. of Canada. Already Thomson Newspapers runs 116 dailies in the United States, more than any other chain operator.

The Gannett Company is the largest U.S. newspaper publisher, putting out *USA Today* and eighty-five other dailies, with a total circulation of 6.3 million. It is the country's second largest billboard firm, owns sixteen radio and ten television stations, and is newly active in Hollywood through GTG (Grant Tinker/Gannett) in producing television programming. Ted Turner's Turner Broadcasting System and General Electric, which owns the NBC television network, are also major actors on the scene.

Silvio Berlusconi dominates the Italian scene through his parent firm, Fininvest. Like Murdoch and Maxwell, Berlusconi is an ambitious operator who has become a strong European presence thanks to friendship with powerful politicians, particularly former Italian Prime Minister Bettino Craxi. Political influence permitted him to circumvent three Italian courts, which ruled that nationwide private broadcasting was illegal. He is a major newspaper publisher in Italy (Il Giornale), a partner in a major new commercial television channel in France (La Cinq), has a program production company for the growing commercial channels in Europe, owns 45 percent of Telefunf in West Germany and has stakes in Spain, Tunisia and Yugoslavia. TV Globo, the domain of Roberto Irineu Marinho of Brazil, is a leading producer of television soap operas around the world as well as owner of Brazil's largest newspaper, O Globo, and a television station in Monte Carlo that broadcasts to Italy. Televisa, owned by Emilio Azcarraga, has a monopoly on Mexican commercial television, with four private channels and five radio stations. Sony of Japan is still relatively small in global terms, but it owns CBS Records, the largest record company in the world, and is in the market for a major Hollywood studio.

True freedom of information requires three conditions: the opportunity to read and watch anything available; a diversity of sources from which to choose; and media systems that provide access for those who wish to reach their fellow citizens. In democratic countries the first condition is generally met. But the media titans are reducing the scope of the other two everywhere as they take over more and more once-independent companies. The new giants are open to whatever will maximize profits, but in pursuit of that goal they are just as ready as any dictatorship to suppress or de-emphasize news or entertainment that might seriously question their power. And far from opening their systems to journalists, authors, dramatists, musicians and citizens groups, the big corporations are working to close them off to idiosyncratic outsiders and ideas. Theirs is a strategy of total control. They buy every possible means of delivery (print, broadcast, films, etc). They strive to use their own rather than independently produced material. Then they convert it to as many forms of media as they control.

A dream sequence tantalizes the lords of the global village: Giant Corporation Inc. owns subsidiaries in every medium. One of its magazines buys (or commissions) an article that can be expanded into a book, whose author is widely interviewed in the company magazines and on its broadcast stations. The book is turned into a screenplay for the company movie studios, and the film is automatically booked into the company's chain of theaters. The movie has a sound track that is released on the company record label. The vocalist is turned into an instant celebrity by cover features in the company magazines and interviews on its television stations. The recording is played on the company's chain of Top 40 radio stations. The movie is eventually issued by the firm's videocassette division and shown on company television stations. After that, rerun rights to the movie are sold to other television stations around the world. And it all started with an article in the company magazine, whose editor selected it because it was recognized as having other uses within the company. The editor of the magazine is given a generous stock option. Every other editor and producer in the empire takes notice.

The dream dramatizes a term popular with firms that engineer mergers on Wall Street: "synergism," the creation of a whole greater than the sum of its parts. As Lee Isgur, a media analyst for Paine Webber, puts it, "The good companies must be integrated." Every major Hollywood studio has recently followed that advice, buying television stations and chains of movie theaters to guarantee outlets for their motion pictures. In 1948 the Supreme Court declared unified studio-theater ownership an illegal monopoly and forced the movie studios to divest themselves of theater chains. That move rejuvenated American movies, introducing independent and foreign films. But we now have a different Supreme Court and a different Justice Department. Monopoly is in, antitrust is out. . . .

Like the nuclear superpowers, the media Goliaths don't want to fight to the death, and surprisingly often they find it convenient to cooperate—always to the disadvantage of the Davids. Even arch-rivals like Murdoch and Maxwell cut deals with one another: On May 16 the two announced a five-year, multimillion-dollar agreement linking Murdoch's Sky Television PLC satellite operation with Maxwell Cable Television. Time Warner is a partner with Hachette and Mondadori in the French and Italian editions of *Fortune.* Berlusconi of Italy has a production project with Lorimar Telepictures, subsidiary of Time Warner, and a similar arrangement for making television programs with Leo Kirch of Germany and Maxwell of Britain. Simon & Schuster buys Hachette's Regents Publishing, and Hachette buys an interest in the big Italian publishing firm Rizzoli-Corriere della Sera.

Many of the media magnates also indulge in another form of synergism: interlocks with financial and commercial operations that are affected by news, opinion and popular culture, and which can be either promoted or protected by the parent firm's media. While Capital Cities/ABC for example, controls the ESPN cable channel, RJR Nabisco, the global food and tobacco company (and an important advertiser with ABC) has a 20 percent interest in ESPN. General Electric, a second-level giant in the media through its ownership of NBC, is a first-rank giant in world military and nuclear reactor production. And Hachette's chair, Jean-Luc Lagardere, is also chair of one of France's largest military defence contractors. . . .

One of the most profitable commodities in the modern world is human attention. Whoever can harvest it in wholesale quantities can make money in kind. In the United States, one Nielsen rating point reflects 1 percent of the country's 90 million television households. One percentage point for a network in prime-time audience share represents more than $30 million in added revenues each year. Nothing in human experience has prepared men, women and children for the modern television techniques of fixing human attention and creating the uncritical mood required to sell goods, many of which are marginal at best to human needs.

The first demand of competitive commercial broadcasting is to freeze the hand that reaches for the channel switch. After years of experimenting with various prime-time programs in the late 1940s and early 1950s, commercial broadcasters found the basic way to maintain second-by-second attention: constant violence, gratuitous sex and deliberate manipulation of split-second change of images and sounds to make an emotional and sensory impact that leaves no time for reflection. American commercial broadcasting has produced much that is important in public affairs, programs with genuine humanistic values; it has also given us entertainment that is harmless and occasionally even uplifting. But most programming conforms to the imperative to freeze the hand that reaches for the switch.

Commercial television has also degraded the electoral process in the United States. National political campaigns are now waged mainly through ten, twenty, and thirty-second commercials; and since television's political dominance began in 1960, a smaller percentage of eligible citizens has bothered to vote in each subsequent election. Another dubious American gift to the world is that enduring national scandal, children's programming on commercial television. Despite the harm done by this mindless menu of violent cartoons and blatant commercialism—harm that has been confirmed by the Surgeon General's office and others—decades of parents' and educators' complaints have been ignored.

Multi-national manufacturers and multinational advertising agencies now have enlarged power to suppress public messages they do not like. [In 1982], Saatchi & Saatchi (the world's biggest advertising conglomerate, remember) acquired the Campbell-Mithun agency in the Unite States. The small agency was servicing antismoking ads for the Minnesota Department of Health, but Brown & Williamson Tobacco Company was spending $35 million then with Saatchi to advertise Kool cigarettes. The Minnesota account was only 3 percent of that, so Saatchi dropped the health department. The parent firm had learned its lesson three months earlier when one of the biggest advertisers in the world, RJR Nabisco, dropped another Saatchi subsidiary because it had create a Northwest Airlines television commercial showing passengers applauding the airline's No Smoking policy. RJR Nabisco, besides marketing food products, makes Camel, Winston and Salem cigarettes.

The linkage between smoking and deaths that now total more than 350,000 a year has been known for more than sixty years. But warnings by medical authorities have been blunted by tobacco ads carried in the media that associate cigarettes with youthfulness, good health, fashionableness, feminine grace and manly vigor. For years, even news stories gave as much weight to the claims of the tobacco industry as they did to the scientific findings of medical authorities. Television did not drop tobacco advertising until forced to by law in 1971. Newspapers and magazines quietly cheered their inheritance of all those advertising dollars. With growing education in the United States and Europe, per capita smoking is beginning to decrease. Consequently, tobacco companies are pressing their commercials in Asia and the Third World, where in recent years per capita smoking has risen 76 percent.

The goal of surrounding every human being with sales promotion every waking moment has now reached even books. Whittle Communications, half owned by Time Warner, plans soon to issue commissioned volumes from major authors like David Halberstam and John Kenneth Galbraith that will carry color ads for Federal Express and be given away to a "select" readership. For a price, Hollywood studios now place brand-name products with the labels showing in motion picture scenes. For example, Reese's Pieces candy was displayed, by contract, in the fantasy film E.T. This tide has reached the Soviet Union, which is selling advertising patches on its cosmonauts' space suits and the sides of space stations. Even the schools are no longer immune. Earlier this year, Whittle Communications began a national campaign to give cooperating districts $50,000 worth of television equipment in return for permission to beam into classrooms a daily twelve-minute "news" program complete with two minutes of commercials for blue jeans, candy bars and other youth products. Even without these classroom sales pitches, by age 16 the average American already has been exposed to more than 300,000 commercials.

The U.N. draft Declaration on Freedom of Information states that "all governments should pursue policies under which the free flow of information within countries and across frontiers will be protected. The right to seek and transmit information should be assured in order to enable the public to ascertain facts and appraise events." In 1960, when the declaration was introduced, it had the support of those who had in mind the controlled information of authoritarian governments. It was assumed that once governments got out of the way, "the free flow of information" and power of the public "to ascertain and appraise events" would be made possible by free-enterprise media. They were correct. The problem today is not free enterprise but the lack of it.

No small group of organizations is wise enough or unselfish enough to provide most of the news, information, scholarship, literature and entertainment for a whole society, let alone most of the world. That can come only from a large number of organizations in a field not dominated by a few, with a variety of newcomers free to enter and compete whenever and wherever existing media fail to reflect the realities and the aspirations of people's lives.

It is time for the nations of the world to meet again and make a new Declaration of Freedom of Information, this time establishing antitrust principles that will apply at home as well as across national borders. An international convention aimed at insuring a diversity of choice in the media could set limits on how many media outlets one person or one mega-corporation could control, just as other international conventions have created rules for marine and air navigation, broadcast frequencies or the dumping of consumer products, where unrestrained activity by a few often damages many. The answer is not some international standard of censorship. It is no gain for freedom to replace national censorship with international censorship. The answer must be directed solely at the size of corporations, not the content of what they issue; at the restraint of economic activity that reduces voices, not at what the voices say. Belatedly, the nations of the world are recognizing that they and their corporations must be restrained from polluting the earth and its atmosphere with chemicals. The basis for all liberty—freedom of information—is also in danger of being polluted, not by chemicals but by a new mutation of that familiar scourge of the free spirit, centrally controlled information.

Chapter 23
The Commission on Freedom of the Press (Hutchins Commission)
1947

Among the more notable contributions to the debate about journalistic responsibility, especially in the context of concerns about the influence of economics, is the 1947 report of the Commission on Freedom of the Press. The Commission is usually called "the Hutchins Commission" after its chair, Robert M. Hutchins, then Chancellor of the University of Chicago.

The commission was initiated and funded by *Time* magazine publisher Henry Luce to study the state and health of the institution of the press in the United states. Its members included highly distinguished representatives from the nation's major universities, government, and the financial community.

Among its chief concerns was the perception that the press was turning away from its general social responsibility to report in a clear, accurate, and comprehensible way the important events of the day. In place of this, the press, according to the commission, was chasing the sensational story, the popular story, the story that was designed to attract rather than inform readers. It was greatly concerned about the decreasing local competition among newspapers and the growth of newspaper chain ownership. Like the authors previously noted in this section, the commission thought that the press was in danger of abandoning its public service charter in order to serve the interests of economic profit.

Instead of simply remarking on the problem, as many others had done previously, however, the commission laid out a very specific program of reforms. It advocated, for example, the establishment of non-governmental press commissions to monitor press performance and arbitrate disputes between the media and the public. It also, somewhat ominously, suggested that if the press were unable to clean up its own house, there was a danger the government would have to take measures to assist it in the endeavor.

As we shall see shortly, the reception by the press to these recommendations was not completely friendly. Many in the media, in fact, were downright hostile to the commission.

Nonetheless, the report remains today a landmark declaration of press rights and responsibilities. It speaks broadly to the general philosophy of public service that ought to guide all journalists in their work and specifically to the various goals that should be the prodigy of that philosophy. What follows is the commission's analysis of the problem and its summary statement of principles.

A Free and Responsible Press
1947

*If there is ever to be an amelioration of the condition
of mankind, philosophers, theologians, legislators,
politicians and moralists will find that the regulation
of the press is the most difficult, dangerous and
important problem they have to resolve. Mankind
cannot now be governed without it, nor at present with
it.*

> John Adams to James Lloyd,
> February 11, 1815.

The problem and the principles
The problem

A he Commission set out to answer the question: Is the freedom of the press in danger? Its answer to that question is: Yes. It concludes that the freedom of the press is in danger for three reasons:

First, the importance of the press to the people has greatly increased with the development of the press as an instrument of mass communication. At the same time the development of the press as an instrument of mass communication has greatly decreased the proportion of the people who can express their opinions and ideas through the press.

Second, the few who are able to use the machinery of the press as an instrument of mass communication have not provided a service adequate to the needs of the society.

Third, those who direct the machinery of the press have engaged from time to time in practices which the society condemns and which, if continued, it will inevitably undertake to regulate or control.

When an instrument of prime importance to all the people is available to a small minority of the people only, and when it is employed by that small minority in such a way as not to supply the people with the service they require, the freedom of the minority in the employment of that instrument is in danger.

This danger, in the case of the freedom of the press, is in part the consequence of the economic structure of the press, in part the consequence of the industrial organization of modern society, and in part the result of the failure of the directors of the press to recognize the press needs of a modern nation and to estimate and accept the responsibilities which those needs impose upon them.

We do not believe that the danger to the freedom of the press is so great that that freedom will be swept away overnight. In our view the present crisis is simply a stage in the long struggle for free expression. Freedom of expression, of which freedom of the press is a part, has always been in danger. Indeed, the Commission can conceive no state of society in which it will not be in danger. The desire to suppress opinion different from one's own is inveterate and probably ineradicable.

Neither do we believe that the problem is one to which a simple solution can be found. Government ownership, government control, or government action to break up the greater agencies of mass communication might cure the ills of freedom of the press, but only at the risk of killing the freedom in the process. Although, as we shall see later, government has an important part to play in communications, we look principally to the press and the people to remedy the ills which have chiefly concerned us.

But though the crisis is not unprecedented and though the cures may not be dramatic, the problem is nevertheless a problem of peculiar importance to this generation. And not in the United States alone but in England and Japan and Australia and Austria and France and Germany as well; and in Russia and in the Russian pale. The reasons are obvious. The relation of the modern press to modern society is a new and unfamiliar relation.

The modern press itself is a new phenomenon. Its typical unit is the great agency of mass communication. These agencies can facilitate thought and discussion. They can stifle it. They can advance the progress of civilization or they can thwart it. They can debase and vulgarize mankind. They can endanger the peace of the world; they can do so accidentally, in a fit of absence of mind. They can play up or down the news and its significance, foster and feed emotions, create complacent fictions and blind spots, misuse the great words, and uphold empty slogans. Their scope and power are increasing every day as new instruments become available to them. These instruments can spread lies faster and farther than our forefathers dreamed when they enshrined the freedom of the press in the First Amendment to our Constitution.

With the means of self-destruction that are now at their disposal, men must live, if they are to live at all, by self-restraint, moderation, and mutual understanding. They get their picture of one another through the press. The press can be inflammatory, sensational, and irresponsible. If it is, it and its freedom will go down in the universal catastrophe. On the other hand, the press can do its duty by the new world that is struggling to be born. It can help create a world community by giving men everywhere knowledge of the world and of one another, by promoting comprehension and appreciation of the goals of a free society that shall embrace all men.

We have seen in our time a revival of the doctrine that the state is all and that the person is merely an instrument of its purposes. We cannot suppose that the military defeat of totalitarianism in its German and Italian manifestations has put an end to the influence and the attractiveness of the doctrine. The necessity of finding some way through the complexities of power associated with modern industry will always make it look as though turning over all problems to the government would easily solve them.

This notion is a great potential danger to the freedom of the press. That freedom is the first which totalitarianism strikes down. But steps toward totalitarianism may be taken, perhaps unconsciously, because of conditions within the press itself. A technical society requires concentration of economic power. Since such concentration is a threat to democracy, democracy replies by breaking up some centers of power that are too large and too strong and by controlling, or even owning, others. Modern society requires great agencies of mass communication. They, too, are concentrations of power. But breaking up a vast network of communication is a different thing from breaking up an oil monopoly or a tobacco monopoly. If the people set out to break up a unit of communication on the theory that it is too large and strong, they may destroy a service which they require. Moreover, since action to break up an agency of communication must be taken at the instance of a department of the government, the risk is considerable that the freedom of the press will be imperiled through the application of political pressure by that department.

If modern society requires great agencies of mass communication, if these concentrations become so powerful that they are a threat to democracy, if democracy cannot solve the problem simply by breaking them up—then those agencies must control themselves or be controlled by government. If they are controlled by government, we lose our chief safeguard against totalitarianism—and at the same time take a long step toward it.

Freedom of the press is essential to political liberty. Where men cannot freely convey their thoughts to one another, no freedom is secure. Where freedom of expression exists, the beginnings of a free society and a means for every extension of liberty are already present. Free expression is therefore unique among liberties: it promotes and protects all the rest. It is appropriate that freedom of speech and freedom of the press are contained in the first of those constitutional enactments which are the American Bill of Rights.

Civilized society is a working system of ideas. It lives and changes by the consumption of ideas. Therefore it must make sure that as many as possible of the ideas which its members have are available for its examination. It must guarantee freedom of expression, to the end that all adventitious hindrances to the flow of ideas shall be removed. Moreover, a significant innovation in the realm of ideas is likely to arouse resistance. Valuable ideas may be put forth first in forms that are crude, indefensible, or even dangerous. They need the chance to develop through free criticism as well as the chance to survive on the basis of their ultimate worth. Hence the man who publishes ideas requires special protection.

The reason for the hostility which the critic or innovator may expect is not merely that it is easier and more natural to suppress or discourage him than to meet his arguments. Irrational elements are always present in the critic, the innovator, and their audience. The utterance of critical or new ideas is seldom an appeal to pure reason, devoid of emotion, and the response is not necessarily a debate; it is always a function of the intelligence, the prejudice, the emotional biases of the audience. Freedom of the press to appeal to reason may always be construed as freedom of the press to appeal to public passion and ignorance, vulgarity and cynicism. As freedom of the press is always in danger, so is it always dangerous. The freedom of the press illustrates the commonplace that if we are to live progressively we must live dangerously.

Across the path of the flow of ideas lie the existing centers of social power. The primary protector of freedom of expression against their obstructive influence is government. Government acts by maintaining order and by exercising on behalf of free speech and a free press the elementary sanctions against the expressions of private interest or resentment: sabotage, blackmail, and corruption.

But any power capable of protecting freedom is also capable of endangering it. Every modern government, liberal or otherwise, has a specific position in the field of ideas; its stability is vulnerable to critics in proportion to their ability and persuasiveness. A government resting on popular suffrage is no exception to this rule. It also may be tempted—just because public opinion is a factor in official livelihood—to manage the ideas and images entering public debate.

If the freedom of the press is to achieve reality, government must set limits on its capacity to interfere with, regulate, or suppress the voices of the press or to manipulate the data on which public judgment is formed.

Government must set these limits on itself, not merely because freedom of expression is a reflection of important interests of the community, but also because it is a moral right. It is a moral right because it has an aspect of duty about it.

It is true that the motives for expression are not all dutiful. They are and should be as multiform as human emotion itself, grave and gay, casual and purposeful, artful and idle. But there is a vein of expression which has the added impulsion of duty, and that is the expression of thought. If a man is burdened with an idea, he not only desires to express it; he ought to express it. He owes it to his conscience and the common good. The indispensable function of expressing ideas is one of obligation—to the community and also to something beyond the community—let us say to truth. It is the duty of the scientist to his result and of Socrates to his oracle; it is the duty of every man to his own belief. Because of this duty to what is beyond the state, freedom of speech and freedom of the press are moral rights which the state must not infringe.

The moral right of free expression achieves a legal status because the conscience of the citizen is the source of the continued vitality of the state. Wholly apart from the traditional ground for a free press that it promotes the "victory of truth over falsehood" in the public arena—we see that public discussion is a necessary condition of a free society and that freedom of expression is a necessary condition of adequate public discussion. Public discussion elicits mental power and breadth; it is essential to the building of a mentally robust public; and, without something of the kind, a self-governing society could not operate. The original source of supply for this process is the duty of the individual thinker to his thought; here is the primary ground of his right.

This does not mean that every citizen has a moral or legal right to own a press or be an editor or have access, as of right, to the audience of any given medium of communication. But it does belong to the intention of the freedom of the press that an idea shall have its chance even if it is not shared by those who own or manage the press. The press is not free if those who operate it behave as though their position conferred on them the privilege of being deaf to ideas which the processes of free speech have brought to public attention.

But the moral right of free public expression is not unconditional. Since the claim of the right is based on the duty of a man to the common good and to his thought, the ground of the claim disappears when this duty is ignored or rejected. In the absence of accepted moral duties there are not moral rights. Hence, when the man who claims the moral right of free expression is a liar, a prostitute whose political judgments can be bought, a dishonest inflamer of hatred and suspicion, his claim is unwarranted and groundless. From the moral point of view, at least, freedom of expression does not include the right to lie as a deliberate instrument of policy.

The right of free public expression does include the right to be in error. Liberty is experimental. Debate itself could not exist unless wrong opinions could be rightfully offered by those who suppose them to be right. But the assumption that the man in error is actually trying for truth is of the essence of his claim for freedom. What the moral right does not cover is the right to be deliberately or irresponsibly in error.

But a moral right can be forfeited and a legal right retained. Legal protection cannot vary with the fluctuations of inner moral direction in individual wills; it does not cease whenever a person has abandoned the moral ground of his right. It is not even desirable that the whole area of the responsible use of freedom should be made legally compulsory, even if it were possible; for in that case free self-control, a necessary ingredient of any free state, would be superseded by mechanism.

Many a lying, venal, and scoundrelly public expression must continue to find shelter under a "freedom of the press" built for widely different purposes for to impair the legal right even when the moral right is gone may easily be a cure worse than the disease. Each definition of an abuse invites abuse of the definition. If the courts had to determine the inner corruptions of personal intention, honest and necessary criticisms would proceed under an added peril.

Though the presumption is against resort to legal action to curb abuses of the press, there are limits to legal toleration. The already recognized areas of legal correction of misused liberty of expression—libel, misbranding, obscenity, incitement to riot, sedition, in case of clear and present danger—have a common principle; namely, that an utterance or publication invades in a serious, overt, and demonstrable manner personal rights or vital social interests. As new categories of abuse come within this definition, the extension of legal sanctions is justified. The burden of proof will rest on those who would extend these categories, but the presumption is not intended to render society supine before possible new developments of misuse of the immense powers of the contemporary press.

The principles in the present situation

The principles we have attempted to state are those general truths which are valid as goals for all civilized societies. It must be observed that freedom of the press is not a fixed and isolated value, the same in every society and in all times. It is a function within a society and must vary with the social context. It will be different in times of general security and in times of crisis; it will be different under varying states of public emotion and belief.

The freedom we have been examining has assumed a type of public mentality which may seem to us standard and universal but which is in many respects a product of our special history—a mentality accustomed to the noise and confusion of clashing opinions and reasonably stable in temper in view of the varying fortunes of ideas. But what a mind does with a fact or an opinion is widely different when it is serene and when it is anxious; when it has confidence in its environment and when it is infected with suspicion or resentment; when it is gullible and when it is well furnished with the means of criticism; when it has hope and when it is in despair.

Further, the citizen is a different man when he has to judge his press alone, and when his judgment is steadied by other social agencies. Free and diverse utterance may result in bewilderment unless he has access—through home, church, school, custom—to interpreting patterns of thought and feeling. There is no such thing as the "objectivity" of the press unless the mind of the reader can identify the objects dealt with.

Whether at any time and place the psychological conditions exist under which a free press has social significance is always a question of fact, not of theory. These mental conditions may be lost. They may also be created. The press itself is always one of the chief agents in destroying or in building the bases of its own significance.

If we now fix our problem in space and time and look at the press in the United State today, we see that the conditions of our society and of the press in our society require new applications of the principles we have stated.

The aim of those who sponsored the First Amendment was to prevent the government from interfering with expression. The authors of our political system saw that the free society they were seeking to establish could not exist without free communication. As Jefferson put it: "The basis of our governments being the opinion of the people, the very first object should be to keep that right; and were it left to me to decide whether we should have a government without newspapers or newspapers without a government, I should not hesitate a moment to prefer the latter. But I should mean that every man should receive those papers and be capable of reading them."

Our ancestors were justified in thinking that if they could prevent the government from interfering with the freedom of the press, that freedom would be effectively exercised. In their day anybody with anything to say had comparatively little difficulty in getting it published. The only serious obstacle to free expression was government censorship. If that could be stopped, the right of every man to do his duty by his thought was secure. The press of those days consisted of hand-printed sheets issuing from little printing shops, regularly as newspapers, or irregularly as broadsides, pamphlets, or books. Presses were cheap; the journeyman printer could become a publisher and editor by borrowing the few dollars he needed to set up his shop and by hiring an assistant or two. With a limited number of people who could read, and with property qualifications for the suffrage—less than 6 percent of the adult population voted for the conventions held to ratify the Constitution—there was no great discrepancy between the number of those who could read and were active citizens and those who could command the financial resources to engage in publication.

It was not supposed that any one newspaper would represent all, or nearly all, of the conflicting viewpoints regarding public issues. Together they could be expected to do so, and, if they did not, the man whose opinions were not represented could start a publication of his own.

Nor was it supposed that many citizens would subscribe to all the local journals. It was more likely that each would take the one which would reinforce his prejudices. But in each village and town, with its relatively simple social structure and its wealth of neighborly contacts, various opinions might encounter each other in face-to-face meetings; the truth, it was hoped, would be sorted out by competition in the local market place.

Those circumstances which provided variety and interchange of opinion and easy individual access to the market place of ideas have changed so radically as to justify us in saying that this country has gone through a communications revolution.

Literacy, the electorate, and the population have increased to such a point that the political community to be served by the press includes all but a tiny fraction of the millions of the American people. The press has been transformed into an enormous and complicated piece of machinery. As a necessary accompaniment, it has become big business. There is a marked reduction in the number of units of the press relative to the total population. Although in small communities we can still see a newspaper plant and product that resemble their Colonial prototypes, these are no longer the most characteristic or the most influential agencies of communication.

The right of free public expression has therefore lost its earlier reality. Protection against government is now not enough to guarantee that a man who has something to say shall have a chance to say it. The owners and managers of the press determine which persons, which facts, which versions of the facts, and which ideas shall reach the public.

This is one side of the shield—the effect of the communications revolution on the right of the citizen to publish his beliefs. The other side is the effect of the communications revolution on the press as the agency through which the members of a free society receive, as well as exchange, the judgments, opinions, ideas, and information which they need in order to participate in the management of that society. The press has become a vital necessity in the transaction of the public business of a continental area.

In local affairs there is still a chance for face-to-face observation to get in its work. Many private groups, formal and informal, throw an extensive web of alternative communication over the country or over parts of it. But there is obviously less opportunity for direct observation and news by word of mouth in a metropolitan region, in a great nation, or in a world society than there is in a village, a small state, or a single country. For the most part the understanding of the leaders and people of China, Russia, England, and Argentina possessed by the citizens of New Hampshire, Kansas, Oregon, and Alabama will be gained from the agencies of mass communications. Hardly less is the dependence on these agencies of midwest farmers for their understanding of a strike in Detroit or a change in the discount rate by the Federal Reserve Board in Washington.

The complexity of modern industrial society, the critical world situation, and the new menaces to freedom which these imply mean that the time has come for the press to assume a new public responsibility.

Through concentration of ownership the variety of courses of news and opinion is limited. At the same time the insistence of the citizen's need has increased. He is dependent on the quality, proportion, and extent of his news supply, not only for his personal access to the world of event, thought, and feeling, but also for the materials of his duties as a citizen and judge of public affairs. The soundness of his judgment affects the working of the state and even the peace of the world, involving the survival of the state as a free community. Under these circumstances it becomes an imperative question whether the performance of the press can any longer be left to the unregulated initiative of the few who manage it.

The moral and legal right of those who manage it to utter their opinions must remain intact; this right stands for the valid kernel of individualism at the heart of all social life. But the element of duty involved in the right requires a new scrutiny; and the service of news, as distinct from the utterance of opinion, acquires a new importance. The need of the citizen for adequate and uncontaminated mental food is such that he is under a duty to get it. Thus his interest also acquires the stature of a right.

To protect the press is no longer automatically to protect the citizen or the community. The freedom of the press can remain a right of those who publish only if it incorporates into itself the right of the citizen and the public interest.

Freedom of the press means freedom from and freedom for. The press must be free from the menace of external compulsions from whatever source. To demand that it be free from pressures which might warp its utterance would be to demand that society should be empty of contending forces and beliefs. But persisting and distorting pressures—financial, popular, clerical, institutional—must be known and counterbalanced. The press must, if it is to be wholly free, know and overcome any biases incident to its own economic position, its concentration, and its pyramidal organization.

The press must be free for the development of its own conceptions of service and achievement. It must be free for making its contribution to the maintenance and development of a free society.

This implies that the press must also be accountable. it must be accountable to society for meeting the public need and for maintaining the rights of citizens and the almost forgotten rights of speakers who have no press. It must know that its faults and errors have ceased to be private vagaries and have become public dangers. The voice of the press, so far as by a drift toward monopoly it tends to become exclusive in its wisdom and observation, deprives other voices of a hearing and the public of their contribution. Freedom of the press for the coming period can only continue as an accountable freedom. Its moral right will be conditioned on its acceptance of this accountability. Its legal right will stand unaltered as its moral duty is performed.

The requirements

If the freedom of the press is freighted with the responsibility of providing the current intelligence needed by a free society, we have to discover what a free society requires. Its requirements in America today are greater in variety, quantity, and quality than those of any previous society in any age. They are the requirements of a self-governing republic of continental size, whose doings have become, within a generation, matters of common concern in new and important ways. Its internal arrangements, from being thought of mainly as matters of private interest and automatic market adjustment, have become affairs of conflict and conscious compromise among organized groups, whose powers appear not to be bounded by "natural law," economic or other. Externally, it has suddenly assumed a leading role in the attempt to establish peaceful relationships among all the states on the globe.

Today our society needs, first, a truthful, comprehensive, and intelligent account of the day's events in a context which gives them meaning; second, a forum for the exchange of comment and criticism; third, a means of projecting the opinions and attitudes of the groups in the society to one another; fourth, a method of presenting and clarifying the goals and values of the society; and, fifth, a way of reaching every member of the society by the currents of information, thought, and feeling which the press supplies.

The Commission has no idea that these five ideal demands can ever be completely met. All of them cannot be met by any one medium; some do not apply at all to a particular unit; nor do all apply with equal relevance to all parts of the communications industry. The Commission does not suppose that these standards will be new to the managers of the press; they are drawn largely from their professions and practices.

A truthful, comprehensive, and intelligent account of the day's events in a context which gives them meaning

The first requirement is that the media should be accurate. They should not lie. Here the first link in the chain of responsibility is the reporter at the source of the news. He must be careful and competent. He must estimate correctly which sources are most authoritative. He must prefer firsthand observation to hearsay. He must know what questions to ask, what things to observe, and which items to report. His employer has the duty of training him to do his work as it ought to be done.

Of equal importance with reportorial accuracy are the identification of fact as fact and opinion as opinion, and their separation, so far as possible. This is necessary all the way from the reporter's file, up through the copy and makeup desks and editorial offices, to the final, published product. The distinction cannot, of course, be made absolute. There is not fact without a context and no factual report which is uncolored by the opinions of the reporter. But modern conditions require greater effort than ever to make the distinction between fact and opinion. In a simpler order of society published accounts of events within the experience of the community could be compared with other sources of information. Today this is usually impossible. The account of an isolated fact, however accurate in itself, may be misleading and, in effect, untrue. . . .

A forum for the exchange of comment and criticism

The second requirement means that the great agencies of mass communication should regard themselves as common carriers of public discussion. The units of the press have in varying degrees assumed this function and should assume the responsibilities which go with it, more generally and more explicitly.

It is vital to a free society that an idea should not be stifled by the circumstances of its birth. The press cannot and should not be expected to print everybody's ideas. But the giant units can and should assume the duty of publishing significant ideas contrary to their own, as a matter of objective reporting, distinct from their proper function of advocacy. Their control over the various ways of reaching the ear of America is such that, if they do not publish ideas which differ from their own, those ideas will never reach the ear of America. If that happens, one of the chief reasons for the freedom which these giants claim disappears.

Access to a unit of the press acting as a common carrier is possible in a number of ways, all of which, however, involve selection on the part of the managers of the unit. The individual whose views are not represented on an editorial page may reach an audience through a public statement reported as news, through a letter to the editor, through a statement printed in advertising space, or though a magazine article. But some seekers for space are bound to be disappointed and must resort to pamphlets or such duplicating devices as will spread their ideas to such public as will attend to them.

But all the important viewpoints and interests in the society should be represented in its agencies of mass communication. Those who have these viewpoints and interests cannot count on explaining them to their fellow-citizens through newspaper or radio stations of their own. Even if they could make the necessary investment, they could have no assurance that their publications would be read or their programs heard by the public outside their own adherents. An ideal combination would include general media, inevitably solicitous to present their own views, but setting forth other views fairly. As checks on their fairness, and partial safeguards against ignoring important matters, more specialized media of advocacy have a vital place. In the absence of such a combination the partially insulated groups in society will continue to be insulated. The unchallenged assumptions of each group will continue to harden into prejudice. The mass medium reaches across all groups; through the mass medium they can come to understand one another.

Whether a unit of the press is an advocate or a common carrier, it ought to identify the sources of its facts, opinions, and arguments so that the reader or listener can judge them. Persons who are presented with facts, opinions, and arguments are properly influenced by the general reliability of those who offer them. If the veracity of statements is to be appraised, those who offer them must be known.

Identification of source is necessary to a free society. Democracy, in time of peace, at least, has a justifiable confidence that full and free discussion will strengthen rather than weaken it. But, if the discussion is to have the effect for which democracy hopes, if it is to be really full and free, the names and the characters of the participants must not be hidden from view.

The projection of a representative picture of the constituent groups in the society

This requirement is closely related to the two preceding. People make decisions in large part in terms of favorable or unfavorable images. They relate fact and opinion to stereotypes. Today the motion picture, the radio, the book, the magazine, the newspaper, and the comic strip are principal agents in creating and perpetuating these conventional conceptions. When the images they portray fail to present the social group truly, they tend to pervert judgment.

Such failure may occur indirectly and incidentally. Even if nothing is said about the Chinese in the dialogue of a film, yet if the Chinese appear in a succession of pictures as sinister drug addicts and militarists, an image of China is built which needs to be balanced by another. If the Negro appears in the stories published in magazines of national circulation only as a servant, if children figure constantly in radio dramas as impertinent and ungovernable brats—the image of the Negro and the American Child is distorted. The plugging of special color and "hate words" in radio and press dispatches, in advertising copy, in news stories—such words as "ruthless," "confused," "bureaucratic"—performs inevitably the same image-making function.

Responsible performance here simply means that the images repeated and emphasized be such as are in total representative of the social group as it is. The truth about any social group, though it should not exclude its weaknesses and vices, includes also recognition of its values, its aspirations, and its common humanity. The Commission holds to the faith that if people are exposed to the inner truth of the life of a particular group, they will gradually build up respect for and understanding of it.

The presentation and clarification of the goals and values of the society

The press has a similar responsibility with regard to the values and goals of our society as a whole. The mass media, whether or not they wish to do so, blur or clarify these ideas as they report the failings and achievements of every day. The Commission does not call upon the press to sentimentalize, to manipulate the facts for the purpose of painting a rosy picture. The Commission believes in realistic reporting of the events and forces that militate against the attainment of social goals as well as those which work for them. We must recognize, however, that the agencies of mass communication are an educational instrument, perhaps the most powerful there is; and they must assume a responsibility like that of educators in stating and clarifying the ideals toward which the community should strive.

Full access to the day's intelligence

It is obvious that the amount of current information required by the citizens in a modern industrial society is far greater than that required in any earlier day. We do not assume that all citizens at all times will actually use all the material they receive. By necessity or choice large number of people voluntarily delegate analysis and decision to leaders whom they trust. Such leadership in our society is freely chosen and constantly changing; it is informal, unofficial, and flexible. Any citizen may at any time assume the power of decision. In this way government is carried on by consent.

But such leadership does not alter the need for the wide distribution of news and opinion. The leaders are not identified; we can inform them only by making information available to everybody.

The five requirements listed in this chapter suggest what our society is entitled to demand of its press. We can now proceed to examine the tools, the structure, and the performance of the press to see how it is meeting these demands.

Let us summarize these demands in another way.

The character of the service required of the American press by the American people differs from the service previously demanded, first, in this—that it is essential to the operation of the economy and to the government of the Republic. Second, it is a service of greatly increased responsibilities both as to the quantity and as the quality of the information required. In terms of quantity, the information about themselves and about their world made available to the American people must be as extensive as the range of their interests and concerns as citizens of the self-governing, industrialized community in the closely integrated modern world. In terms of quality, the information provided must be provided in such a form, and with so scrupulous a regard for the wholeness of the truth and the fairness of its presentation, that the American people may make for themselves, by the exercise of reason and of conscience, the fundamental decisions necessary to the direction of their government and of their lives.

Chapter 24
John C. Merrill
1924-

While the Hutchins Commission saw the market system as the primary source of potential journalistic malfeasance, it suggested that it might be necessary for government to take action to help the press live up to its implicit social mandate. That suggestion, however, was laid out in a constitutional mine field. No matter where you stepped, you were in danger of setting off a First Amendment explosion. Even the hint that government might be required to "help" the press do its job returns us to the specter of governmental control that the First Amendment and its underlying philosophy are meant to prevent.

For this reason, many in the profession saw the Hutchins Commission report as an assault on journalistic freedom and autonomy. Even stripped of the possibility of government intervention, the press councils and press codes suggested by the commission amounted to outside interference in the ongoing process of freedom of expression that lies at the heart of the journalistic enterprise, according to some critics, including the powerful *New York Times*.

One of the preeminent contemporary spokesmen for this position is John C. Merrill, professor emeritus at the University of Missouri. During his career, Merrill has focused largely on a defense of the independence of the individual journalist. Merrill sees in the shadows of the social responsibility doctrine a real threat to expressive freedom. Journalists, he argues, must seek ethical guidance from within themselves, not from the codes of organizations, commissions, or councils.

However, it could be argued, and Merrill implicitly acknowledges, that while one may have to begin at one or another of these extremes—either allegiance to a code of social responsibility or adherence to a philosophy of purely personal autonomy—that ultimately these things need not be mutually exclusive. Conscientious journalists may, and must, respond personally to the tough questions about their journalistic and social obligations. It is not enough merely to follow. They must fashion a personal commitment to a set of journalistic values that arise out of their own understanding of truth, popular sovereignty and freedom of expression. This does not, however, preclude one from developing a system of professional ethics, a moral compass, that embodies the vision of the Hutchins Commission. One can stake a personal claim to these goals.

The Imperative of Freedom
1974

I ncreasingly one hears reference to the responsibility of the press and less and less about its freedom to react independently in a democratic society. Not only has the concept permeated the authoritarian countries, where it is an expected development, but in recent years it has made notable incursions into the press philosophy of the United States and other Western libertarian countries.

The book, [Fred S. Siebert, Theodore Peterson and Wilbur Schramm] *Four Theories of the Press* [Urbana: University of Illinois Press] published in 1956, attempted to put in intelligible language this new concept of the press which had been developing at least since World War II. It dealt with "social responsibility" as a press theory alongside the theories of communism, authoritarianism and libertarianism. And from this book the new "theory" has made its way, largely unchallenged, into innumerable books, articles, speeches and academic dissertations. On the surface this new emphasis appears noble. Writers and speakers enthusiastically expound its virtues. And, of course, it is difficult for anyone to take issue with any concept which is wrapped in the glittering garments of "people's freedom" and "public good" and "social responsibility."

Although journalists, statesmen and academicians have for years (actually centuries) been thinking in terms of "responsibility" as well as freedom for the communications media, there had really been no significant effort to place the concept as a serious theory—parallel in importance to "libertarianism"—until 1947 when the Commission on Freedom of the Press, headed by Robert Hutchins, discussed it in *A Free and Responsible Press* [Chicago: University of Chicago Press]. Previously, it had been thought that responsibility was somehow a personal concept or somehow automatically built into a libertarian press, or that various of the media units would interpret "responsibility" in their own ways. Actually, it had generally been felt that the multiplicity of interpretations was what actually constituted not only a free press, but also a responsible press. At least it was felt generally in the Western world that a "free press" in a democratic sense was responsible per se to its social system.

But the Hutchins Commission thought differently. After seeing a very clear danger in growing restriction of communications' outlets and general irresponsibility in many areas of American journalism (the criteria for responsibility, of course, set up by the Commission), it offered the ominous warning that "If they [the agencies of mass communication] are irresponsible, not even the First Amendment will protect their freedom from governmental control. The amendment will be amended." Another blast: "To the extent that the press does not assume its responsibility, some other agency must see that the essential functions of mass communication are carried out." (Would this be only for those of the media which do "not assume their responsibility" or for the entire press? The Commission did not see fit to get into that.)

Two basic assumptions (and conclusions) stand out in the Hutchins Commission Report: (1) That the press has a responsibility (defined by the Commission) to society; and (2) That the libertarian press of the U.S. is not meeting this responsibility, therefore a need for a new press theory exists.

For a while, it seemed that the majority of United States publishers were quite excited over the Commission's report and the implications which they read in (or into) it; but by 1950 the issue had largely settled down, the journalists perhaps thinking that the best policy was to ignore it. Certain ideas inherent in the report, however, had taken root in journalistic soil which was already well-fertilized with the philosophy of Welfareism and egalitarianism and a readiness to accept ever greater governmental power.

Here is what a press scholar wrote about the Hutchins Commission report in the 1960's:

> In 1947 the Commission on Freedom of the Press—thirteen men, of whom most were scholars and none was connected with the mass media—reported the results of several years' deliberations on freedom and responsibility in mass communication. Their central theme was not the need for a rebirth of competition, but for a greater sense of responsibility on the part of the owners and personnel of the mass media. They said that the people would surely demand regulation of a press that did not meet more fully the needs of society for mass communication services. The fullest, most orderly, and perhaps most basic statement of the problem and of suggestions for change among American analyses, the report was attacked heavily by the press as unfair, badly informed, and unfriendly to freedom of the press. Much of the world of the press was to mellow somewhat in its attitude toward the Commission; some publishers even came to agree with most of its report.

Some Implications of the Theory

Just what does "social responsibility" mean as used by the Hutchins group in 1947, nine years later in *Four Theories of the Press,* and by many others who have become attached to this new theory? It is really difficult—or even impossible—to answer such a question largely because its proponents do not seem to know the answer themselves. At any rate, it is interesting to try to assume what they might mean. One thing is certain: they do not mean "libertarianism" (for they see social responsibility as a theory growing out of libertarianism), nor do they mean media autonomy or editorial-determination of what is responsible (for that is what we theoretically have in libertarianism already).

Proponents of "social responsibility" see their theory closely related to the libertarian press system, but they see it as going beyond the free press theory, in that it places many moral and ethical—and conceivably, legal and other—restrictions on the press. It is a restrictive theory although its devotees do not stress this point. Instead of emphasizing "freedom," it stresses "responsibility" to the society of which the press system is a part.

If this responsibility is not forthcoming, voluntarily, then in time it will be absolutely necessary that it be imposed on the communications media by the government. According to the Hutchins group, press freedom is limited by a social responsibility to report facts accurately and in a meaningful context. Since such thinking inevitably leads to the advocacy of a regulatory system to watch the actions of the press and to keep it functioning "properly," the Hutchins Commission suggested that some type of government regulation might be needed to assure that the press accept its responsibility.

The social responsibility theory implies a recognition by the media that they must perform a public service (of some specific "responsible" kind—that, presumably, they are not already performing) to warrant their existence. The main parts of the Commission's report which seemed to have antagonized many American editors and publishers were those that intimated possible government involvement in the press system. Also there was the basic arrogance of this self-appointed "commission" which set up its own standards for press responsibility and then found the American press unable to meet them.

This "theory" of social responsibility has a good ring to it and has an undeniable attraction for many. There is a trend throughout the world in this direction, which implies a suspicion of, and dissatisfaction with, the libertarianism of press-related journalism. Implicit in this trend toward "social responsibility" is the argument that some group (obviously a judicial or governmental one, ultimately) can and must define or decide what is socially responsible. Also, the implication is clear that publishers and journalists acting freely cannot determine what is socially responsible nearly as well as can some "outside" or "impartial" group. If this power elite decides the press is not responsible, not even the First Amendment will keep the publishers from losing this freedom to government, we are told.

Nobody would deny that the press, in one sense, would be more "responsible" if some type of governmental supervision came about; indeed, reporters could be kept from nosing about in "critical" areas during "critical" times. The amount of sensational material could be controlled in the press, or eliminated altogether. Government activities could always be supported and public policy could be pushed on all occasions. The press could be more "educational" in the sense that less hard news (crime, wrecks, disasters, etc.) would appear, while more news of art exhibits, concerts, speeches by government personages and national progress in general could be emphasized. In short, the press would stress the positive and eliminate, or minimize, the negative. Then, with one voice the press of the nation would be responsible to its society; and the definition of "responsible" would be functional in a monolithic way—defined and carried out by government or by some non-journalistic power.

Many persons will object to this line of analysis and will say that "social responsibility" of the press of a nation does not necessarily imply government control. I contend that ultimately it does, since if left to be defined by various publishers or journalistic groups the term is quite relative and nebulous; and it is quite obvious that in the traditional context of American libertarianism no "solution" that would be widely agreed upon or practiced could ever be reached by non-government groups or individuals.

The only way a "theory" of social responsibility could have any significance in any country is for the governmental power elite to be the definer and enforcer of this type of press. Since in any country the organization of society—its social and political structure—determines to a large extent what responsibilities the press (and the citizen) owe society, every country's press quite naturally considers itself (or might logically be considered) as being socially responsible. . . .

It is certainly not contended here that all information coming to the public from all mass communication outlets in a libertarian society is reliable, honest, complete, fair and "socially responsible." Nobody really knows just how much of it is—or if any of it is. Since, in a nation such as the United States, there is no ready definition for "social responsibility," there is really no standard to which our media seek to conform—even though, without a doubt, they would all conceive of themselves as socially responsible.

Their very pluralism, their very diversity is the base of their nebulous idea that in our society they are responsible. This is based on the concept of autonomy. Responsibility to our society implies a continuance of this very pluralistic (and autonomous) communication—with all of its virtues and evils—and a constant guard against any encroachments by government on any level to "define" what is "responsible" to society and further to align the press to its definition.

This concept of "press autonomy" seems much sounder (and easier to grapple with) than "social responsibility." All press systems can claim to be responsible to their societies, but the idea of autonomous media injecting a variety of opinions and ideas into the social fabric is one which only the libertarian system can reasonably claim. Libertarianism, or press autonomy, then, if it is to be considered as a separate theory must embrace the right of, or at least the possibility for, some press units to deviate from others to the degree that they will be considered "irresponsible." When the term and concept of "irresponsible journalism" disappears from the United States—or even comes close to disappearing—then will be the time when journalistic freedom and autonomy are dead....

Postscript: The imperative of freedom

In spite of the philosophical synthesis just discussed, the theoretical focus of this book should not be blurred. Freedom is the central issue; journalistic autonomy is the highest value, and the person who submits to extra-self determinism gives away himself, forfeits his very essence and authenticity. This, of course, is fundamentally an existential stance; and in emphasizing the importance of freedom it is quite valid to say that this book advocates an existentialist journalism. For the journalist there is, indeed, an imperative of freedom. Freedom is the very source of personhood; it is the wellspring of ethics; it is the foundation that supports the related concepts of rationality, commitment, integrity and responsibility.

The free journalist who cherishes his authenticity and his integrity has one dedication: a dedication to his freedom and the viability of his freedom. This whole book has attempted to stress the importance of freedom or journalistic autonomy—not only for the individual journalist, but also for the individual media and the press systems themselves. With the potent pressures that are exerted on media systems and journalists, it is a wonder that we have as much journalistic freedom as we do. Certainly we have seen that escaping from freedom is a very strong human desire; and regardless of how important freedom and autonomy are to some people, not everyone considers such states desirous or even necessary. Freedom, of course, is not an imperative for everybody; this certainly must be conceded. As Erich Fromm has pointed out, freedom can even be a burden and a person can have a very basic "instinctive wish" for submission to the dictates of someone else or to some group.

But the journalist is in a special position. If he abdicates his pursuit of autonomy and freedom, he largely projects his stance on his whole audience; in a sense he expresses his disdain for individualism and selfhood and joins in tacit support of collective mentality, institutionalized morality, and personal and political slavery. He certainly has the "right" (stemming from freedom) to give up his freedom and accept slavery, but this really gets him nowhere except in a position where further free choices become extremely difficult if not impossible. For the free man who wishes to remain free can never will that restrictions be placed on his freedom. But even the freedom-loving journalist is in danger of losing his freedom to the forces which surround him.

The journalist works under the persistent pressures which often cause him to adapt to the "social good" and to institutional expediency. Being a member of a group and accepting institutional responsibility tend to suppress conscience and true existential consciousness. It is not easy for the institutional and professional journalist to retain his authenticity. A journalist, Robert Stein, has written that "journalists are going to have to rely on their own values more rather than less, not only in interpreting the news but in deciding what it is." Stein is appealing to the journalist to express his real authenticity to a greater degree and indicating how easy it is for the journalist to be swallowed up by his group. He puts it this way:

> As publishers, broadcasters, editors and reporters work under the constant demands of deadlines and competition, their private values tend to be pushed further and further into the background until, in some cases, particularly at the executive level, they disappear completely. For years I have been fascinated by what happens to individuals (including myself) when they gather around a corporate table. Institutional responsibility seems to act simultaneously as a narcotic that suppresses conscience and a stimulant that bring out every bit of low cunning that can be used to profit the organization.

The freedom-loving journalist will, of course, fight constantly against such depersonalizing submission to groupism. He will promote in himself the basic Nietszchean theme of saying "yes to life" thereby becoming more noble and heroic—and more authentic. The ideal journalist would be something of a Nietzchean Superman—a person who has learned to transcend himself, to rise to, and beyond, his highest potential. He would be a "higher man"—a law unto himself, a center of virtue, and powerful, happy person of exuberant self-expression and self-confidence. A key concept of Nietzsche, consistent with his existentialist orientation, is his passionate belief in the worth of the individual and his view of the hero as the person who does not submit to authority—or at least fights constantly against it. Karl Japsers reinforces this position. The true existential person, he writes, is the one who on his own initiative gains "possession of the mechanism of his life"; if he does not, Jaspers sees him as "degraded to become a machine" that surrenders to "the apparatus."

To stay free is the primary imperative of the authentic journalist. Only the free journalist can be a truth-seeker. As Luka Brajnovic says, "Defending and divulging the truth is the first postulate of press freedom." The Yugoslav philosopher, now teaching in Spain, stresses the importance of truth—not "artistic" truth, but truth based on evidence, on exactness which comes close to objective reality. Of course, the free journalist may lie, may not be willing to correct errors, may distort, and may intentionally provide misconceptions, says Brajnovic; but the unfree journalist cannot be dedicated to the truth; the truth is not in his journalism because the importance of truth is not part of his national philosophy. This is perhaps a little strong—and unfair—to the existentially "free" journalist working in a controlled society (and this could apply to Brajnovic himself), but as a basic generalization, it is undoubtedly valid. And surely Brajnovic is right when he says that to seek the maximum truth, the journalist must seek the maximum freedom—for himself and for his own medium and media system.

Brajnovic strikes the Kantian note when he writes of "human dignity" being a check on the use of freedom. "We are the owners of our own destiny because we possess freedom," he says. He also contends that this dignity places just limits on freedom for the simple reason that man does not live isolated in society; all members have this same human dignity. And this human dignity he refers to, just what is it? We told that the "moral man" has it. And who is this moral man? The man who does not succumb to his instincts or to his passions; who does not change his opinion without justification; is not a flatterer or renegade. Brajnovic calls all of these characteristics "monstrosities" which negate dignity, as well as the rights and the liberty of man.

This freedom is not only checked by human dignity of the moral man but also by a sense of journalistic responsibility. No good will be served here by exhaustively going back over what has been said about responsibility and freedom in earlier chapters. But it is probably worth reemphasizing the view that responsibility for the journalist should be personal responsibility. The concept of "social responsibility," however good it may sound, is one which the libertarian journalist should approach with great care. The current emphasis on "social responsibility" in journalism may well be nothing more than a subterfuge under which elite groups or persons go about trying to make the press system over in their own image. Self-realization demands a rejection of the whole concept of social responsibility—except that sense in which it might be taken to mean that personal responsibility which a free and rational journalist determines for himself. The existential responsibility to one's self and for one's own actions is the responsibility of a free person and a free society.

Conclusion

The professional life of a journalist is delimited to a large extent by the constraints of time. Nearly all stories could be more thoroughly reported, more clearly written, more thoughtfully produced if there were only another hour, another day to do them. The need to generate a broad array of accurate and detailed stories under the unforgiving pressure of deadlines too often forces serious discussion of journalism's moral dimensions to the edges of the workday and to the occasional lull in the rhythm of the news cycle. Given the pace, it is in some ways remarkable that in most news operations, the top editors assemble daily to wrestle with the *should* component of the next edition. But those planning sessions, too, are hemmed in by time constraints and by a full plate of technical and logistic details demanding a hearing.

Taking serious time on the job to reflect on the history of the profession, its intellectual and philsophical roots, is a luxury most in the business simply cannot afford. It is, nonetheless, a history that shapes everything the journalist is and does. The wisest of those who have spoken about the problems and promises of journalism have done more than merely influence the way the business currently operates. They have defined the way that the best reporting should be done.

The most fundamental duty of American journalism—that of providing the free flow of information essential to democratic self-government—has largely been upheld. The First Amendment has borne up well against two centuries of assault from many fronts. This is true despite the many well-chronicled shortcomings, and even though critics from left and right are often correct, from their respective vantage points, when they cry, "Unfair!" It has often and correctly been observed that more reporters consider themselves liberals than conservatives. Just as often and just as correctly, critics from the left have noted that American journalism is, at bottom, a capitalistic enterprise and continues to behave as one. For all that, we have a press that, on its best days and even on most of its average ones, takes seriously its assigned job as democratic watchdog. Indeed, the most outrageous journalistic sins of sensationalism and invasion of privacy come from taking that assignment too seriously.

There remain, certainly, hundreds of questions concerning both new problems and continuing dilemmas. Journalists of the twenty-first century may well work for huge multinational conglomerates and FAX their stories directly into selected, market-determined homes and businesses. The implications of emerging technologies are profound. An old problem, the financial influence on all aspects of news, has yet to be resolved. Readers and viewers have historically been unwilling to bear the full cost of the information they receive, and they demand a considerable measure of entertainment even to pick up the paper or turn on the set. Massive government subsidies, even if they were available, would cripple news gathering. Thus, largely unregulated private enterprise seems to be essential to the news media's most important role, even though the corrupting influence of money has been obvious for more than a century.

The essential point is not that only some of the important problems have been solved or even that some may never be fully solved at all. The point is that journalism in the very best sense of the concept is essential to what we are and what we hope to become. It can and does enrich and ennoble those who write the news and those who read and view it. It is about the possiblities of journalistic excellence that the writers in this book have spoken, directly and indirectly. For both the working journalist and the journalist-in-training, this book is a series of identifying marks on the landscape, bits of thought to help them find their way though the inevitable thickets and tangles of trying to observe, to understand and to explain the human condition in a meaningful way.

Suggestions for Further Reading

What follows should not be taken as an exhaustive catalog of everything ever written about the topics raised in this book. Instead, it is an idiosyncratic and highly subjective list of works the editors have found to be important or illuminating. Some are classics, others are very recent. Some have been hailed as masterpieces; others have been seen as seriously flawed. The list is intended to provide the next level of guidance to those readers who found something in the essays that warrants further thought.

In the area of politics, studying the free-press clause of the First Amendment is almost an academic discipline in itself. For the eighteenth century, all journalism historians owe a debt of gratitude to Leonard Levy, even those who disagree with his argument (advanced in *Legacy of Suppression*, 1960) that the Founders intended a much more limited press freedom than that which we accept today. Among other important works, Levy's *Freedom of the Press from Zenger to Jefferson* (Indianapolis: Bobbs-Merrill, 1966) provides an important survey of the era and draws attention to many writers otherwise nearly lost to history. One of them, John Thomson, a Jeffersonian thinker too long ignored, is especially worth noting. Thomson's remarkable book, *An Enquiry, Concerning the Liberty, and Licentiousness of the Press and the Uncontroulable Nature of the Human Mind* (New York: Johnson and Stryker, 1801), makes a compelling case for a free press on political grounds, and sets up the argument of the great libertarian thinker of the mid-nineteenth century, John Stuart Mill.

The two most powerful champions of free speech early in the first half of this century are Zechariah Chafee Jr., *Freedom of Speech* (New York: Harcourt, Brace and Howe, 1920), revised and republished as *Free Speech in the United States* (Cambridge, Ma.: Harvard University Press, 1941), and Alexander Meiklejohn, *Free Speech and its Relation to Self-Government* (New York: Harper, 1948).

Two Supreme Court free-speech cases are so important they deserve special attention. The 1919 Abrams case is examined in detail by Richard Polenberg in *Fighting Faiths* (New York: Viking, 1987). More recently, the critically important Times *v.* Sullivan libel case is explored with insight and grace by *New York Times* columnist Anthony Lewis in *Make No Law* (New York: Random House, 1991).

A good contemporary case for free speech and what it means to our society is made by Rodney Smolla in *Free Speech in an Open Society* (New York: Knopf, 1992). Readers are also directed toward John Keane, *The Media and Democracy* (Cambridge, MA: Polity Press, 1991).

For more on very early considerations of the problem of truth and the nature of reality, look at Plato's dialogue, *Theatetus*, in which Plato answers Protagoris's subjectivity. Bacon stands historically between Plato and the British Empiricists. Students are encouraged to read in the original the works of George Berkeley and John Locke, the rationalism of René Descartes and Baruch Spinoza, and finally the great skeptic who seriously weakened all notions of objective reality, David Hume. See especially Hume's *Enquiry Concerning Human Understanding*, first published as *Philosophical Essays Concerning Human Understanding*.

While epistemological discussions may have become tumultuous during and after Hume, "science" nonetheless quickly moved on with demonstrable real world success, and it is in the attempt to apply the methods and rule of science to the social world that we begin to discern the roots of objectivity as a standard for journalistic practice.

For a thorough discussion and critique of the rise of objective journalism, including the role of the scientific movement and other elements in its development, see Michael Schudson, *Discovering the News* (New York: Basic Books, 1978). For a briefer discussion, see Richard Streckfuss, "Objectivity in Journalism: A Search and Reassessment," *Journalism Quarterly* 67:973-83 (1990), and Dan Schiller, "An Historical Approach to Objectivity and Professionalism in American News Reporting," *Journal of Communication* 29:46-57 (1979).

All journalists and journalism students should read Walter Lippmann's *Public Opinion* in its entirety. Lippmann's philosophy is heavily influenced by pragmatist thinking of the first quarter of this century. But more than any other writer, Lippmann brought social theory to journalism, advancing both and tying both areas to public policy. Other important works by Lippmann include "Two Revolutions in the American Press," *Yale Review* 20:433-441 (1931); *The Phantom Public* (New York: Harcourt, Brace and Co., 1925), and *Liberty and the News* (New York: Harcourt, Brace and Co., 1920).

Sociology and mass communication studies began in the early and mid-1900s to consider the variety of organizational, professional, and ideological influences on the reporting of news, demonstrating from a different perspective the difficulty of untangling notions of objectivity and impartiality from the social roots of journalistic practice. Breed's "Socialization in the Newsroom" is only one of the best and earliest examples, but there are many more, including David Manning White, "The 'Gatekeeper': A Case Study in the Selection of News," *Journalism Quarterly* 27:383-90 (1950); and David Weaver and Cleve Wilhoit, *The American Journalist* (Bloomington: Indiana University Press, 1986). Other noted works in this area include Herbert Gans, *Deciding What's News* (New York: Random House, 1979); Todd Gitlin, *The Whole World is Watching* (Berkeley: University of California Press, 1980); Gaye Tuchman, "Objectivity as Strategic Ritual: An Examination of Newsmen's Notions of Objectivity," *American Journal of Sociology* 77:660-79 (1977), and *Making News* (New York, The Free Press, 1978); and Leon Sigal, *Reporters and Officials* (Lexington, Ma.: D.C. Heath, 1973).

For those who found the leap from Adam Smith to Karl Marx too great to take comfortably, two classic works help fill in the gap. The first is Thomas Malthus, *An Essay on the Principle of Population* (1798, rev. ed., 1803). The second is David Ricardo, *The Principles of Political Economy and Taxation* (1817). Both have been reissued frequently.

For more specifically on media and economic problems, see Bagdikian's earlier and longer work, *The Media Monopoly*, now in its fourth edition (Boston: Beacon Press, 1993), along with Robert Picard, James Winter, Max McCombs and Steve Lacy, *Press Concentration and Monopoly* (Norwood, N.J.: Ablex, 1988).

The muckrakers are endlessly fascinating. A recent and sympathic look at them is Walter M. Brasch, *Forerunners of Revolution: Muckrakers and the American Social Conscience* (Lanham, Md.: University Press of America, 1990). The muckraking tradition in contemporary America is examined in David L. Protess et. al., *The Journalism of Outrage* (New York: Guilford, 1991).

Other worthwhile works by noted curmudgeons and press critics include all of A.J. Liebling's *The Press* (New York: Ballentine, 1964) a collection of his "Wayward Press" columns from the *New Yorker*. No examination of the American press is complete without H.L. Mencken, who published many collections of his newspaper and magazine writings during his lifetime. More recently, Marion Elizabeth Rodgers has made her own collection of what she sees as Mencken's greatest work and published it as *The Impossible H.L. Mencken* (New York: Doubleday, 1991).

For a different theoretical perspective on the same issues, students should consider a "critical studies" or Marxist analysis of media economics. A basic, contemporary starting point might include some of the works of Herbert Schiller, including *Culture, Inc.: The Corporate Takeover of Public Expression* (New York: Oxford University Press, 1989) or *Mass Communication and American Empire*, 2nd ed. (Boulder: Westview Press, 1992), and an anthology of American and European work such as Michael Gurevitch et. al. eds., *Culture, Society and the Media* (London: Methuen & Co, Ltd., 1982).

For an extended discussion of the philosophy underlying the concept of social responsibility by one of the authors of the Hutchins report, William Ernest Hocking, see Hocking's *Freedom of The Press* (Chicago: University of Chicago Press, 1947); also consider the classic journalism text, first published in 1957, *Responsibility in Mass Communication*, 3d ed. by William Rivers, Wilbur Schramm and Clifford Christians (New York, Harper & Row, 1980).

The questions of women and minorities in news are, not surprisingly, frequently considered as part of the broader concerns of the portrayal of women and minorities in the mass media generally—in entertainment programming, in advertising and so on. A current bibliography of women and the mass media is John A. Lent, ed. *Women and Mass Communications* (Westport, Ct.: Greenwood, 1991). Among the best of the journalism-specific books is Kay Mills, *A Place in the News* (New York: Dodd Mead, 1988).

See also Marolyn Martindale, *The White Press and Black America* (Westport, Ct.: Greenwood, 1986).

New technologies are beyond the scope of this book, but the fundamental problems that satellites and fiber optics pose for the conscientious journalist should be familiar by now: Who will pay the billions of dollars it will take to deliver the news and entertainment of tomorrow? Consumers will pay money for some kinds of information, often the more salacious the better, and advertisers will pay for the chance to pitch their soap and beer to those consumers. But who pays to make sure the city council is playing fair on a rezoning question, and who pays to find out if an incumbent Senator sold a crucial vote for a contribution to the re-election war chest?

Index

About the Editors

STEVEN R. KNOWLTON, Assistant Professor of Journalism at Pennsylvania State University, worked for more than twenty years as a reporter and editor for six different newspapers around the country and for United Press International and as a press aide on a presidential campaign. His most recent book is *Popular Politics and the Irish Catholic Church* (1991).

PATRICK R. PARSONS is Associate Professor of Communications at Pennsylvania State University. His recent publications include *Milestones in Cable Television USA* (1990) and *Cable Television and the First Amendment* (1987). He has written at length on ethical issues for journalists and on their roles in society.

ISBN 0-275-94537-5

90000>

HARDCOVER BAR CODE